Worthy

A MEMOIR

Worthy

A MEMOIR

DENICE TURNER

University of Nevada Press ▲▲ Reno & Las Vegas

University of Nevada Press, Reno, Nevada 89557 USA
Copyright © 2015 by the University of Nevada Press
All rights reserved
Manufactured in the United States of America
Design by Kathleen Szawiola

Library of Congress Cataloging-in-Publication Data
Turner, Denice H., 1964–
Worthy : a memoir / Denice Turner.
pages cm.
ISBN 978-0-87417-968-2 (paperback) — ISBN 978-0-87417-975-0 (e-book)
1. Loss (Psychology) 2. Grief. 3. Self-esteem. 4. Mothers and daughters. I. Title.
BF575.D35T87 2015
818'.603—dc23
[B]
2014042411

The paper used in this book meets the requirements of American National
Standard for Information Sciences—Permanence of Paper for Printed Library
Materials, ANSI/NISO Z39.48-1992 (R2002). Binding materials were selected for
strength and durability.

FIRST PRINTING

23   22   21   20   19   18   17   16   15

5   4   3   2   1

For Lan, who taught me to stop being nice

CONTENTS

ONE Separations 1

TWO The Smallest Key 8

THREE Jar of Hearts 18

FOUR Angels and Demons 27

FIVE All Is Well! 38

SIX S.O.B. 47

SEVEN Fascinating Womanhood 58

EIGHT An Ecstasy of Weeding 71

NINE The Distorting Mirror 83

TEN The Bridge Builder 101

ELEVEN Troubles 120

TWELVE Lath and Plaster Disaster 135

THIRTEEN The Room of Blood and Bones 152

FOURTEEN Harold 172

FIFTEEN Cecilia 184

SIXTEEN Principles of Internal Medicine 195

Acknowledgments 211

Worthy

A MEMOIR

Separations

My mother's heart weighs 370 grams. Her brain, 129 grams. She is 166 centimeters tall and weighs 75 kilograms. Her hair is 10 centimeters long. Her uterus and ovaries are gone. There is a metal stent in her left anterior descending coronary artery. Her liver is 1,230 grams, her kidneys 90 grams apiece, spleen 100 grams. From the autopsy, I even know that the thickness of the subcutaneous layer of fat in her abdominal wall is 1.8 centimeters. All of her organs have been carefully removed, weighed, analyzed, and—I assume—returned to their original locations.

The language in the report does the same work as the scalpel and skull chisel, toothed forceps and rib cutters. It severs the human being from the body, reduces the body to the sum of its parts. My mother's organs are not "her" organs; they are *the* scalp, the right and left lungs, the hair, the skin, the larynx filled with sooty debris. The words carve her into manageable pieces, organize her into internal and external features. I notice that if I try to substitute the word *your* in the report—*your* skin, your lips, your abdomen, your hands, your breasts, your cause of death—the document gets dangerous. Too close, too heavy, the words fill my stomach and chest, churning up something like panic. *Your* turns the body on the metal gurney into my mother.

The autopsy confirms what the melted television in her bedroom already revealed. That the room was a nightmare of heat and black smoke. Her clothes were thick with soot, the side of her body nearest to the bedside table covered with second- and third-degree burns. Her skin was blistered and red with patches of peeling. Her earrings were melted; her glittering acrylic fingernails were blistered. Still, she appeared to be sleeping. There was no sign of panic or attempted escape, no indication that she was aware that the oxygen in her blood was slowly being replaced with carbon monoxide. The work of the document is not to offer insight, but assign liability. What happened? Who is to blame? Who will have to pay, and how much?

The unflinching terminology in the autopsy is my mother's language, not mine, verbiage loaded with Greek and Latin prefixes, suffixes, and stems. A registered nurse and physician assistant, she would have understood the document completely, and I suspect she would be fascinated by her own report. Even now, I can imagine her sitting across the kitchen table from me, sipping a mug of Swiss Miss with tiny marshmallows, sketching alveoli and capillaries, speculating on why her alveoli had begun to collapse well before her bedroom filled with smoke. And I can picture her intrigue and surprise—and maybe her derision—at not diagnosing her own heart or liver disease.

My brother staunchly refuses to look at the autopsy, and I can't blame him. Driving to the first of what are sure to be many court hearings about the disputed trust to which we are now heirs, he cautions me to do the same. "We need to leave her death alone," he says. "There is nothing but darkness there, no reason to dwell on it."

Maybe he is right. But maybe her life wasn't always so dark. And silence was part of the problem.

I READ ONCE that death rends the world in two. There is a world before and a world after, and you can never go back to that innocent world again, where things are stable and people are permanent.

When my mother died, I thought I would respond with a magnificent display of grief, but I didn't. Stepping into the new, gray world where people left and never came back felt as if it were happening to someone else. The phone rang and I heard my sister-in-law's voice begin to say something and falter. The words "your mother is gone" seemed to have traveled a long way only to become incomprehensible. Detached from the significance of the words, I turned the information over in my head, the same way I might consider the position of Venus. There was the fact of its existence, a pinprick of light. The pinprick was related to me somehow, but not clearly so.

"There was a fire."

This second bit of information is strange too, but abstract and irrelevant. Like the heat and density of the sister planet, I simply can't conceive of it, and so I don't. The distance between me and the tiny voice on the other end of the line stretches until it occurs to me that I should ask questions—measured, rational questions, like "When did it happen?" and "How do you know?" Something tells me that I should probably be feeling something huge and unwieldy, but the calm, rational person who answered the phone takes the call as if it were part of a consumer survey. "Ms. Turner, can you rate the quality of the service you received on a scale from one to ten?" "Oh, a ten," says the even voice on the line. Definitely a ten.

I nod thoughtfully, *well, these things happen,* but beyond that I'm at a complete loss. My husband will get home from work in a couple of hours, and I suppose I'll tell him about it then. I've still got boxes to fill for the garage sale, after all. But I am running low on boxes, and suddenly I feel so tired. It occurs to me that maybe I should take a break, or possibly a shower. But the kitchen is in chaos, and the junk drawer needs sorting. And I'm still on the phone. But with nothing to say. It does not occur to me that the appropriate response is "We'll be right there."

I pause, holding the phone in a sweaty grip, trying to think of the right way to end the conversation. I want to say something thoughtful that will acknowledge the pain in the uneven voice on the other end of the line and the enormous courage it must have taken to call. But it's so hard to think, and she's so far away. Finally, I stammer the only thing that seems real to me: "I love you, Jeanne." And then I hang up.

After I put down the receiver, everything feels heavy. The silence, the space between the cupboards and the bar, my arms and legs. All of the air in the house has become thick and hard to move through, like a dream where I need to run but my legs refuse to budge. I make my way into the living room where I decide to sit and wait—for what, I'm not sure. Outside, spring has finally arrived in our frigid little corner of northern Utah. The valley bathes in green, and jagged limestone mountains jut skyward, still capped in white. But it is not beautiful. The air is too blue, too hot, too blinding against the mountain peaks. And it's so hard to breathe. Finally, I call my husband, who surprises me with his ability to know just what to do. Before I know it, he is home, pulling me into his broad chest, ready to take me to the Ogden sheriff's station, fifty miles away, where my family is waiting.

HALFWAY THROUGH THE MOUNTAIN PASS, a cluster of cars with flashing hazard lights blocks all four lanes of highway, and our progress grinds to a halt. The implication of the scattered cars comes to me slowly, as if trickling down through a morphine haze. Someone has veered into incoming traffic, forcing cars on both sides of the road to divert. A crumpled car sits askew in the median next to a dented white pickup, which faces diagonally into traffic as if confused. A lumpy figure lies on the shoulder of our lane. All of my senses are muted. There is no sound as far as I can tell, no wail or flash of emergency vehicles, just a few people standing near the crumpled cars, pressing at cell phones urgently. One of them picks up a thin, mangled bicycle wheel and carries it toward the figure by the roadside.

The tragedy is shocking and immediate, and yet it seems as distant as the fire. A woman bursts from the car in front of us and runs toward the figure on the side of the road. Kneeling, she pulls back a plaid blanket, crosses her hands on the lumpy form, and presses hard. At regular intervals, she leans in as if she might bring the figure to life with a kiss. She works the chest some more, pressing, waiting, pressing again. Sirens wail up and EMTs surround the body. One bends toward the woman, whose shoulders have begun to sag. The man takes her place, pumping, waiting, pumping, while the woman looks down, disheveled. A gurney appears, and two men shift the body onto it, shroud it in a white sheet, and lift it into a waiting ambulance. Later, we learn that three people died in the wreck: a young mother, her twelve-day-old baby, and a man who had been training for a bicycle race. For the time being, all we know is that the canyon is closed.

By the time we backtrack around the mountains to the sheriff's office in Ogden, my family has been briefed, interrogated, and, without their knowledge, digitally recorded. In front of the station, a dark-haired KSL news anchor speaks earnestly into a camera, and I make a mental note to hit her if she asks me anything.

Inside the building, my father, brothers, and sister wrap up a conversation around a small conference table, presided over by a burly officer.

My father looks blankly at the center of the table, his face white. "She had been acting strangely for months, maybe longer," he says. "I should have known."

WE ARRIVE at the house to find a crime scene. Yellow tape maps a wide perimeter. Armed police officers guard the front entrance. I stay close to my sister, Michelle, threading my arm through hers, and survey the structure, at least twice the size of any other home in the neighborhood. From where we stand, it's impossible to tell how extensive the damage might be. A broken upstairs window gapes like an open mouth, its teeth broken, and the slightest hint of black surrounds the opening. A few shards of smoky glass surround our feet, but otherwise everything looks normal. Looking at the high pink stucco, I imagine one or two darkened rooms. Beyond that, my imagination fails completely.

Shadows deepen on the front lawn as the sun settles below a sea of rooftops. In the fading light, I spot a small red plastic wreath and an unsteady potted plant, ready to topple in the uncut grass between the hedges. "That's where they tried to revive her," Michelle whispers. "The EMTs. The neighbors left the flowers."

I mark the distance from the door to the small shrine, imagine men struggling down the broad cement steps with a figure swathed in a bedspread cocoon. The scene in the canyon provides the rest of the details. A kneeling figure, a crumpled body, a rhythmic thumping. One and two and three and four and five. Two breaths. One and two and three and four and five. Check pulse. A pause, a shrug, a waiting ambulance.

A voice shatters the scene. "Are you the family?" The word "the" spills into the air, as if the referent might be the house. One of the officers has emerged from the shadows to talk to us, and I am relieved to hear my father answer him. "Yes," he says, steadying himself and stepping forward. "I'm the husband."

The man nods. "We can't let you go into the house until the investigation is complete. Until then, we will have a twenty-four-hour patrol in place."

We ask how long the investigation will take, but he doesn't know. Two or three days, maybe a week. We are welcome to stand in the driveway as long as we like, he says, but it's as far as we can go.

PIECED TOGETHER, the story goes something like this:

Just after 11:00 AM, a passing motorist notices smoke coming from an air-conditioning unit in an upstairs window of my mother's house. He flips a U-turn, calls 911, and runs to a neighboring house to ask for help.

The neighbor calls my mother's phone. When no one answers, she runs around the house trying to find an open door or window. Unable to get in, she pulls a garden hose toward the home and tries to spray the smoking window. When police arrive, she tells them that my mother has antiques, an elevator, "a white poodle old dog," and a beautiful singing voice in church.

Units from the Roy City and Weber County fire departments appear minutes behind the police. A cloud of thick black smoke spills from the house as firefighters break down the front door.

Four men climb the stairs toward the source of the heat, where flames crawl along the hallway. The men put out the fire and find more flames in a gutted-out bathroom. They extinguish those and search the adjoining bedroom with a flashlight.

In the darkness, the men make out the shape of a woman lying on her back in bed. The men pick her up and hobble down the stairs in the dark, putting her down twice to get a better hold. At the front door, they realize that they have inadvertently grabbed a blanket that keeps slipping. The men wrap the blanket around the woman and use it to carry her down the cement steps.

A driver for Weber Fire spots the men struggling with the blanket and runs to help move the figure onto the front lawn. He checks for a carotid pulse, inserts an oral airway, and gives respirations and administers CPR while other rescue workers apply an automated external defibrillator and monitor for a pulse. After ten minutes, he confirms that she is dead.

Two police officers arrive at Thiokol to relay the news to my father and take him to the police station. As soon as my father spots his supervisor in the hallway, he says, "It's my wife, isn't it." It isn't a question.

As firefighters remove the last hose and ventilation fan, one of them notices a small blue zippered purse on the front steps. Thinking it might be a medical pack belonging to one of the other units, he picks it up before noticing the charring around the edges. Unable to tell where the bag came from, he shows it to a Weber County deputy who orders him to put it back where he found it.

Crime scene investigators wait until the last of the fire trucks leaves. They photograph the contents of the bag, order a search warrant, send for an arson dog, and secure the house.

No one tells us about the small zippered purse.

No one tells us about the money or jewelry.

No one tells us about the note.

T W O

The Smallest Key

Still numb from the news of the fire, I wander around Dillard's look-ing for something to wear to the viewing. It's been at least three years since I've worn a dress, much longer since I attended church. A "jack Mormon," I'm not sure if women still have to wear panty hose in the chapel. Being a jack Mormon in Utah is sort of like being a jackalope—a hybrid nuisance in a place where people shoot jackrabbits and taxidermy them, adding a set of tiny antelope horns.

Like my mother, I grew up in Tremonton, Utah, a dusty agricultural town north of Salt Lake, the last stop westward before the marshes of the Bear River Basin succumb to the parched hills of Promontory, where men in felt hats and linen waistcoats once raised glasses to the Meeting of the Rails. There were people who stayed put and people who didn't, right things and wrong things. You were Mormon or you weren't. Seasons consisted of summer and winter, with some sleight of hand in between. Without meaning to, I ended up staying—not in Tremonton, but close enough to hit it with a high-powered rifle—but became an outsider all the same.

As my non-church attendance made my mother mopey, I try not to think about it as I thumb price tags and fabrics in the department store. As I move between clothing racks, my reflection winks in and out of the tall mirrored columns. I am wearing the same attire I've worn for years: titanium vest, stone-washed jeans, and a long-sleeved green cotton top, which I switch with equally dull cotton tops. Unstyled since the fire, my short hair hangs limp under a gold corduroy derby my sons have dubbed my "potato chip hat," an accessory that allows me to neglect my hair whenever I'm running low on time and give-a-shits.

8

I can't say what I'm running low on as I walk around the store, caring and not caring about what I buy. My unimaginative wardrobe is partly a product of graduate school, which has usurped any funds I might squander on fashion, but I also just don't enjoy shopping like I used to. Once I felt my faith starting to slide, I hungered for new experiences. I got a pilot's license and traded Sunday school lessons for writing seminars. Preoccupied with wind and words, I started looking like I'd been held hostage in a Patagonia warehouse.

The department store makes the world feel safer since the fire. There are the usual distractions: bone-white mannequins and loud prints, glass-topped cases and clustered accessories, colognes and miracle creams. While I don't feel much like buying a dress I will never wear again, it is my mother's farewell, her viewing and funeral. And I owe her a proper appearance, if nothing else.

Holding a black skirt, I pause next to the nylons wondering if I can make myself put them on. Disembodied legs kick gleefully across rows of crisp packaging, and I feel suddenly dizzy. For a wild moment, I think I might fall down or throw up. I don't know if it's the severed torsos or the suggestion of my mother's legs and abdomen, ensconced in nylon and spandex, but I feel as if my own legs might give way.

Desperate, I cast around for a chair, but there's nowhere to sit—nothing between the carpet oasis and glittering columns. Reaching for a rack of purses, I rest my head in my hands and wait for the room to stop spinning. From somewhere, Sinatra sings "Fly Me to the Moon," while I breathe, eyes closed, trying to marshal my reserves. Finally, I grab a package of black panty hose, and take it to the register.

At home, I snap on the waist-high stomach-suckers before kicking them off. They only look stupid rising above the black A-line skirt riding low across my hips, and the waistband makes me feel jittery and pinched, like the years I tried to do all the right things without much success. I slip on a jacket over a black sleeveless tank so it won't be obvious that I'm not wearing garments, sink my bare feet into a pair of dusty black slip-ons, and silently apologize. *Sorry, Mom. It's what I've got.*

Downstairs, my husband, Lan, and our two sons are sorting out their own wardrobe issues. God knows where they dredged up the suit for our fifteen-year-old, but it looks as if it belongs to someone twice his size.

Our older son, just sprouting a strip of hair along his jawline, fares better than the rest of us as he recently bought a suit for a school dance. But, like the rest of us, he owns no dress shoes. Lan wears a forest green sports coat I bought for him years ago, which in no way matches the black and gold tie he ended up with after lending the boys his other two. Holding the two ends of our younger son's tie, Lan explains how to tie a full Windsor as if reminding himself how to do it.

In happier moments, I blame Lan for our split with the Church. He had been the first to order a beer at a restaurant, which prompted me to cry all the way home and insist that I drive, since he was bound to be radically impaired. Meanwhile, I'd accepted the waiter's offer of a complimentary brandy as I figured it was only a mouthful. The pattern we established was one in which he forged ahead while I disapproved, largely oblivious to my own rogue inclinations. Now, watching him reworking skewed ties in the kitchen, I feel as if I may split apart with sheer gratitude. The men I love most in the world, preparing to follow me straight into hell.

THE VIEWING is a predictably maudlin cocktail party, minus the drinks. Photographs of our family have materialized on tables in the church hall, haphazardly framed and tinged with smoke. Pretty sure I'm supposed to line up somewhere, I linger near the casket waiting for cues while the boys retreat to a row of pink chairs at the far side of the room.

Incongruous against gauzy curtains, my mother's coffin gleams like a new sports car, lit by the late afternoon sunlight spilling in through the window. Atop its taupe and gold exterior, birds of paradise leap from among purple roses. We are in the Relief Society room, a space normally reserved for Mormon women, but hollowed out to accommodate mourners now. Next to the door, Gordon B. Hinckley's "Proclamation to the World" presides like a Lutheran thesis, urging world citizens to adopt Traditional Family Values, which are what you get if you insert God's injunction to be fruitful and multiply into episodes of *Leave It to Beaver*.

It's an ironic viewing as there's no body to view. Next to the casket, my mother's face beams from a Glamour Shots portrait, brown eyes sparkling from behind bejeweled frames, brunette curls brushing her cheeks. The woman in the portrait is the mother I knew in recent years, modest and mightily devoted to Church principles. And yet I find myself longing for the mother I knew as a teenager: the freethinking physician assistant who simultaneously worried and inspired me. In my favorite photo—which I notice is not at the viewing—a strand of sapphire ostrich feathers hangs low over the neckline of her blue chiffon gown, its tight bodice and full circle skirt showing off her impossibly thin waist. She'd picked out the dress for a school dance when she was fifteen, but I'd never seen her wear it until I was a junior in high school.

I can't remember why she ditched her garments that night—if she was headed to the Utah Woolgrowers Convention in Salt Lake City, where her father was about to be named Sheepman of the Year, or if she'd donned it for a New Year's Eve dance—but I never forgot how she looked. Scandalous and dazzling. The strand of feathers the only thing between her shoulders and God.

As the room fills with mourners, I watch how Michelle works the room, amiably in charge, grasping hands and extending warmth, clad in heels and hose and a calf-length broom skirt. My father is similarly engaged, accepting hugs, alternatively crying and joking with the people who walk through the door.

Trying to channel Michelle's native kindness, I drink in condolences and shake hands. I ask after cousins, careers, and golf. But the whole thing feels as if my siblings and I have wandered into the same bad dream. We nod at introductions, hug people we don't know, listen to people tell a story that makes sense to them: our mother's passing was a blessing for someone in so much pain.

But as the evening wears on I feel increasingly annoyed by the script. I don't believe the fire was a blessing. I don't feel reassured. I am deeply confused by the details and not a little pissed off. And I am sick of people who can't seem to tell the difference between my mother and me.

"You two were always so much alike."

And very different.

"You are just like your mother!"

You have no idea who I am.

"Isn't it comforting to know that we have the Plan of Salvation to help us through times like this?"

Not really, no.

As the crowd thins, a woman breaks from a conversation with my mother's sister, Cherre, to grasp both of my hands. About my age, thin and freckled with straight shoulder-length red hair, she seems vaguely hippyish, even though it's clear that she fits among the other women in midcalf skirts with shirts worn under dresses that would otherwise be sleeveless. While other people regard me with long faces, she practically bubbles over with joy.

"I'm Andrea," she says, warming my hands in hers.

I pull my hands away, not caring if she senses my resentment. The woman had been my mother's psychologist, and a woo-woo one at that, practicing some kind of bullshit energy medicine that involved peering into the spirit realms. My mother had always been a little put out with reality, and her fantasies flourished in response to the woman's treatment.

Determined not to indulge her cheeriness, I offer a dry, "Hello," trying to be civil.

"You must be the daughter who flies!" she says, smiling, her yin-yang earrings bobbing up and down with excitement. "I could always sense such a strong connection between you two. I knew your mother so well!"

I stifle the urge to slap her.

I hardly knew her at all.

MORNINGS AFTER THE FUNERAL all start the same. I wake with a start as news of the fire unravels the thin seam of dreaming. People say that my mother is *gone,* which seems qualitatively different from being *dead.* At the service we mourned a box—who knew what was inside it? Like the quiet assurances of the spirit world, we took her gone-ness as reality, although we had no evidence of it aside from the police line still strung around her home like morbid crepe paper.

Squinting at the clock, I mark the time, 6:15. Next to me, Lan rests on his back, his chest rising and falling in the dim light, graying temples marking our two decades together. Our marriage has been like Florida: marked by sudden squalls, but mostly temperate in recent years. Trying not to wake him, I slip out of bed, pull on a ratty striped bathrobe, and head downstairs. Outside, the Bear River Range, formed from Cretaceous upheaval and flecked with sage and canyon maple, casts a dull shadow against a slivered sunrise.

Were I to mark the places I know best on a map, they would form a crude parallelogram: my childhood home in Tremonton twenty-six miles to the west of our home, my mother's house in Roy an hour's drive to the south, my grandfather's ranch at Monte Cristo, an easterly ride into the pines, and the place we live now, Providence, Utah, God's country. An oasis of grass and willow, sandwiched between Logan and Paradise.

Bypassing half-filled boxes that never made it to the garage sale, I snug up my bathrobe and slide up to the sink to make coffee. I discovered the magic beans in my thirties, about the same time I discovered the magic grapes that made wine.

I knew my mother disapproved, but she never really confronted me about it, unless it was to point out that the coffee I drank had much more caffeine than, say, the TaB she had enjoyed since I was a toddler and used to buy by the cartload.

Our quibbles about sanctioned and nonsanctioned beverages were silly, and they drove an unnecessary wedge between us. But coffee was the least of our problems. I did not lose my mother the day rescuers failed to revive her, but in a thousand other ways that built up over time. By the time I sat at her funeral, I wasn't sure who I was mourning or if I was mourning at all. I had spent most of my life trying to win her approval. When it became clear to me that I was not going to get it, I bought a small airplane with a student loan and lit out for a doctoral program in Reno, Nevada. For the last three years, Lan and the boys had fended for themselves while I flew back and forth, taught literature, and finished my coursework. If she was impressed, fine; if she wasn't, fine; but I was finally going to do something big. Something adventurous and relevant. But then she was suddenly *gone,* and I'd barely passed my comprehensive exams.

Standing at the window as the coffee machine bubbles and pops, I survey the backyard, wondering offhandedly if I ought to till the garden. Aside from a row of brave garlic and a raspberry patch that is still a fortress of brown sticks, nothing appears to be growing except for the bright patches where the dandelions will soon be sporting yellow beads.

From what I understand, I am grieving. There are supposed to be stages. Denial and anger and a few more I do not recall. The stage I am in doesn't feel like a stage at all, but an extended pause, between the past and the present; between the person I was before and the one I am now. The only emotion left to me is irritation. For the Church and its countless silly rules, for my mother and her cracked-up family, for the weird and myriad excesses and excuses that convinced me that she did not care about me.

The irritation I feel is safe and reassuring, as familiar to me as the sour smell of sheep or the lines on my palms. I can hardly remember a time when irritation did not wink into my consciousness, embedded, it seemed, in my genetic code. It was one of the things my mother and I had in common. We did not cry. We gritted our teeth and threw dishes. At least *I* threw dishes. Now that she is *gone,* I am grateful for the irritability that comes to my aid, the resentment that keeps me from the one thing I cannot bear, which is my regret. Regret that I did not pay more attention to what was happening to her; regret that we never had a close relationship; regret that I stopped trying. Regret that I did not see a rotten end coming.

My mother's funeral, after all, was not the first time we had mourned a box. Deaths were so bizarre and violent in her family that hers seemed downright dull in comparison. None of us saw the body of her brother, Johnnie, after the .45 slug carved a path through his chest. We did not see her brother Monte after a bullet from a .38 entered his skull, nor the body of Monte's wife, who died next to him with gunshot wounds to her chest. Four years ago, I had been thinking about my uncles and made a bold prediction in my journal: "Endless fighting, chronic illness, yawning depression and violent death haunt the family, and when my mother dies she will be the fourth to do so prematurely."

Kicked out by my subconscious before I'd had a chance to censor it, the sentence stayed scrawled on the page, where it embarrassed me. Where I grew up, you didn't mention "yawning depression," unless you wanted to be laughed out of town. The same thing went for violent death. People died—that's the way it was. With guns, maybe, and you shut the hell up about it, too. My mother used to accuse me of being an overly emotional girl with a flair for the dramatic, and so the sentence's parallel clauses and ominous prediction had made me wince, even though all of it was true. And even though my therapist had thrown up her hands at my battered intuition ("For god's sake, trust yourself!"),

I bracketed my assertions with a neurotic backpedal: "Maybe I'm just being melodramatic."

The extended pause in which I wait for the coffee to brew and consider the barren garden is one in which my mother's heartache winks like a star I can't see. Her illnesses and untimely death are part of my inheritance. But my stunted intuition whispers that I've inherited more than I know: that her brothers were not just violent, but perilously sad, that my own edginess and self-doubt have something to do with their sadness, and that there was more to my mother's pain than the ragged complaining of nerve endings. And I feel like I need some time. Not just to mourn, but to sort out what on earth I've inherited.

EVERYONE INHERITS SOMETHING. I, for instance, used to inherit Michelle's clothes, which I'm pretty sure she inherited from somebody else, since my mother was as thrifty as she was poor when we were little. Lace, if there was any to be had, sprang tired and limp from well-worn dresses, and I got used to the telltale bulletproof squares on my knees that indicated where my mother had ironed on patches, which did not bend when you ran, and held fast even as the rest of the fabric steadily disintegrated.

The things you inherit are products of place and time and social class and culture. Like the cutoff jeans I used to wear to float fat inner tubes down the canal, which were not Daisy Dukes but more like capris, cut down past the knee and rolled twice, because we took modesty seriously. Few things horrified our god-fearing community more than the bra-less, halter-top-wearing women we saw on TV. My mother sewed our clothes and mended them and got what she could for free in an attempt to make us look fashionable. In my second-grade photo, I am wearing a stifling double-knit polyester dress with a wide, erect collar that looks as if I might attach an astronaut helmet if I so desired. Brown and gold parabolas burst between orange flowers, starbursts, and dots, framed by gold suspenders sewn into the dress, and I grin, teeth askew, sporting a dutifully ratted bouffant, bangs cut blunt across my forehead. My look betrays the whims of an era, but it is also reveals a certain amount of care and creativity and resourcefulness. And genetics. Like my mother, I have dark brown eyes, fine brown hair, and olive skin, but I do not have her long braids or wool skirts or black patent shoes and ankle socks, because those were products of another time.

If you look closely, you will notice that the things you inherit suggest specific values. Take the sheep camp that resides in our barn. A cross between a covered wagon and a camper, the wagon had sheltered my grandpa Chournos as an impoverished Greek immigrant. It marked his change in fortune, rescued him from the copper smelter and railroad. It symbolized frugality and independence and a certain braving of elements. It bequeathed the romance of the early West, the promise of prosperity in the New World. It spoke of my grandfather's character: sparing and practical and gruff. What you saw was what you got. The rubber wheels weren't *pretty;* they were more functional than the wooden wheels. The story that seeps through its oak bows, thin mattress, and tiny cookstove is one of rugged self-sufficiency, working hard and working alone, the hard-won promise of board and bread.

You don't have to be given a thing directly to have inherited it all the same. Like my grandfather, I own sheep. Not ten thousand, thank god. But when Providence City threatened use-'em-or-lose-'em animal rights, I figured we better put something on the acre plot behind our house and sheep were the obvious choice. And so, as the fields behind our house turn into tidy subdivisions, our tiny herd remains, where families with young children can stand on newly polished redwood decks and watch our sheep fornicate.

Trickier to spot than the things you inherit are the ideas you inherit. Ideas that determine what is normal, what is right and what is wrong. Like coffee. Whether it is a morning beverage or a moral sin all depends on the context. And this context won't feel like a context at all, but reality. The sheer invisibility of an idea's strangeness is how you know you own it completely. Witness my confusion when I first started visiting non-LDS churches: for example, those crazy Episcopals, swinging balls of incense and wearing crosses, dudes strutting around in dresses, ha ha. Because *Mormonism* was so normal. It did not matter how quirky my own inherited beliefs were, or if they were incompatible with a hundred other beliefs, because they were so powerfully true.

The things you inherit—the ones you will fight over—may not be expensive, but they will always have stories attached. So far, I have inherited my grandma Chournos's wedding ring, which my mother cajoled from her mother before she died so her sister Cherre wouldn't get it. The ring had not been the first my grandmother owned, but it had been the most elaborate: three fat diamonds set between garnets in white gold. My grandmother bought the ring for herself, since my grandfather didn't buy gifts. For him, it was enough to give her fat rolls of cash and permission to buy something nice. And so it was hard to say if the ring was a symbol of love or neglect.

Like the stories on which they are built, legacies are never trouble-free. Some are more harmful than others, and it takes a strong stomach to look one squarely in the eye. Coming into my mother's legacy feels like inheriting the keys to Bluebeard's castle, where I am welcome to use all of the keys except one. If I want to, I can spend all day opening doors, letting the light fill the musty rooms filled with riches, fine jewelry, and textiles. I can fling the windows open wide from the balconies, gawk at the vast, rolling property, and gasp to think that everything I see is mine. But I will be constantly aware of the smallest key, the one I have been forbidden to use, and I will turn it over and over again in my hand, wondering where it leads, and I will become bored with the things in the other rooms, and I will not be able to stop snooping until I come to the tiny door that leads to bones and blood and bits of hair.

THREE

Jar of Hearts

T ight-lipped and professional, investigators gather the last of the crime scene tape and leave my father to his ruined home. He can, they say, expect a full report in a month or two. Heaven knows what it must have felt like to be him at that moment—to have your life turned back to you so disastrously, to be so suddenly and starkly alone. But I have an image of him standing on the wide front steps looking sort of bereft, holding a cell phone and wad of keys, worrying about what the police might have found, preparing to call his children and tell them it's time to come home.

Within the hour, I arrive at the house with Michelle and my brothers. Our father arms us with flashlights. "The investigators wanted me to tell you that the heat in the bedroom was upward of eight hundred degrees. A few more minutes and it would have exploded. Don't plan on saving anything from up there."

I nod stalwartly and step into the doorway, struck by the safeguards my imagination had so far provided. I had expected a darkened bedroom; I had not expected a fully blackened *house,* infiltrated by the systemic ways of smoke. It is as if the home were a giant lung that had inhaled a lifetime of tar and lead and benzene and butane; a failed organ in which dioxinlike compounds bathed everything in carcinogenic black grease, blasting the brightly papered walls, reducing every starry thing my mother ever loved to sooty obscurity.

Inside the house, my feelings abandon me. Anything tender or sorry or sad retreats before the long slender beam of my flashlight, is held at bay by the acrid punch of melted plastics and spent glues, by the rolled molding carpets, still bleeding from the blast of the fire hoses. Shocked by the sensory overload, I muster professional detachment of the sort my mother had championed as a physician assistant. She did not flinch when my brother, Nick, showed up at her office after a motorcycle accident with his skull poking out. Hell, she'd once made him wait until she was done cooking Sunday dinner before she sutured his hand, sliced to the bone by a slippery transmission. I never once saw her get nervous or teary or grossed out over something like a little blood and bone. Life was oozy and gruesome sometimes, and you didn't get worked up about it. So I don't. I scan the house as indifferently as I can, surprised that I seem to be doing ok.

Taking the winding staircase next to the door, my father leads us through the vaulted upstairs living room, stopping at the door of the museumlike room that my mother had decorated to celebrate her love of medicine. "Well," he says. "You can see what happened to all of her stuff."

If I hadn't seen the room without the soot, I would have thought some deranged soul had put it there for sheer horrific effect. A cross between an old-fashioned doctor's office and a laboratory, the room boasts an antique examination table and wheelchair, a full-sized skeleton flanked by a chorus of skulls, hundreds of vials, and shelves of anatomical models. All dusted with black, and creepy as hell.

Something races around my chest at the sight of the stethoscopes and anatomical models, threatening to undo my trusty detachment. If I ever felt close to my mother, it had been during her Medex training, so thrilled was she to show me how to shoot up a grapefruit or explain the oxygenation of blood. At one point, she had put two lamb hearts in a quart-sized Mason jar, filled it with formaldehyde, and sealed the lid. I couldn't think of a thing in our house that was more wondrous. I traced the blood's journey from vena cava to ventrical and took the jar to Show and Tell, pleased to show my third-grade classmates that the heart—a real heart—wasn't anything like the tidy symmetrical hearts we cut out of construction paper and glued to our desks. A real heart was creased and lopsided and brownish, not as dark as the liver or as smooth. A real heart was homely and shot through with holes. A real heart was not soft and sweet, but rubbery and steadfast and tough. Like my mother. Like me.

What I took from my mother's medical training was that the body was made up of organs that all did their jobs more or less independently as they took directions from the brain. And if I knew anything, it was that the brain was in charge of the heart and not the other way around.

Amid the blackened vials, forceps, and bones, the Visible Woman stands guard next to the Visible Man, the Barbie and Ken of internal beauty with wide popping eyeballs. I learned about the human body as my mother took the Visible Woman apart and reassembled her, explaining the role of each organ. No matter how I tried, I never managed to put the model back together successfully, not once. Looking at her now, I still don't think I could reassemble her. And I certainly can't reassemble my mother, not metaphorically, not hypothetically, not imaginatively, not at all.

My father continues down the hallway, stopping to show us each room as if he were a guide on a twisted tour. Dutifully poking my head into each one, I am almost glad to see the ruined objects. If anything had come between my mother and me, it had been her abominable home, filled to the gills with anything she deemed "clever!" "fun!" or "special," which was just about everything she saw.

My mother's wild acquisitions were enabled by windfalls from her father's estate. I didn't really care that she spent her inheritance recklessly— it wasn't mine, after all. What I minded was the fanaticism with which she clung to her things, as if the symbols of certain ideals were imbued with the ideals themselves: as if the painting of Joan of Arc lent you bravery, or the huge inlaid globe made you well traveled, or the eight-foot painting of Jesus Christ made you pious. The weepiness with which she regarded her Lenox Rose china, the veneration of anything that remotely suggested her upbringing, all of it, drove me up a tree. If she had ever looked at my children or me with such affection, I could not recall it. If she looked at us at *all,* I might have forgiven her. But she hadn't, and I hadn't.

I hadn't always hated the home. I'd moved away by the time my parents bought it and barely gave it a passing thought. But the longer my parents lived in it, the more I detected something wrong about it. It wasn't the structure itself, or the small fortune invested in its furnishings. It was the weird synergy between my mother and the home, as if she wasn't sure where she left off and the structure began.

Then there had been the tipping point when my mother just seemed to flip out. Refusing to be happy until the home was larger, she begged my father to double its size. One kitchen turned into two, three living rooms turned into four. An elevator appeared like a wide central artery. Her bedroom, which boasted a small bathroom, sprouted another, morphing into a pillared suite that resembled a Greco-Roman bathhouse. The crawl space above her bedroom bloomed into a loft; the southern edge of the home moved farther south; the western walls moved farther west. The small formal sitting room gave birth to a towering annex, graced by a ten-foot stained glass angel. Formerly nondescript bedrooms became theme rooms: the Egyptian room with its seven-foot sarcophagus, the Victorian dressing room that might have been lifted from the set of *Phantom of the Opera,* the fifties room with its soda fountain and jukebox, the princess room with its virginal canopy, rococo wardrobe, and more white lace knitting than I cared to think about.

Pausing in the hallway next to my mother's bedroom, my siblings and I take stock of each other. We have touched nothing, and yet our clothes and faces bear dark smudges. Our shoes, black now, are beyond cleaning. Michelle seems small and delicate, my brothers, young, as if they've become the two small boys in mustard-colored shirts elbowing each other in a studio portrait. But although we feel small, we also feel old, aged by grief in this world that is hungry and dark.

Glasses smudged and askew, clothes dappled with black, my father looks like a little kid just ambushed on the playground by a herd of bullies. "I don't know," he says. "But there's got to be an envelope around here with some money in it. Seven or eight thousand dollars. I've checked the safe, but it's not there. Your mother begged me to take it out of my retirement. She said she just couldn't go on without some pocket money."

That she needed *thousands* of dollars for "pocket money" doesn't surprise me—things always got extreme where she was concerned. But finding the money in the charred chaos seems like a lost cause.

"I found a credit card receipt from Macy's, totaling about four thousand dollars. I can't tell you what it was for. Anyway . . ."

He takes a breath and nods at silvery wallpaper, charred and peeling around a brightly framed painting of a lion protecting a lamb. "This is where the flames started coming down the hallway. I was so afraid that it might have been my wiring, but the police said it probably started in the old part of the house. Over here."

We follow him into our mother's bedroom, where he points to a small adjoining bathroom, reduced to a charred hole. "Or here," he says, pointing to the nightstand where a tall black V has chewed through the wallpaper. Then he nods to the bed. "That's where they found her."

Standing in the black hole, a dull ache spreads through my body. The bed is the hardest to face, not because of the soot, which we have become accustomed to, but because it features the only place untouched by soot—the one bright space where our mother had been.

Holding onto each other, we stand in silence. There is nothing to do but bear witness. No words to say. None. And for my part, no feelings. It is as if I have gone to a place that is beyond crying, a place where I have become too weathered and worn and grownup for such things. And if there is a part of my body that manufactures tears, I can't say what it is.

MY MOTHER HAD BEEN SICK. How long, I did not know. Had it been a few years? Longer than a decade? Her first memory had been one of searing pain. No one knew why the little girl was screaming, or why her temperature had skyrocketed. Her mother had rushed her to the hospital, where the family doctor diagnosed a brain abscess, shot the three-year-old through with antibiotics, and quietly explained that the disease was almost always fatal. Her mother spent three days at her side in a prayerful bedside vigil before her fever broke. The story was one that got told and retold in our home, as it reaffirmed our faith in God and modern medicine. What one couldn't cure, the other one would.

And then it seemed as if God and medicine failed her simultaneously. No one could say when it happened, exactly—when we were in college?—but it was as if she'd struck some horrible Faustian bargain. She developed every illness you could think of and no identifiable illness at all. She hurt everywhere, all of the time, day after day. Doctors looked at her, shrugged, and sent her home with a slip from a white prescription pad. When someone finally labeled her condition fibromyalgia, she was practically jubilant, since she had the dignity of an actual condition.

The diagnosis told us everything and nothing. Her pain had no obvious source, and without a source there was no way to treat it. The most she could do was chase symptoms, which were so quirky and widespread that it was hard to know where to begin. The research on the syndrome did little for her besides populate a list of possible concomitant conditions: sleep disorders, trauma, cervical abnormalities, stress, infection. No one could even say for sure if the pain was physiological or psychological, since there seemed to be components of both. It was as if the brain had turned tyrant, manufacturing pain just to punish the system, picking up false cues from a peripheral nervous system that had gone haywire, the body at war with itself.

BUT IF HER BODY WAS AT WAR WITH ITSELF, her mind and heart seemed utterly unified, especially when it came to her career. Closing my eyes, I try to picture my mother when she was happiest. Days she collected bright stethoscopes in every color, pairing them with shoes, blouses, nail polish. Nights she came home trailing Moonwind perfume, kicking off peacock or rose-colored pumps, her hair pinned with silk flowers, to declare that it just wasn't right for a person to get *paid* for having such fun.

When I was little, I felt nothing but pride for my mother. She had been a nurse and was going to be something like a doctor. At the same time, I could hardly miss the veiled disapproval. It wasn't just my father's mother, who found flaws in her housekeeping, or his brother, Earl, who told my father, "If you let her go up to that university, you will lose her." It was also my best friend Kim's mother, who glanced up from a recipe with a strangely cocked eyebrow to ask me who did the cooking at our house. And, there was Mormon Church president Spencer W. Kimball, who called upon women to quit their jobs: "Come home from the typewriter, the laundry, the nursing. . . . Come home, wives, to your husbands. Make home a heaven for them."

It wasn't until my freshman year in high school that I realized I might have to choose between allegiances. We were studying Church history in seminary that year, and I was thrilled to be the same age Joseph Smith had been when God the Father and Jesus the Christ first appeared to him, thus heralding his role of prophet for the Restored Church.

Brother Anderson read the account of the vision and paused to see if we'd been paying attention.

"What," he asked, "is the meaning of the story?"

When no one said anything, he reread the ending, channeling the Prophet's words. "When the light had departed, I had no strength; but soon recovering in some degree, I went home. And as I leaned up to the fireplace, mother inquired what the matter was. I replied, 'Never mind, all is well—I am well enough off.' I then said to my mother, 'I have learned for myself that Presbyterianism is not true.'"

What, he repeated, was the message?

I raised my hand and said something about God answering prayers of the faithful. That Presbyterianism wasn't true seemed a little too obvious. "No," he said, shaking his head. What mattered most was that the Prophet's mother was *home*, waiting to give support to her son who was about to become the prophet of the Restored Church.

Without meaning to, I snorted loudly. It was the most ridiculous thing I'd ever heard. Whether or not the Prophet's mother was *home* had nothing to do with the fact that God Himself had just arrived. I waited for my classmates to snicker as well, but the room went icy and still.

Brother Anderson assumed his most pious tone. "Mocking the words of God's anointed has always been a sign of wickedness and pride. The righteous have always been ridiculed. You should think twice about which side your laughter puts you—with the faithful, or against them."

I OPEN MY EYES and the nightmarish bedroom comes back into view. If my mother second-guessed herself, I hadn't known it. When I told her about the incident with Brother Anderson, she shrugged it off. Some people just weren't all that enlightened. But I had felt sick and confused. If Brother Anderson was right, then my mother was an abomination. If my mother was right, then the Prophet was wrong, which made things feel shaky, indeed.

The funny thing was that our house *had* felt like a heaven when we were little. Under our mother's tutelage, the once-a-week family meetings advocated by Church leaders took on a new flair. Lessons on prayer and obedience morphed into lectures on germs and viruses. Once, she brought home a placenta, still warm from the looks of it, to explain the biological changes that occurred during pregnancy. I didn't look at Michelle, who was certainly blue with unease, or my brothers, who must have wished themselves invisible as they gazed at the bloody mass in the cake pan, but I thanked her wordlessly and made a silent vow never to have children.

Standing at the foot of my mother's bed, I can't imagine how someone so strong and smart when it came to the body could sleep through her own asphyxiation. Next to me, Michelle and my brothers stand silently mired in their own thoughts. I'm not sure any of us had a decent relationship with our mother once she moved to Roy, where her house of finery and pain supplanted the joyous unkempt home of our childhood.

Following our father up the stairs to the loft, I brace myself for what had been the hottest room in the house. If my mother bewailed anything about her life, it was only to say that she'd been lonely as a child. Isolated from others by the sheer remoteness of the mountain ranch and four years younger than her closest sibling, she grew up in a starkly divided world. There was the home in Tremonton and the cabin on the mountain, the work of men and the work of women, the Church and the Outfit. All meticulously ordered and compartmentalized.

My mother's version of her childhood changed with her mood. Sometimes she waxed nostalgic about the glories of a ranching life long gone. Other times she seethed about being cut off from the adventures of men, who rose before dawn to saddle horses and ride out onto the range. When she begged to go, she was largely ignored, except by her brother, Johnnie, who insisted it just wasn't right. "Where's a man gonna pee," he'd look at her and drawl, "if a girl comes along?"

Alienated from just about everybody, my mother was free to imagine whatever she pleased. A few colorful scarves made her the Queen of Sheba. A collection of bottles and cans transformed her into a grocery store owner. Once, I'd found a page pulled from a notebook that listed her childhood games, as if she might forget what they were: a stack of books made her a librarian; extra pads of Union Pacific stationery made her a schoolteacher. In spaces behind the swinging doors of the flour bins, in closets and laundry chutes, in the attic and cellar and dirt spaces under the house, my mother invented allies and found friends, manufacturing worlds in which she mattered.

At the top of the stairs, my mother's childhood blooms in gloomy detail. Between the toothy, blown-out black windows, two dressmaker's dummies appear to hold hands, one in a white wedding dress, the other in a Mormon Battalion uniform. Under the low, slanted ceiling, a trunk spills sooty costumes, tiaras, and lace, while a cluster of tiny desks play school by themselves, heaped with 1950s grammar and story books. And everywhere, dolls. Hundreds of them: Stacked on shelves and sitting at tea, playing the tiny organ, waving or standing demurely with vacant eyes, their dresses dark doilies, pink faces melted and darkly deformed.

From behind me, I hear a choked sob and turn to see Michelle cradling a doll our mother had owned as a child. Stroking the soot-covered satin, she dabs at the inky black face, not caring that her pink polo will turn hopelessly black if she does. The doll's face shines a little from under the soot, but the bands holding her body intact are already beginning to snap. Michelle looks at me, her face crestfallen and white.

"She was broken, Neece. She seemed so strong and secure, but she was broken inside. And we didn't know how to help her."

Watching Michelle, I am surprised to see that she has a fully functioning set of emotions. Clutching the doll, she allows her heart to break apart, to mourn, to see the small girl our mother had been, confiding in the doll in lieu of a friend. Unlike Michelle, I feel pressed against something invisible, a barrier that shields my heart, buries it behind glass. My brain accepts the sadness of the scene, but I do not feel its full impact. At the fringes of consciousness, I allow my irritation to smolder, let my anger protect me from the lonely child our mother had been, lurking at the fringes of the Outfit, the little girl arranging dolls and desks, as alone at the end of her life as she had been in the beginning.

FOUR

Angels and Demons

Walking down the steps from the loft, I can't decide which is worse, seeing the house or not seeing the house. I felt as if I needed to face my mother's home head-on, since I would have maintained a haunting image of the bedroom whether I saw it or not. But I could have done without the melted faces of her dolls, the shrine to her childhood destroyed, along with the rest of the sooty artifacts. A person could get too much information.

Which is why I did not put up a fight when the mortician wouldn't open the casket. Michelle had waged an impressive campaign to see our mother one last time, but he had refused. The body, he said, had been too damaged to hold the embalming fluid. I'd already had a fairly disturbing mental image before he'd added the detail, and so I'd asked why he'd bothered to embalm her at all. And he'd shrugged and said "State law."

I had been annoyed by the man's lack of emotion—any gently bobbing feelings of sympathy seemed to have been rolled flat by years of watching people sob—but I was not upset that he refused to show us our mother's body, seeping with chemicals and butchered by the autopsy.

Scanning my mother's bedroom with my flashlight one last time before we go, I am surprised to see a painting of an angel standing guard against a dark wall like an afterthought. The thick, baroque frame bears the telltale smudges of soot, but the image itself, a foil-enhanced Giclée from the looks of it, is curiously soot free in comparison to everything else. All told, the image is almost as tall as me.

"Where'd that come from?" I say, waving the light toward my father. "I've never seen that before."

27

"Oh," he says, turning to me, his voice thick with affection or irritation or both. "I found that under the bed. Your mother knew I'd go tilt if she bought one more painting. But she just couldn't help herself."

I size up the bright bronze halo and golden wings, fitted bodice, and pillowy blue virago sleeves, and exhale. My mother's shop-and-hide pattern had been legendary. Knowing that my father had always been concerned about money, she squirreled things around the house as if he wouldn't notice. And most of the time, he didn't.

Her mother had done the same thing. Married to a man who was as sparing as he was successful, she knew not to expect gifts. In the world in which he lived, you did not buy things to demonstrate your faith or wealth or love. You got what you needed and not one thing more.

But my grandmother needed more. His love, for one. And barring that, nice things would just have to do. While he was alive, she stockpiled clothes and shoes and purses. After he died, she stockpiled volumes of Reader's Digest Condensed Books, magazines, unopened videos, and hopeful mailers from Publishers Clearinghouse. When she died, she left behind her legacy of love and faith, along with thank-you letters from George W. Bush and Newt Gingrich, who showed their appreciation for her donations with glossy autopenned eight-by-tens. She left behind canned fruit from the 1970s and closets full of sheet music and blouses. She did *not* leave behind nearly $600,000 that her accountant could not account for. She left a legacy of trying to help all of the right people. But she also left a sad longing to share in the kind of success her husband had enjoyed. If she couldn't do it with sheep, she would do it in sweepstakes.

My grandmother's gullibility and misguided investments made sense to me. She'd grown up poor and spent sixty-three years pleasing a man who had the money to buy her niceties but never did. Why not spoil yourself a little? Try to make your own fun? Try to be a good American if nothing else?

Unlike my grandmother's periodic splurges, my mother's reckless spending made no sense to me. She grew up in a world of plenty. She had a professional identity and a doting husband. What more could she need?

My mother's spending made my father anxious and moody. Especially as money from my grandfather's estate began to dry up, and my mother maxed out all of the credit cards. The subtly strained question we'd heard all our lives—"But where are we going to *put* it, Helen?"—had ratcheted up in pitch and texture in recent years, so that it sounded more like a man pleading with his wife to *put down the knife* than a request to stop buying Care Bears.

I take a last look at the angel. Eyes closed, body inert, she dangles like an ornament, passively floating above a violet void, brown hair falling to her shoulders, teasing the top of a bejeweled neckline, dreaming or possibly praying above the charred carpet. At the bottom of the frame, a flash of gold from a placard catches the light: *Cecilia.*

"Well," I say finally, looking up from the painting. "I guess it's kind of cool. If you like angels, that is."

He sighs. "She went crazy about angels the last year or so. If something had an angel on it, she had to have it." He shakes his head. "I got so sick of angels."

There's more we might say to each other, but we don't. Distanced by time and competing demands, we've learned to avoid certain questions. Like when and how the tenuous fibers binding our family together began to unravel. He had my mother to contend with; I had my doctoral work. And so it's a little awkward for both of us, thrown together as father and daughter again, unsure how to negotiate this strange place where angels bloom amid the wreckage.

"Well, Dad," I say. "I don't know what else you're going to be able to save, but it looks like Cecilia survived the fire just fine."

BY THE TIME I get home, the last spray of sunset stretches multifingered over the valley. The boys are out with friends; Lan is at a trade show in Las Vegas. My first evening alone since the fire. Worried about leaving, Lan had tried to cancel the trip, but I insisted he go. What was there to do after all but hang around while I moped? He'd already spent thousands of dollars on the event, and it was going to be one stupid night. We'd spent about half of the last three years in separate beds while I flew back and forth to school. The boys would be around, the cat would be underfoot, and I was fine, fine, fine. And glad, actually, to have a little time to myself.

Pouring myself an unapologetically large glass of merlot, I curl up on the couch, trying to decide what to do. I don't read for pleasure anymore, since graduate school turned reading into an ice pick-and-tweezers ordeal. I can't remember the last time I watched television. Looking at the assorted remote controls, I doubt I can figure out how to turn the new system *on*. So I sit on the couch as the room turns dark, waiting for the wine to work its magic.

The angels my mother collected in recent months trouble me, but I can't say why. She had sets of Hindu god plates, for heaven's sake, and at least a hundred Nativity sets—three in which the Holy Family had been represented by pious black bears. And she hid things. So what if the biggest angel I'd ever seen had been lurking under her bed? She bought things because they were clever or beautiful or painfully nostalgic. Her things had to be larger than life, a little more ornamented, a little more outlandish, a little better than normal. Madame Alexander dolls: more expensive than run-of-the-mill drugstore dolls. Petit fours: more decadent than sheet cake. Pendleton skirts and sweaters: finer than regular skirts and sweaters. Ditto for real silver silverware, real crystal, fine china, and all of the multicolored plastic cups shaped to look like the stratosphere.

So, angels. A little bit more than human; a little bit better than human. Beings without faults. Intermediaries between God and human beings. Ministers to humanity, messengers, beings with the power to save you from peril or comfort you in your darkest hours. And, in the Mormon way of looking at things, probably someone you know. Joseph Smith had proclaimed that all angels *had* belonged to the earth or *would* belong to the earth, which meant they had or would be human. Which also meant that my mother could come back to me as an angel or a spirit lingering between realms. And I didn't want to see her either way.

Growing up, I knew that the world was teeming with invisible agents: spirits waiting to receive earthly bodies, spirits of ancestors who had gone before, fallen spirits that would never become flesh, having botched it in the War in Heaven.

I knew about the war in the same way I knew my ABCs, as it was a linchpin of our faith. My favorite version was the one my mother read to us when we were little, George Bickerstaff's *Before I Was Born*, a 1966 picture book in which earthly mothers swept floors in bubble-flip hairdos and scarves, and the line drawings of Michael and Lucifer looked kind of like George Harrison and John Lennon.

The way the war played out, according to Bickerstaff, was that the heavenly hosts squared off in tunics and bare feet behind Lucifer (who would become Satan) or Michael (who would become Jesus), their respective flags flying behind them: "Force" and "Freedom." Lucifer had proposed forcing everyone on earth to behave (which was sort of like communism, if I thought about it), while Michael had argued that human beings should be free to choose between good and evil (though why there was evil to choose from in the first place was never explained). When Lucifer lost, he was cast out of God's presence, along with a full third of the heavenly host. How much power these spirits had was unclear. I only knew that they had been let loose on the earth, where they tempted people to make rotten choices.

Knowing that spirits roamed the earth thrilled and terrified me as a child, and so I lay in bed at night mentally rehearsing how to cast out a bad spirit in case one showed up. In order to determine the nature of an apparition, you had to ask for a handshake. If the spirit declined, it was a good spirit. If the spirit reached out and its hand passed through yours, it was evil. As a fallen spirit would fall for the handshake trick every time, you could raise your right arm to the square in a special ritual gesture that made it look as if you were about to tell the whole truth and nothing but the truth, and command it to leave in the name of God.

My whole worldview depended on the knowledge that God answered prayers, and if that involved showing up in person or sending an angel with a flaming sword or golden plates it meant that you had something special to do. Apparitions did not mean that you were unhinged; they meant you were relevant. Visits from evil spirits weren't particularly desirable, but visions and voices were perfectly normal and patently okay, if not secretly sought after. Which is why I devoted a fairly large chunk of my teenage years to praying for a sign from God that I had a purpose in life. For reasons I could not fathom, the powers of good (or evil for that matter) seemed flatly uninterested in me, and the most I got was my own thoughts bouncing back to me in a silent and solitary inner game of squash.

The reality of the spirit realms meant that the line between a vision and a psychotic episode was sort of up for grabs. I knew all about physical illness, but mental illness was so much speculative fiction. The most solid people in the world heard the still, small voice, bore witness to the legions of angels protecting the temple, wrestled with the powers of evil—figuratively and not so figuratively. And so I was able to dismiss the signs of my mother's crumbling psychological health, which was far more terrifying for me to contemplate than the fact of her aching body.

AS DUSK TURNS TO DARKNESS, questions about my mother's mental universe whiz through my head like a series of wrong numbers or a dinner guest who refuses to drop an irritating conversational thread. How much had her waking world been textured by hallucinations? By spirits bright and terrible beyond my imagination? My own demons had been metaphorical, but my mother's had taken on a local habitation and a name.

My mother did not tell me about her demon or her voices. These details were supplied after the viewing by my father, who shifted awkwardly and exhaled deeply, admitting that he had started to catch our mother midprayer, her arm raised to the square, trying to keep some horrible presence at bay. Too exhausted or protective to say anything, he hadn't told anyone but my brothers, whom he enlisted to help give her blessings. And I might have been irritated that no one asked for my help if I wasn't so glad not to know.

I blame my mother's delusions on Andrea. What bothered me wasn't just that the therapy sessions were so bullshit-weird—a cross between a faith healing and a séance—but how my mother spoke of them as if her life had finally acquired grace and purpose. My mother had always been interested in her "mission in life," a Mormon idea that we had been given a special work to perform on the earth, and in Andrea's care curiosity flowered into full-blown obsession.

In time, I got used to my mother's new fixation on God's purposes, but I never got over the patient-client relationship, which flatly stunk. As sporadic as sun dogs, my mother's attention was nigh impossible to earn. And yet Andrea, whom my mother called her "magic lady," seemed to be becoming her very best friend. The daughter that, perhaps, I was not. A little better than the real thing. A little more intuitive. A little more angel-like.

I did not share my misgivings about Andrea with my mother, since her self-esteem seemed wholly wrapped up in the drivel the woman dished out. And so I shut my mouth and seethed during the wonderfulness mantra: Andrea said that she had been one of God's elite in the pre-existence! Andrea had helped her reconnect with her dead father! Andrea read her body's energy like Braille! Andrea had sensed a bitter male presence, still trapped within her! Andrea said that her powers of intuition and spiritual perception were getting stronger! Andrea said that she had a special mission to fulfill!

And so on.

Andrea could give my mother things I could not, suffused as I was with ordinariness and motherhood and interests that failed to inspire her: dirt and airfoils and (gawd) the *environment*. No matter what I did, I could not reflect back to my mother an image of herself that was splendid enough to make her want to spend time with me. But Andrea. Andrea could. And what was more, Andrea *would*.

The more my mother mused about her mission in life—which became grander with each session—the more I countered by extolling the mundane: the glories of muskrats and carbon and corn. When she invoked the spirit world, I praised the physical world.

By then, I was mostly pissed off, having spent the better part of my life monitoring my behavior for presences unseen. The injunction to keep a journal, for instance, was good enough on its own, but Mormon Church president Spencer W. Kimball insisted it be an inspiration "for the ages"—available "for the angels to look upon." If that wasn't daunting enough, the journal was supposed to supply a rendering of "your true self rather than a picture of you when you are 'made up' for a public performance." As if writing for angels and babies unborn wasn't spectacularly public by definition.

Going to graduate school had been my way of reclaiming my brain, without the meddling gaze of Church authorities or children yet unborn or—dear god—the Heavenly Hosts. By the time my mother's demon showed up, I'd quit listening. And not just any demon, but one bent on destroying her family.

SITTING ALONE ON THE COUCH, I try to suppress images my mind wants to supply of my mother's imaginative world. I doubt she had used the word *demon*. An avowed fan of novelist Dan Brown, my father had supplied the term. Still, *fallen spirit* doesn't make me feel any better. Sizing up my half-full glass of merlot, I'm pretty sure there's not enough alcohol in the house for me to consider what haunted my mother. And there's this: I don't feel much like finishing the wine anyway.

If my mother's days had gotten fuzzy, if the spirit realms bled into her waking world, who knew how terrifying her days had become? Her hallucinations would have been as real as the stacked sugar bowls and barberry hedges. As real to her as me. And what was worse? That some dark presence was winking its way into her consciousness, or that her own mind was turning on itself, producing imagery consistent with the stories we believed? If her imaginative world rattled me, it must have frightened her—and so her obsession with angels might not have been a sign of greed but a gathering of talismans. And the image of her walking through her darkly whimsical home, dreamlike and alone, voices trailing after her, familiar or fiendish or both, is more than I want to think about my first night alone after the fire.

I try to squelch the panic that surges up from my sternum by focusing on the dull realities of the room. The *realities,* damnit: the empty leather wingback and wide, wide front window, flat olive walls and alder wainscot, the reliably straight lines on the gold and green rug. Slowing my breath, I catalog every prosaic detail, refusing to let my mind wander: the worn leather armrests of the tweedy brown couch, all of the familiar trappings of the house we'd fled to in order to save our marriage.

My mother said our house was a gift from God. It was the same logic she used when she talked about her house in Roy: we had been granted a house of healing. By then, Lan and I had been through the marital wringer. He'd fallen in love with another woman years before. I was recently obsessed with a married man. Each of us had an affair. My mother and I had been walking through the pasture at dusk one afternoon, sunlight spilling through her coarse black hair, when she said "The Lord wants you to have this place. You deserve it for all you've been through." And I thought, *God wants unrepentant adulterers to have farmhouses?*

To mend things, Lan and I enlisted the help of a matronly counselor who listened to our stories in turn. When we finished, I cast a sidelong glance at Lan, who looked back at me, perplexed. Then I turned back to the therapist. "He started it."

I meant it to be funny, but she missed the humor and signed us up for more sessions.

Months later, she looked up from her clipboard. "I probably don't need to see you regularly anymore," she said. "If you like, you can come on an as-needed basis from here on out."

Grinning at Lan, I punched him in the arm. "Hey, Honey, we're healed!" I said, emphasizing the word *healed* as if I had just performed a faith healing.

"Except you," she continued. "You need to deal with your mother. Until you do, you're going to be a mess."

The sentence made me feel like I'd just swallowed socks. I searched Lan's eyes: *Was* I a mess? For a moment, it looked as if he might say something before he thought better of it. Then he kissed my cheek, picked up his coat, and left.

RISING FROM THE COUCH, I walk to the living room window and press my forehead to the glass. When we moved in, I removed the latticework so I could paint it, but I never put it back, pleased to see the mountains without having to peer past the quaint crosshatching. Eventually, I removed all of the screens from the home so it buzzed with moths and black flies, depending on the season. I left the doors and windows wide open, swept up seedlings and soil, as if doing so would save me from what was happening to my mother.

The therapy sessions I started that year revealed a girl so desperate for attention that she might have had sex with anyone. During a particularly bleak dark night of the soul, I ripped a wide hole in the screen of the guestroom window, trying to make out the moon more clearly, gasping for air, aching and wild for something my marriage could not supply, knowing even then that the vibrant woman who had been my mother was gone.

As much as I hate to admit it, Andrea was probably my fault. My mother had called to tell me she would be undergoing some surgeries for her sleep apnea. When I asked how she was feeling, she said, "Oh, I don't know. I'm so tired of hurting, and I miss working so much. I've tried antidepressants, but they don't seem to work."

In all the years my mother had grappled with pain, I'd never heard her mention *depression*. Feeling powerless and scared, I grasped at the only thing I could think of. "Why don't you go see someone, Mom? Our therapist saved our marriage. I still go now and then."

Her voice turned suspicious. "What do you need a psychologist for?" she asked, adding a line from *"Crocodile" Dundee* in a mangled Australian accent: "Don't you have any mates?"

I didn't, but wasn't going to say so.

"Well," she continued. "I'd go to see someone, too, but it wouldn't do any good."

"Why is that?" I asked, baffled.

"Because I learned all of that stuff in school. A therapist couldn't tell me anything I don't already know."

Three months later, she found her Magic Lady.

WHILE I WORKED through my demons with my therapist, my mother confided in Andrea. Even now, in our too quiet house, I can feel my frustration resurface amid the panic racing around my heart, tinged with the pathos of lost time and love. And so I hold on to the alder trim, anchoring my attention to the flowerbeds bathing in the dim porch light, the well-clipped grass and roped clematis.

It wasn't *that* your loved ones could hang around, in the Mormon scheme of things; it was what they did that bothered me. I had no sooner pressed my cheek to my dead grandmother's cheek, when I heard the mortician begin the afterlife talk for the assembled children. "Did you know," he said, oozing sincerity, "that from where your great-grandmother is now she can see you? And when you do what is right she will be happy, and when you do what is wrong she will be sad."

I don't know what my mother had thought of the spiel—it was her mother after all—but I had been furious. In the space of thirty seconds, the mortician had turned the most caring, woe-besot woman I had ever known into the Dream Police. According to the little speech, my grandmother was not the deeply human woman who worried about children or hummed on an elbow while her rolls turned black in the wood-burning stove. She was a mechanism of surveillance in a religion so neurotic about the free agency it championed that it did everything in its power to fix every one of your choices.

Standing at the window, I shiver. I do not know where imagination blurs into hallucination, where intuition becomes delusion, where memory overshadows reality, where the thin line of sanity stretches and snaps. I do not believe that my mother is watching me from the spirit world, or that her eyes are glossed over with sorrow for her wayward daughter. I do *not* believe that spirits hang out in your living room, waiting to test you or torment you. And yet I notice that I am clutching my cell phone. Why, I don't know. So that if my mother shows up I can call someone? The only thing I know for sure is that if she does appear, I'm not about to shake hands.

FIVE

All Is Well!

The next morning, I put on a cauldron of coffee, surprised by the panic I'd felt the night before, as if my mother were going to materialize in the living room, sad-eyed and horribly burned. If I were going to imagine her at all, why not see her as Andrea had? As angelic and buoyantly transcendent? During the viewing, the bobbly redhead had pulled my father aside long enough to announce that my mother had appeared to her in spirit, white-clad and joyously free from the pain of mortality.

I don't know how my father took the news, but I wanted to smack someone. In the first place, the irony was hard to miss: a psychologist trilling about an experience that bore all of the markers of a psychotic episode. But what I really resented were the story's implications. Of all of the people my mother might have visited in spirit, she chose to see her *therapist*?

Seen through the gauzy goggles of my upbringing, the vision meant one of two things: One, that my mother had cared more about Andrea than anyone else (and god knows this could have been true). Or two, that the woman was just more spiritually attuned than the rest of us. Consumed with postfire petulance, however, I would argue that in addition to possessing zero tact, my mother's shrink is batshit crazy.

Still irritated by the vision, I slip on some frayed shorts and head outside. It's not that I have some morbid wish to imagine my mother in a Dantean nightmare, but her death was a *tragedy* for god's sake, and so it would be nice if people would let us feel bad about it.

Every story I'd ever read as a young woman was mind-bogglingly triumphant—even those filed under "grief" in the Church libraries. Teen literature featured youngsters momentarily distressed by the loss of a chinchilla or grandmother only to find reassurance in a strategically placed scripture. Stories for adults followed the same pattern. If grief dared to find its way onto the page, it was invariably eclipsed by enthusiastic testimony-bearing, as if true mourning—so unruly, vast, and weird in its manifestations—signaled a lack of faith. Once, I'd read an article in the *Ensign* by a woman who lost her seventeen-year-old son while she was away on a Mormon mission, and her lack of emotion was positively eerie: her son's death was part of Heavenly Father's plan; it was an honor and privilege to serve the Lord; and such trials gave us the opportunity to count our blessings.

Looking at the strip of cheatgrass sprouting along the fence, I feel stuck. I can't grieve and I can't cheer up. If anything, I feel the panicky urge to *do* something. Were it not for advisers who have assured me that my dissertation can wait, I'd be up in my office now, shoring up my theoretical framework, adding sources to my bibliography. It's not that I'm dying to write a lengthy academic treatise, but that the looming months scare me to death. If I don't stay busy, I'm sure I will burst.

Leaning down, I tug at some wayward cheatgrass before scouring the shed for a shovel. The handle feels solid and reassuring as I work at a patch of green near the apple tree. Before long, I've forgotten all about the coffee brewing in the kitchen. What I need is a clear patch of soil, a place to start over, somewhere I can plant sunflowers or gangly clematis.

Conceived during my screen-removing phase, the garden had been my idea. We'd lived in the lanky white farmhouse less than a month before I rented a sod cutter and took out half the back lawn. The garden was symbolic: a swipe at renewal. But it was also good old-fashioned labor. What else was there to do when you made a mess of things besides plant zucchini?

As I work, I feel the sun boring into my neck and forearms. Sweat pools between my breasts. Thoughts about my mother come and go, but they are manageable, assuaged by the rhythm of the shovel. Step jump pull. Step jump pull. Grief avoidance in three-four time.

Vaguely, I wonder how my brothers and sisters are doing. We were raised on pioneer stories of hardship and pain, but live in a culture where it's shameful to admit either one. When President Gordon B. Hinckley lost his wife of sixty-six years, for instance, Dieter Uchtdorf urged Church members to see his service and not his grief. To illustrate, Uchtdorf described an exchange between Hinckley and a woman who had recently lost her husband: "Work will cure your grief," the prophet had said. "Serve others."

While the advice seems sort of unhinged ("My mom died, have some cake!"), I notice that I am in fact working.

By midday the grass along the fence line is gone, as are any rebel traces of green amid the raspberries. In lieu of lunch, I swing by the hardware store for some seeds—snap peas, snow peas, lettuces, scallions, radishes—anything that can survive a sudden freeze or random acts of snow.

Back at home, I put the seeds on the porch and wrestle with the tiller until it sputters to life. I can't remember the last time I ate, but I'm not hungry. If deceased relations can spy on you from the spirit realms, my progenitors are proud as punch.

When it came to soldiering on, no one came close to my grandma Chournos, a woman whose losses rivaled those of anyone I ever knew. While my mother pursued her career, my grandmother bequeathed to me her quiet company along with her mistrust of "bellyaching."

My mother insisted that I was special to her mother, but I couldn't tell if I was or not. We spent time together because we were thrown together. When I needed money, I got sent to her house to earn it. By the time I was ten years old, I knew her floorboards, cupboards, windows, and pantries by heart. I scrubbed the floors of the cabin on the ranch at Monte Cristo, wiped down the outhouses, swept out the cellar, and scoured the dishes. During the hour and a half drive to the cabin, we barely spoke. Ours was an arranged alliance. In a signature move both charming and alarming, she waited until I was safely stowed in my seat before hollering "Let's peel out!" and hitting the gas, launching us onto the highway in a spray of gravel. Then she plopped in an eight-track tape and fell silent, powering her purple Cadillac around the hairpin mountain turns, listening to Roger Whittaker coo that he did not "believe in If anymore."

Now and then she commented on something as we passed, like the water-skiers on Pine View Reservoir. "Look at them people," she'd say, her voice shot through with scorn. "Playin'."

MY GRANDMOTHER'S MISTRUST of recreation stemmed from a past in which it did not exist. Her's had been a rugged life that did not accommodate whininess, wimpiness, or (god help us) leisure. You planted, you cultivated, you harvested, and if your potato plants got ate right down to the ground by hoppers, so be it. You maintained a fierce resolve to buck up, cheer up, carry on, no matter what. The worst thing you could do was feel sorry for yourself. Once, I asked if she had ever cried in front of Grandpa. "Well," she'd said. "Maybe some at first, but not after that. Nobody likes someone who's boobin' all of the time."

A descendant of Mormon pioneers, my grandmother prided herself on the fortitude. A hundred and sixty some-odd years ago, Brigham Young had said "Put 'er there," and so her grandparents had, having left places with the word *green* in them—Gillar's Green and Collin's Green—or with names like Rainhill, for places like Dry Lake, Piss Ant Flat, and The Barrens. The rolling hills of Cheshire and Lincolnshire became the rocky quartzite ledges of the Wasatch Mountains, towering in ragged peaks to almost twelve thousand feet. The Irish Sea became the Great Salt Lake, brackishly foreshadowing the desert beyond, rippled by basin and range.

My grandmother inherited an unforgiving place, along with the injunction to make it bloom like the rose. Her father made bricks for the beet sugar factory until he could purchase the family farm: twenty acres of sagebrush-strewn desert. By the time I came along she had become much like her Ma: big-boned and unflappable, a woman who personified work and faith and gumption more powerfully than anyone else I knew. If fire started raining from the skies, she might have regarded it with interest before saying: "You know, it could be worse." She was famous for contradicting herself and swearing that she hadn't. Endowed with a mix of no-nonsense playfulness, she advocated upholding the laws of the land as she racked up speeding tickets; reprimanded you for swearing and punctuated her own surprise with "sonofabitch!"

If I asked her about herself, she knit a yarn of self-deprecation and wry humor that completely effaced anything like sorrow. If I asked about hardship, she extended examples. If I asked about heartbreak, she'd shrug and say, "Well, everyone's got their troubles."

The stories she told of her childhood were simultaneously dull and depressing. But she told them with such pluck and pride that you would have thought that herding cows and thinning sugar beets on a stomach full of boiled flour balls was big fun for a five-year-old. During the 1970s pet-rock craze, which thrilled my eight-year-old heart no end (because: capitalism), she regarded my hand-painted gravel family with amusement before claiming to have owned the first pet rock. "My friends all had baby dolls," she said. "But we were too poor for something like that, so I got myself a river rock and wrapped it in one of Ma's wool blankets."

Her one childhood toy was not a toy at all, but she carried it along while she herded cows all the same. I could not imagine hefting a stone around in a blanket, not just because I'd never yearned for a baby doll (and had abandoned my Betsy Wetsy, which Michelle thankfully adopted), but because it seemed like so much effort. Once, she told me she had spent a sleepless night worrying that she'd left the doll out in the rain. Ma, she said, was sure to whup her hide for ruining the blanket.

"What happened?" I'd asked, suddenly mindful of her childhood hide.

"Oh," she said. "I found the blanket and washed it and put it back in the cupboard."

While I made a mental note of the most anticlimactic ending to a story ever, she frowned. "The government took the age off kids," she said, as if the comment made perfect sense. "You know, the age they let 'em work for wages."

I had no idea what she was talking about, but didn't dare interrupt, as it might seem rude. "It's when kids are small that they learn to work," she went on. "Not when they're grown up and have laid around all their life."

Proud that I had not laid around all my life, I nodded earnestly, until she concluded: "And that's the trouble with boys and girls today."

STRANGELY HOMESICK for my grandmother, I chop an uneven line in the freshly tilled soil with a hoe. When people in our town started keeping gardens in the 1970s, after Mormon Church president Kimball extolled the importance of self-sufficiency, she was flatly confused.

Why would you cultivate tomatoes you could buy at the store? That I am planting lettuce in order to *feel better* would be as mysterious to her as the day I brought a camera to the ranch at Monte Cristo to capture the majesty of the mountains. Why would anyone take pictures of their *job?*

Our world was composed of brute realities that glorified work and disregarded emotion. What we knew of God was that He required absolute obedience, sacrifices and separations, tests of faith and endurance. If you could not meet these trials with a cheerful heart, the least you could do was muster a measure of grim-faced determination.

Childhood was an inconvenience. You got by until you could do something useful. When my grandmother spoke of her parents, it was as if they sprang forth fully formed as small pioneering adults. A "big lady," her own mother had birthed eleven children by the time my grandmother showed up. And her Pa, a looming no-nonsense man, had demons of his own.

Orphaned when he was eight and unable to get along with his stepfather, my great-grandfather took refuge in the railroad camps, where he survived by procuring supplies for men who taught him to chew tobacco, play cards, drink, and gamble.

I knew about my great-grandfather's trials from my grandmother's personal history, which relayed her dad's story in all caps: "HE ALWAYS SAID THE LORD HANDLED HIM AND IT WAS PRETTY ROUGH." Her father suffered from what he called "tremble spells," which could be relieved only by prayer. As a child, she often found him bent to his knees before God, pleading to be relieved of the forces that tormented him.

What I took from the story was that bad behavior got punished. Persistence, on the other hand, along with long-suffering and unwavering obedience, got rewarded with perks such as health in the navel and marrow in the bones. All you had to do was work hard and walk circumspectly before God, and your demons were bound to vanish.

Physical discomfort was expected, and as a sign of hard work, even respectable. That your skin turned a deep brown from cultivating sugar beets under an unrelenting cloudless sky, that your body stooped double from harvesting granite, that your legs became a network of varicose veins from one pregnancy after another—these were signs that you fulfilled your duties without question or complaint.

Emotional distress, on the other hand, was deeply suspicious, a sign that you lacked faith or harbored some dark secret in your past. My mother's suffering, for instance, could be traced to sins for which she had never repented. Which is how one of her family members put it to me just before she died.

BURYING A ROW OF SNAP PEAS, I fume. It's not just the presumption of sin that bothers me, but the logic. In order for it to work, my mother would have had to out-sin virtually everyone I could think of. I knew people who lied their asses off, people who scooted off to South America with the life savings of retirees, clergy who fondled children, for god's sake, who never developed debilitating pain. And there was me: adulteress, scotch-swigger, and blackjack enthusiast. A mother who left her children to pursue a PhD. A woman with a nipple ring, nose screw, flower tattoos, and a case of irritable God syndrome. If anyone deserved to be divested of health and happiness, it should be me.

If anything, my mother was obsessed with doing things *right*. In spite of her pain, she made hundreds of care packages for Mormon humanitarian efforts in the Dominican Republic and Africa. She sewed leper bandages and spent her days pitched in front of the BYU channel, pumped full of medicines that allowed her to function, frustrated with herself for not being as stalwart and strong as her mother.

She lived a scant three and a half years after her mother died, and spent most of them castigating herself for slacking off: Her mother would not have been such a wimp! Her mother would not have taken a nap in the middle of the day! Her mother had worked hard every day of her life and never once felt sorry for herself!

It did not matter that I told her that grandma did indeed doze off in the afternoons and that sorting out her mother's pills was like playing truth or dare. My mother was sure that her mother possessed some fortitude she lacked—was special to God in ways she wasn't.

But how good did my mother have to be? How hard did she have to work? How many receiving blankets did she have to sew for God to say, "It is enough"?

BY LATE AFTERNOON, I stare out at a garden with eight perfectly spaced rows of seeds, white strings against the bare earth. Plant a radish, get a radish. Plant a story and who knows what will turn up? Given a different century, my great-grandfather's story would have been one of childhood trauma. Given some compassion, my mother's decline would be senseless and sad.

Vaguely, I am aware that I haven't really cried. Oh, I've been a little misty-eyed, but it's as if I'm mourning something *in general.* I felt sorry for my father's desolate face and cockeyed glasses, sorry for the high-pitched detour his voice had taken when he tried to say the word "sweetheart" while picking out the casket ribbon. I felt sorry for Michelle's quivering shoulders, sorry for the urgency with which she'd begged the police to bring her something from the burned home *to hold.* I felt sorry for my brothers standing stalwartly at the viewing, sorry for my sons waiting miserably under a print of Jesus in Gethsemane. But I have not felt sorry for myself. I have not felt the immediate and personal loss of my mother. And so I do what I know: pick up and move on.

One of the most beloved Mormon films, *Legacy,* follows the early members of the Church as they get thrown out of one settlement after another en route to Utah. In one scene, the Tabernacle Choir sings "Come, Come, Ye Saints" as a line of handcarts and wagons trundles through a downpour. There is no dialogue, just the measured, blended voices of the choir, urging the saints onward over the sound of creaking wheels and heavy footsteps. "Though hard to you this journey may appear, Grace shall be as your day." As the wagons move forward, the camera pauses briefly to show a woman, kneeling in the mud, a lifeless bundle clasped to her breast. You cannot hear the woman cry, and who knows if she does? Head bowed to the earth, she places the bundle in a shallow opening as dark skies threaten more rain and the voices dim to sotto voce: "and should we die before our journey's through. . . ." Pulled to her feet, the woman embraces a man standing behind her. The voices behind the scene hum rather than sing the next line of the hymn, which you know to be "Happy day. All is well!" The scene fades into a shot of grimy shoes, tattered skirts, and mud-caked wagon wheels, which carve muddy ruts across the tiny grave, crushing the small bouquet of flowers, placed there by an unseen hand. The camera pans to a long line of wagons crawling across a montage of diverse landscapes. Just when it seems the saints can trudge no longer, the Salt Lake Valley comes into view. Triumphant music washes over the scene. "All is well! All is well!"

SIX

S. O. B.

I don't know how other people grieve, but I've found that what I do is wander around the house looking for shoes to throw away. This strange pattern, which started in the garden, has taken me on a whirlwind cleaning and de-junking spree.

Nothing is safe. The garden has become an antiseptic, weed-free zone with budding, perfectly spaced rows of peas and lettuce—vegetables we don't actually eat, but watch politely until they overripen and then throw to the sheep on the other side of the fence. It's the idea of growing my own food that appeals to me. Somewhere I've romanticized an idea of living off the land, but I participate in it only insofar as I watch the sheep nuzzle through corn stalks while I polish off a bag of corn chips.

I treat the things in our house the way I treat the vegetables: wait until there's too much of a good thing and start tossing. Vegetables over the fence, clothes and shoes and books to charity. The problem with the pattern since my mother died is how extreme it is. By the time I finish cleaning the basement, it's not just clean; it is *empty:* corner to corner, shelves and drawers, everything. It looks like we're selling the place.

Southward, my father is cleaning and sorting as well—haggling with insurance adjusters who spent a whole day just counting blouses, hundreds of which still had price tags on them. The art appraiser had walked off the job after the first hour, overwhelmed by the hundreds of prints and paintings. The last time we talked, my father had announced that the insurance company had agreed to award $20,000 for the dolls alone.

I don't need a therapist to observe that our house is becoming the inverse of my mother's: a Spartan model home that gives off the *impression* of human habitation. Nothing remains that is not absolutely necessary. Need a place to sit? The couch can stay. A bed? Fine. Anything nostalgic or otherwise cute or sweet or sentimental or marginally damaged or dinged or smudged has disappeared. I've allowed myself one small shelf of memorabilia, but that's it. Other mementos—if they survive at all—are there by request, or by supreme effort, or hidden within my boys' bedrooms. Which I have offered to clean.

Every item in every drawer and closet has been pulled out and sized up for dismissal. The toolbox is so maniacally ordered that the Phillips screwdrivers line up according to size. And no, they are not mixed in with the flathead screwdrivers. I control the placement of tools in the same way that I control my emotions, lining them up and sticking them in all the proper places.

In addition to maniacally ordering our house, I'm embarrassed to report that I've begun dream-cleaning other people's houses. This morning, I awoke from a scenario in which I was sorting through an old woman's jewelry, trying to decide what to give away, vaguely concerned that I may have killed her when the shotgun went off. (Yes, I was cleaning it.) Last week's installment of dreams featured me hanging on tight to the upper limbs of a weeping willow, throwing down things that didn't belong there: a socket set, feathered hat, and various orphan rings of keys. My subconscious is on Freudian holiday.

I will admit to assuaging my grief with blame—criticizing my mother's excesses while engaging in my own wacky compulsions. Like the afternoon I ended up in therapy detailing all of the reasons I would refuse to accept any of my mother's belongings.

I had not planned on calling my therapist. I felt guilty about spending the money, and besides, what could she tell me that I didn't already know? That I was going to feel rotten for a while?

But then I'd been standing in the kitchen in the same place I'd learned about the fire, and I'd been bowled over by a feeling so vast and empty and wrong that I felt I might throw up. I couldn't lift one more thing, couldn't clean one more drawer. I could barely see beyond the back of the barstool I gripped with both hands. By the time I'd managed to find the phone book, I could hardly control my fingers, let alone my voice; and when someone answered, it shattered.

The room was the same one I remembered from our marriage-counseling days, soft-lit and adorned with prints of the American Southwest. There was the familiar Kleenex-topped coffee table along with the brown leather couch where I'd pronounced our marriage healed.

By the time I got there, something had rescued me from the feeling in the kitchen and I rallied my old hurts: my mother's things were markers of pathology; she loved them better than her very own children. And so my father could burn the rest for all I cared.

"Well," my therapist said after I finished the rant, pressing her fingers together under her chin. "You took her shit; you might as well have some of her stuff."

AS PER HER INSTRUCTIONS, I drive down to my mother's house and rummage through the soot-infused things with my father. As part of the ongoing restoration of the home, a gigantic iron dumpster has appeared in the driveway. Black-dappled drywall and pieces of furniture poke up through pillows and padding and clothes and carpeting, as if the house belched a couple of rooms out of an upstairs window.

While I position six freshly hosed-off palm trees into the back of my Ford Ranger so they won't blow out on the way home, my father rests his elbows on the truck bed, barely concealing his amusement. It's not just that I'm taking some things off his hands that seems to delight him, but that I'd been so determined not to.

The items I've chosen are deliberately frivolous—like the palm trees. There is no story of success lurking in the fronds, no implied message, no subtle to-do list. The trees are no more momentous than the leopard-print pillows, the basket-weave trunk, the ottoman with long golden tassels and embroidered elephants, or the something that might be a bear skin.

Plopping a cherrywood end table over the palm tree, I pause to consider a three-foot statue of Michelangelo's David, who I've decided can defend our garden against marmots.

I feel like I ought to wrap the strapping young man in a blanket. He is, after all, practically naked. The version I've got has sprouted a tiny sculpted loincloth, as he is living among Mormons, but he still looks sort of vulnerable.

"You know," my father says, interrupting my thoughts and gesturing toward the garage. "I've got those oil paintings of Grandpa and Grandma Chournos in there if you want them."

I give him a good-natured scowl. "You know what I think of those, Dad."

"I don't know," he shrugs, and I can't tell if he's kidding or not. "You might like having portraits of your grandparents around."

When I say, "I only want the one of Grandpa if it's still got the marker on it," he breaks into a sheepish grin.

"Now, Kid, that came right off."

THE PAINTINGS had caused a stir at the house a year before. Up to my elbows in soapy water, I had been scrubbing pots and pans after Sunday dinner, vaguely aware that that the cookware did not just bear the day's lumpy remains but greasy residue from meals gone by, as if no one bothered to use soap anymore. Were I paying attention, the grease might have struck me as troubling. I might have also noticed that my father had begun to look harried, that my mother had started to disappear right after meals, and that she'd stopped preparing them long ago. How long had it been since my mother had cooked? I didn't know. Chalking one more thing up to illness was how I skirted reality, normalizing things that should not have seemed normal at all. Immersed in the task at hand, I barely noticed the tension building downstairs until it culminated in a shout. "Hey, honey, you might want to come see this!"

Still holding a dishrag, I'd hurtled the few stairs to the sunken living room to find Lan gesturing toward a painting of my grandfather. The words MY FATHER, NICK CHOURNOS, engraved on a brass placard, had been enhanced by another title, scrawled in black permanent marker: "S.O.B."

My mother had several paintings of her parents, all of which I disliked. It wasn't that I harbored contempt for my grandparents, but that I mistrusted the worshipfulness attached to the images. No one else had earned the distinction of being cast in oils and framed next to Friberg's "Prayer at Valley Forge" and "Light of Christ." And so I disliked the paintings in the same way I disliked the prints of virtually every scene in the Bible.

As much as I disliked the paintings, I wouldn't have scribbled on them. Panicked, I looked at Lan. None of my siblings or their children swore. As I harbored a gift for profanity that could peel wallpaper, and as I had more or less passed this gift on to our children, I could only imagine that one of them must have done it.

We called the boys over, but they looked as surprised as we did. I fastened my eyes on the younger one, who glared back at me with why-do-you-always-blame-me irritation. While I waited for one of them to fess up, my father cut in to the tense little huddle. "What's going on?"

My eyes darted from the boys to my father and back to the frame. "I'm sorry, Dad. I just don't know how *that* got there." Nodding toward the initials, I waited for him to come unglued.

"Oh." he said. "I did that."

I couldn't tell if he was ashamed or proud. There was something bordering on defiance in his voice, something half-amused and deeply distraught.

"Your mom was going on about him the other night," he said. "About how he was so disapproving and distant. You know how he was."

I did. My grandfather was about as affectionate as a cherry pitter. The man I knew had mellowed with time; but my mother spent most of her life afraid of him. When she was eight years old, he stormed out of the house when his eldest daughter, Cherre, eloped with a boy he despised— a temperamental boy from a "no good" family, which was another way of saying "poor." Terrified, my mother had cowered at the top of the stairs as her father's rage shook the house. She heard him bellow, "You don't let your prize ewe go to any old ram!" just before the door slammed. Work on the range had excused his absences before, but for the next six years he almost never came home. And so my mother grew out of braids in his absence, powerless to stop the stifled sobs of her mother, surging and retreating behind a locked bedroom door.

"Anyway," my father continued. "Your mother just snapped. She started yelling that her dad was to blame for her failing health and Monte and Johnnie's suicides. I tried to calm her down, but that only made it worse. So I grabbed the marker—it was the only thing I could think of to do. I wanted to write it right across his face, but she wouldn't let me."

My father laughed, but the words "right across his face" had come out strained, as if he still harbored the impulse to do it. We snickered along with him, but I could not ignore the feeling that things were coming to a head somehow. His eyes were tired and battle-weary. In them a memory of marching full-tilt down the stairs with my mother at his heels, demanding that he stop. But all he could see was his own fist, curled around the marker and aiming for the canvas, wrestling with how much of the iconic image he needed to black out.

CLOSING THE TAILGATE, I picture the details of each painting: my grandmother standing at the wood-burning stove, stirring something in a cast-iron pot; my grandfather leading a gray mare across a mountain meadow.

"Sorry, Dad," I say. "But you'll just have to give those heirlooms to somebody else. I don't want anything to do with them."

"Well," he smiles. "I kinda thought you would say that."

"Think about it, Dad," I say. "Did you ever see one picture of *your* parents in the whole house—or anyone else in your family? It's like you didn't even *have* parents. But huge commissioned oils of hers? Really?"

"Well, I guess that's true," he says. "She was pretty taken with her family."

"She was more than taken with her family, Dad. She was . . . I don't know, obsessed. Remember the fight she had with her sister, Cherre, over who got their parents' wedding photo? And the portrait from their fiftieth anniversary? That thing showed up on a redwood easel in the living room. But your children—you? There are maybe half a dozen snapshots of us on that measly shelf in the kitchen."

He nods. "Well, she always said that you worship what's on your walls."

"Which only makes it weirder," I say, relieved that he's letting me fume. "It wasn't *that* she had paintings of her parents. It was their proportion to everyone else."

THE PROBLEM with my grandfather's story was that it had become so convoluted over time that there wasn't anything real of it left to hold onto. The version I learned as a child went like this: Grandpa Chournos was born to a poor family in a little place called Greece. Then he moved to America, where there was Opportunity. When he got to Utah, he worked hard and got rich. By the time I was old enough to walk the perimeter of his original homestead property, he had amassed over a hundred and thirty thousand acres, scattered from the parched eastern rim of the Great Basin to the high desert peaks of the Bear River Range of the Rocky Mountains.

In Tremonton, he was nothing short of a legend. There was a steady stream of interviews and newspaper articles, and awards—Rancher of the Year, Utah Sheepman of the Year—all of which glorified him as the rugged western manifestation of the American Dream. In 1975, *National Geographic* ran a story that made sheep-shearing out to be a warm, family-oriented affair. As the grand marshal for the Box Elder County Fair Parade, he led the procession on a white appaloosa.

Of course, the real story was a whole lot grittier, and I got an earful of it before I was ready to appreciate it. As a mongrel preteen with zero ability to feather my bangs like Farrah Fawcett, I got shuffled off to work at the ranch at Monte Cristo, where I stayed with my grandparents. As it wasn't clear to my relatives if I was human, let alone female, my grandfather gave me a job trapping gophers for a buck a tail.

Living at the cabin taught me that my grandfather was two different people: one when my grandmother was around and one when she wasn't. When she was there, he sat sullenly at the table near the wood-burning stove. If he spoke to her at all, it was to bark orders or complain about the food. If there was a night she didn't "dry it all up" or "burn it all to hell," I wasn't aware of it. When she wasn't around, he talked like a regular person.

The first night my grandmother left me at Monte Cristo with him, I perched uneasily on a folding chair in the kitchen, wondering who he was going to yell at, since I was the only one around and it was all I'd ever heard him do. He warmed some lamb chops in a frying pan and we finished them in silence. There was no television, and the generator hummed into dusk, powering the one yellow lightbulb.

Feeling awkward, I finished the dishes and prowled through my grandmother's collection of novels, bypassing the assorted romances, from which my grandmother had torn the covers, as if doing so would shield me from heaving breasts and titles like *Seduction in the Sahara*. I picked up the only book that was by neither Louis L'Amour nor Janet Dailey, *The Story of the Trapp Family Singers,* and started to thumb through the pages.

"Those pocket gophers," my grandfather began in uneven English, and I glanced up, startled that he seemed to be talking to me. "They get at the roots, eat up the vegetation. Kill a whole tree, ruin a whole damn meadow that way."

I nodded, unsure what to say about it. "Pretty bad, huh?" I offered loudly, mindful of his hearing aids, and burrowed back into the tensions building in Austria.

"When I first got here, we don't have the gophers so much," he said, almost as if he were speaking to himself. "But then, I started with nothing. No fencing, no buildings, just those camps down there and a few ewes."

I glanced back down at the book, since he had just expended more words on me than I had heard him say to anyone. Outside, the twin pines on either side of the cabin towered toward a night sky strung with stars, enfolding the tiny log home in prickly fingers, their bodies sparkling with golden sap.

"In Davia," he said, "we got nothing. No jobs there, no money there. Just some sheep and goats we keep under the house."

I kept expecting him to stop, but he kept me in stories for almost three hours while I watched the clock tick off the minutes past bedtime. The West he described was not the one I'd learned about in Sunday school, where the Mormon pioneers got to the Salt Lake Valley and set up homes and streets and irrigation ditches in wide and tidy straight lines. It was a harsh place, where men got sick and starved and died in railroad and mining camps. At one point he paused as if forming an image just outside the screen door: "Hard on everyone, worst for the Chinese."

My great-grandfather had been seeking his fortune in America when he sent for his sons to join him. Along with his younger brother, George, my seventeen-year-old grandfather endured storms and seasickness before getting off the boat in San Francisco and making his way to Magna, Utah, a town booming from the open-pit copper mining in Bingham Canyon. In the six years he worked the mine, his father collected every paycheck, doling out just enough for the boys to survive. Fed up with being unable to spend his own hard-earned money, my grandfather left the smelter and went to work for Union Pacific.

He never said how long he stayed with the railroad, only that it was imbued with bedbugs and hunger. "The train with the bread, it don't stop you know," he said. They just throw those sacks of bread onto the tracks. We almost starve to death."

While I imagined hungry men grappling for bread, my grandfather got to the part of his story I loved best: the day he answered an ad for a sheepherding job. Before he knew it, a man named J. B. White had hired him to oversee three thousand ewes. After five years, White offered him an interest in the business: 10 percent of the profits and a few dollars a month besides.

I thought that was the end of his financial worries, but it wasn't. Once word leaked out that he had a few hundred dollars to his name, his father demanded the money for return fare to Greece. Staring at nothing in particular, my grandfather finished the story in a way I never expected. "He took everything he had and mine too, and never came back here anymore. And that left me here almost broke, you might say it. And I stayed with those sheep."

MY FATHER AND I stand silently in the garage. Neither of us can figure out my mother's fixation on her parents. When I first told her about her father's impromptu soliloquies, she had been proud. He had chosen one of *her* children to bequeath his stories to, which seemed to endow our family with a kind of specialness. But I detected something like envy as well, as if I had blundered into something she had longed for all of her life.

I did not realize how deeply hurt she had been until I unearthed an interview of her father in the Utah State University archives during my graduate work. I thought she would be delighted to hear his unmistakable growl ten years after his death, but as his thick dialect rolled through the room, she burst into tears.

"My father never spoke to me like this. Not once, not ever." Her voice wavered and then persevered. "What I would have given for him to treat me like one of his friends!"

Shutting off the recording, I hugged her. But I was more stunned than sympathetic. In all my life I'd never seen her so distraught. She stood in a red floral print blouse and cream slacks, shaking, tears falling through tattooed eyeliner. The misery she endured was thick and systemic, and the only person who could assuage it was gone.

What we loved best about my grandfather's story was how work got rewarded. We never saw the dark themes of exploitation and abandonment. And so it was hard to say who the real S.O.B. had been. My grandfather, who left his daughter when she was eight years old? Or his father, who left him in America without a penny to his name?

Survive or die. Those were the rules. Sons were labor and daughters were expensive. Children were not friends; they were a means to an end. A way of securing a little meat in the world. And if you were lucky, a fortune.

"WELL, DAD," I say, taking one last look around at the storied wreckage in the garage. "It looks like I'm loaded. My therapist ought to be proud."

"You know," he says, wandering aimlessly back through the garage as if he might off-load something more. "Most of this stuff is junk. There will be lots more to pick from when the stuff the insurance company sent off to get cleaned comes back."

"Oh, no," I say, flashing him my brightest grin. "I don't want to get healed up prematurely."

He looks up from the debris and smiles. Humor: our great deflector. A gift I received from him. Whenever things came to a head—when our mother refused to let us leave the table until we had finished our liver, when tempers flared over what I would or would not wear—he defused the tension by making up stories, or lining up everyone's empty water glasses and tapping out a tune on them with his fork, or singing some ditty in his hallmark tune-challenged way. I can't remember if his antics made my mother laugh, but they always worked on me.

"Well," he says, turning serious. "Your mom was writing a letter to you before she died. Did you know that?"

My spark of levity vanishes. A letter. My mother wrote letters only if a friendship was in peril or her family happened to be hauling out lawyers and pistols, or if she felt like something vitally important needed to be set straight. The last letter I had written to her had read like an agnostic manifesto. So I can only assume she was writing a rebuttal, a ploy to get me back to church.

"I don't know if she ever finished it," he says. "If it's here, I haven't seen it."

"That's okay," I say, surprised to feel a wave of regret. While I'd rather not read a treatise on the relative merits of church attendance, a letter meant she had been thinking of me. It would be my last link to her, evidence of—I don't know—a connection. "Let me know if you find it."

Encouraged, he walks toward a stack of boxes. "I've got some of her papers and journals here, too, if you want them."

Looking at the boxes makes me feel tired. "Maybe I'll pick them up some other time," I say, meaning never. Or "sometime" meaning in a few decades—like in a movie where the main character cracks open a mysterious diary on her deathbed.

"Well," he says. "They're just right here," gesturing to a box teeming with colored folders, manila envelopes, and intermittent loose papers.

Despite my misgivings, I peer inside. Haphazardly tucked in with everything else, a single sheet of paper pulled from a purple legal pad rises above the chaos. On it, my mother's cursive curls along the page, running sideways as if she's run out of room, her sentences punctuated at intervals by shorthand. There is something about the intimacy of her script, the page smudged with black, that I can't bear to look at, and I turn back to my father, trying to smooth out the break in my voice.

"I don't know, Dad. Maybe later. Not now."

"That's okay, Kid," he says. "They'll be right here when you want them."

SEVEN

Fascinating Womanhood

I t doesn't take long for me to realize that I should have left my mother's
things alone, since they pack a sensory punch that brings forth actual
tears. The items I rescued on my therapist's advice turned out to be fat
stink bombs, infused with a stench that permeated our home with a
rugged, Boy Scout campfire scent—which is not at all like a respectable
campfire scent, as Boy Scouts will pitch everything into a fire, plastic and
piss and tires and Twinkies, if not each other. The beaded pillows had
adorned our guest bedroom for less than an hour before the smell of char
and ash swallowed everything, and I tossed the lot into the dumpster. I
banished the rest of the things—throw rugs and palm trees and statuettes
and wicker trunks—to the back porch, where they merge with the view
of the barn and pasture, so that stepping outside feels sort of like stepping into a dream sequence in which Indiana Jones and Charles Ingalls
discover they are brothers.

I barely have time to mull over the implications of weird items before my
father calls to ask if I will come help him clean out the basement. While the
cleanup crews can throw things out, they can hardly decide what to keep,
and, for better or worse, everything in the basement is just fine—including
my wedding gown and prom dresses from my virginal days of yore.

As much as I enjoy time with my father, the summons makes me
surly. After driving back down, I let myself into the house and pull up a
barstool to sulk. Recently mopped and scrubbed, the kitchen is a golden
sanctuary amid the rubble, but it does little for my mood. I really don't
want the dresses, but I also don't have anything better to do. Unless
I want to dive into my research (which I don't) or line up my books
according to size (which I do).

I barely have a chance to start brooding when I hear a muffled voice from upstairs, "Is that you?" And Michelle bounces in with a broad smile. "Lighten up, Neece!" she says. "It's not so bad. Look at all this stuff we saved just for you!"

Holding out a lacy metal belt, she grins as if I had just won the Daily Double. Made from hundreds of tiny silver links, the belt forms a broad V that shimmers under the fluorescent lights, sleek and cheap. "We knew you'd be upset if we didn't let you have it."

I take the belt in my hands, letting the links slip through my fingers. "Jeez, Michelle, do you think she actually wore this?"

"Um, I think so!" she chirps. "But I don't want to know where."

The belt looks familiar and I put it aside, noticing that Michelle has also retrieved a matching set of metallic earrings and necklace, which she has displayed on a dishtowel as if to tempt me.

Immune to my surliness, she produces a gray leather bag from behind the bar. "Oh, yeah, and we're giving this to you, too. Don't say no; you'll hurt our feelings."

I know what's in the bag without opening it. "Oh, for crying out loud, couldn't you have thrown that out?"

"This bag of treasured heirlooms? No way. You'll thank me someday."

"Oh yeah?" I say, taking a peek inside. A flash of sheer purple fabric confirms the contents, and I zip the bag shut. These treasured heirlooms had wreaked havoc with more than one marriage.

"Well," she says. "You have to admit that we saw more of our mom than most kids do!"

She flashes a look of feigned horror and winces, sure that we are conjuring the same image: our mother belly dancing in front of the full-length living room windows, weight pressed to the balls of her feet, hips shimmying to *Zorba the Greek,* finger cymbals chopping the air like fierce, arrhythmic clams, a dictionary balancing precariously on her head.

I was barely sprouting breasts when she donned her first costume, and had been shocked to discover that she had a torso, and was even more shocked that she didn't seem to mind displaying her torso for visitors. The wide coin belt and silver sequined bra, festooned with beads that fell in loops from one cup to the other, had been one of two outfits she wore interchangeably, depending on her mood. I had regarded the hobby with equal parts fascination and unease, concerned about the bellybutton jewel for reasons I could not articulate, unsure whether to be alarmed or impressed.

"I'm just saying that there's stuff I'm willing part with," Michelle continues, gesturing toward the metallic V as if it were one of several prizes I might win. "Come on, be a sport."

Michelle's ability to produce cheerfulness on cue as if it were a stash of secret coins she kept up her sleeve baffles me no end. I've seen her break and rally, seen her tremble with tears, but I've not seen her angry, not once, since the fire. I can't tell if she's a saint or the soul of repression, but her playfulness is hard to resist. "Fine," I say, hanging the chain low across my hips. "You happy now?"

"See, Neece?" she beams. "It's you! You were meant to have it."

I look at the silver shimmering against my battered khaki shorts and dinged-up legs. "Of course," I say. "It goes with everything I own."

"Oh, and these," she adds, holding out a pair of mammoth earrings. "We thought you should have these too."

My defenses hijacked, I burst into laughter. "Oh, shit, Mush—they're peacock feathers!"

"Yes," she says. "The finest. We didn't want you to feel like you didn't get any of the good stuff."

"*Any* of the good stuff?" I say, threading the posts through my earlobes. "It looks like I am getting *all* of the good stuff. You're going to be sorry you gave these up."

"Oh, don't worry," she says. "There's more where that came from. Wait until you see the Xena: Warrior Princess collection."

ASSURING MICHELLE that she can keep whatever happens to be in the Xena collection, I follow her to the basement, where the quantity of my mother's belongings is matched only by my father's space-making genius. It's not *the* closet, but closets. Catacombs of closets. Cubbyholes stuffed to the gills. One bursts with lawn ornaments and silk flowers, another with bedding. For better or worse, everything in the basement escaped the black tar, so we start with the clothing: dresses and pantsuits and coats: pink and aqua and cherry red. Leather, mostly, and fur. Full-length, creamy white furs; plush brown and black.

Prowling through the closet, we sink into our own thoughts, pausing occasionally to point out some furred or beaded wonder, our conversation consisting of variations on "Remember this?" and "Can you believe *that?*"

Noticing my mother's emerald prom dress, I pull it from the rabble, admiring its tiny waistline and wide hoop skirt, the way the chiffon gathers over a bustle of green satin roses. Meanwhile, Michelle assesses my prom dress: a clumsy fuchsia reenactment that we had sewn ourselves. The biggest difference being that mine had generally failed to slim my barrel-like torso. Like my mother, I had gone to the prom dressed as Scarlett O'Hara, but a Scarlett who had made too many trips to the Hostess aisle. It was one of the things I always hated about being a teenager—how people invariably noticed how *tiny* my mother was in relation to "such a big daughter!" And while "big" could have meant *grown,* I knew it meant *fat.*

Tastefully white and modest, my wedding dress hangs next to Michelle's, flattened by the force of countless shimmering formals. I had selected the long-sleeved Victorian gown partly because of its bustle, which my mother thought was "just so fun!" before she and the sales clerk fussed about finding a seamstress to add more fabric along the back and shoulders to make it suitable for the temple. Meanwhile, my grandma Chournos thumbed through back issues of *Bride,* while I'd scanned the forbidden dresses with slim sleeves and spaghetti straps or—heaven forbid—no straps at all.

The throng of sequined gowns is not surprising, given our mother's penchant for anything that sparkled—who knew when you might need something fancy? But there's no accounting for the surplus wedding dresses hanging next to ours, adorned with tall lace collars and long white trains, princess sleeves and beaded appliqué, as if we harbored secret sisters.

Wide-eyed, I turn to Michelle and shrug. We grew up with extras of everything—wheat, honey, clothing, blankets, coats, and shoes—since we wanted to be prepared for anything: wars, rumors of wars, governmental collapse, apocalyptic chaos, plagues, pestilence, the moon turning to blood. So, extra wedding dresses. Why not?

"Well," I say without trying to conceal my sarcasm, "I guess you never know when you might have a marital emergency."

Sizing up an intricately beaded train, Michelle says, "I guess so," when it hits me that her arrival in the world *had* constituted such an emergency. Thanks to Michelle, our mother had never been fitted for a white wedding gown. Instead, she'd ended up in the Chapel of Love, dressed in a slim-fitting gray wool suit with a flash of fur on the lapel.

My mother was fourteen when she met my father, and her dad didn't like him any more than he had liked Cherre's boyfriend, Junior. The way my father told it, a Chevy pickup screeched to a stop outside his house one Halloween. Inside the cab, his best friend grinned next to two young women. My father barely managed to make eye contact before his pal hit the gas. Standing on the running board as the truck picked up speed, my father forced himself through the open window, landing in a heap on my mother's lap.

The two dated on and off for years despite my grandfather's disapproval. A headstrong teen, my mother did as she pleased, knowing that her father was too busy to pay her much attention. And then, during the summer of her junior year, she missed a period.

As they huddled in a borrowed Buick while the first leaves of summer turned gold, my father did not offer my mother the elaborate wedding she'd dreamed of, but what amounted to a grubby handful of magic beans. He might be a skinny kid from East Garland, but he would not abandon her. He could get a job; she could finish high school. They would start a family together. It would be hard at first, but they would find a way to get by.

EXAMINING THE EXTRA wedding dresses, an idea flits through my mind that starts to dismantle the happiness I felt in the kitchen. If there were a way I could stick the idea back in a drawer, I would. If I could line it up along with the drill bits and PVC fittings—if I could detach myself from it and turn it over in my hands, I might be able to tolerate it—but it's so self-evident, so profoundly sad and unbearable, that I wish I were anywhere but here, standing in a grotto full of gowns, unable to ignore my mother's history, told in beads and sequins like a glittery Morse code.

It's not the dresses themselves that bother me, but the idea that she'd bought them to satisfy a deep ache. The extra wedding gowns serve no practical purpose, and yet, as objects of desire, they are glaring. My mother lamented her unceremonious marriage and seemed to mourn her curtailed youth, even as she credited my father for saving her. She used to say that she would have run off with anyone to get away from home, to fill the bottomless sensation she described as "love-starved." Even as a child I knew that a dress was more than just fabric. A dress—especially a fancy one—made you lovable.

MY MOTHER did not talk about her life as a teenage mother, except to say that not being able to go home broke her heart. As soon as he learned she was pregnant, her father disowned her. While her classmates attended the senior ball and made plans for college, she took night classes and nursed her bulging stomach. Now and then, when her dad was out with the sheep, she asked my father to drop her off at home, where she stole an hour or two with her mother.

The covert meetings worked fine until her father arrived unexpectedly one night. At the sound of his pickup slowing to a stop on the gravel, she sprinted toward the far bedroom, where she let herself out the window and dropped into the snow. With Michelle boinging around inside her, she ran two miles to her sister Cherre's house, where she called my father.

When I asked my grandmother about it later, she insisted my mother had overreacted. Surfing through a brown stone ashtray full of pills, she scowled a little and shook her head. "Your mother didn't have to go and jump out that window like that. Nick wasn't going to hurt her or anything."

Growing up, I saw nothing of the frightened teenager who leapt from a window to avoid a confrontation with her father. By the time I came around, she had made an uneasy peace with him, and she was fearless and feisty and ashamed of nothing, least of all her own body. Maybe she felt she had done penance for her pregnancy by marrying and having her family as she was supposed to. Maybe she was insecure and I just couldn't see it. But she just seemed incapable of shame. She professed the same beliefs as everybody else, used the same respectful platitudes when she talked about Joseph Smith and Jesus Christ, and yet she positively radiated sexuality in a place where nothing was more terrifying to the locals.

Between my mother's extravagance and the Church's propriety, I got so many competing messages about sex that I was a constant jumble of wild thoughts and emotions. At my first Chastity Night—a meeting designed to warn youngsters of the dangers of promiscuity—the speaker warned us that he was going to be Very Specific before launching into something like a vocabulary lesson. There was something called "petting," a term that sounded dumb to me, since it conjured up images of fondling cats; "intercourse," a chunky, mechanical term that sounded as if someone was about to do something completely uncalled for with an erector set; and "heavy petting," which seemed like something between a soft handful of fur and an actual linking of parts. The message I got from the devotional was this: 1. Being pure was essential to God's eternal plan. 2. If you got touched, your purity all went away. And 3. If your purity went away, nobody would want you.

Back at home, I consulted Michelle as I worked on my Personal Progress goals. Didn't she think that the Cleanliness requirement was a little too easy? After all, you only had to take a shower, and you could check off the whole dumb category. I giggled, proud of my cleverness, while she stared at me, serious. No, she assured me, it was more complicated than that. How complicated it was, she wouldn't say, but I guessed from her silence that there was something hugely interesting about it. Maybe it was like the germs our mother told us about when she went back to school: there were things that made you unclean, and you wouldn't even know it.

Even though our mother prided herself on being straightforward about the body, she lapsed into the same unhelpful tropes that everyone else used when it came to sex. I was in first grade when she initiated The Talk, prompted by my trying out a word I learned at school that rhymed with *duck;* but all the talk seemed to confirm was that if you loved somebody enough then a baby would occur, like clouds blooming in a clear blue sky. It wasn't until third grade that scattered comments on the playground converged in my head like a train wreck to suggest that something like penetration was involved, which was the grossest thing I could imagine.

If we spoke about Things at home, we did so in cryptic allusions. My mother never told me that she had been pregnant when she married. That I learned from Michelle, who explained the reason behind our parents' marriage in the same low voice she'd used to reveal the truth about the Easter Bunny. When my mother did finally allude to the fact that Something had occurred, her clinical vocabulary flew right out the window: "Someone must have really wanted your dad and I to start our family!" she'd say, meaning God. Or, "Michelle must have been really impatient to come down!" referring to the preexistence, where one waited to receive one's earthly body. By the time I was dating, her rendition got a tad more specific, but more baffling than ever: "We didn't even have sex, and there she was!"

WHILE MY MOTHER WAS VAGUE, her mother was worse. My grandma Chournos may have disapproved of books like *Seduction in the Sahara,* but she bought them in bulk all the same. The only time she got anywhere near the subject of sex, I caught the faintest hint of a smirk before she said, "My sister, Lapreal, told me that I better bring a sock to bed on my wedding night. And I thought, 'Why on earth would I need to bring a sock to bed?'"

I wondered the same thing, but was not about to ask her about it since I did not want to seem naive.

My grandmother passed on the tradition of noninformation to her youngest daughter, who figured things out on her own, along with some help from the *Playboy* and *Sexology* magazines her brother, Johnnie, stashed around the house. What she didn't learn from the magazines, she said, she learned from him.

The message I got from my mother's story—a message she seemed to miss entirely—was that her father's rejection mirrored the kind of rejection she should expect from God. I may have been a little slow to grasp things sexwise (ok—a *lot* slow), but I knew this to be true: nothing was worse than sexual misconduct. Okay, there was *murder,* the unpardonable sin, but that was pretty much out of the question since no one I knew wandered around all day tormented by thoughts of killing other people. Sexual fantasies, however, could pop up unbidden like acne, and it was one's sworn duty to squelch them. I learned early on that thinking a thing was as bad as doing it ("As a man thinketh in his heart, so is he"), which made me wonder why you didn't just go ahead and do it in the first place. Unless you happened to be my mother, thinking about sex did not make you pregnant. It did not make you an outcast, and it did not get you thrown out of your house. Only iniquitous actions could do that. And if you were shunned or disowned or abandoned, you deserved it.

From what I learned at church, I couldn't tell if the body was sacred or profane—if true love and passion were cut from the same cloth, or if they were enemies. Few things were worse than touching someone you-knew-where, or touching yourself for that matter. Nothing was more shameful than premarital "relations." And yet, once you got married, those same relations were glorious, sacred, and holy—if not fanatically required. We knew the rules: bare shoulders and bare knees were out, unless you were showering or possibly swimming. Skirts were to hang four inches below the knee. Bare torsos were an abomination, swimming or not. And yet the body was also this wondrous thing we'd inherited as part of our Heavenly Father's plan.

I took rules about modesty seriously, as if they had been written by the flaming finger of God, while my mother seemed to regard them as polite suggestions. While Church authorities yodeled about the horrors of bare midriffs and called upon women to reject swimwear that didn't cut a fat straight line across the hips and thighs, my mother bought a blue and white polka dot bikini that hooked to her body with a thin white string. Most of the time she dressed as modestly as everyone else, donning a puffy-sleeved Gunne Sax dress for work or church. Then, without warning, she'd shed her garments and show up at a church dance in a strapless formal with a full circle skirt.

MY MOTHER made me nervous. Not just because she occasionally ditched her garments and wore a belly-dancing outfit around the house, but because of something else. A feeling perhaps? An intention? From the moment I got my first crush in fourth grade, I sensed something about my mother that was as heartsick as I was. I could not see the countless overtures that earned her a compliment here, a wink there, but I felt them. I knew she was in love with my father, as evidenced by the wonky dance routine she used to perform with him in the living room to "Knock Three Times," but it sometimes seemed like she was in love with everybody else, too.

My alarm for my mother's flamboyance went well beyond Church precepts to the very core of my being, where I learned to disregard it. What do you say, after all, when your mother says, "I could make any man happy," and means it? Or: "The law of polygamy was meant to allow for multiple *marriages,* not *wives.*" The context for this comment was usually that polygamy had been divinely inspired, but that people had been too narrow and petty and otherwise selfish and jealous to accept it in full.

With such beliefs, my mother had precisely zero women friends. Although my parents struck up friendships with dozens of couples, the connection between the women was always strained. Aside from one couple that managed to stick it out with them for decades, my parents went through friends like they went through cans of instant mashed potatoes: they'd meet some people, double date for about a year, and then the man's wife would reach the absolute end of her rope with my mother's "charm" and blow a gasket. At which point my mother would spend a week or two fuming and crying and crafting a long typed letter that explained everything and fixed nothing.

My mother's preoccupation with charm came from a chunky pink book that was something like a Bible to her. She once told me that the book was "controversial," and so I'd pulled it from the shelf when nobody was looking, thrilled by the promise of subversion. But I barely got through the first chapter, "The Ideal Woman from a Man's Point of View," before I realized that the book was not controversial at all, but summed up everything I knew to be patently True.

By drawing upon works by literaries such as Charles Dickens, the book's author, Helen B. Andelin, delineated the traits a woman needed to win and keep a man. There was something about being Angelic, which meant acquiring traits like worthiness and inner happiness; and something about being Human, which included traits like radiance, flirtatiousness, and femininity. As far as I could tell, the whole point of the book was Thou Shalt Be Charming. And if you were not utterly charming—and if your marriage ran aground or splintered on the hard edges of disinterest or disillusion—it was your own fault. The book featured a diagram of a woman split right down the middle by the demands of both ideals, which is what I learned from *Fascinating Womanhood.*

My mother followed the formula to a T (except for the fact that she was gainfully employed, which the author discouraged). But she did not just extend the flirtatious and feminine qualities of the Ideal Woman to my father; she extended them to all men, as if doing so would mend something deeply frayed inside her. There was something overboard about her interactions, something needy that seeped through the confidence she radiated. It was as if every man, particularly if he were successful or striking or dark-eyed, was a stand-in for the one man she could not please; and she gravitated toward the pure power of attraction as if her life depended on it.

The way I dealt with all of the messages, implicit and otherwise, was to become so neurotic that I crawled right down inside myself and shut out all the lights. The human body—my human body, at least—was no longer the wondrous machine my mother had described to me as a child. A body, I realized, was the enemy, something you had to watch at all times in case it wanted to do something wicked. Mine, for instance, was constantly hungry, and I'd already had to confess to the bishop for touching myself. Curled in a sleepy ball in our tweedy brown loveseat after church, I woke from a nap surprised by a sudden longing in my inner thighs, as if my pelvis had a mind of its own. Massaging this feeling only made it worse, and so I gave up in frustration, wondering if I'd participated in the "impure actions" my friend Curtis had alluded to the last time we talked on the phone. He repented of his, he said, and I figured I'd have to repent of mine, too, though I couldn't figure out for the life of me what boys might be up to when no one was looking.

I confessed my sin and secured a conditional forgiveness, based on my promise to never do it again. But I had been so rattled by the bishop's soberness that, had my sexuality been a cat gently circling my leg, I would not have stroked it or fed or nurtured it, but driven it up the canyon where, if all went well, it would be devoured by coyotes.

While I fretted about approval from God, my mother foraged for approval from friends, who were mostly male. When she and my father went out with other couples, she mainly tolerated the women, who seemed to bore her. The only man she actively despised happened to be our bishop--which also made me nervous.

By the time I was fifteen, I was subtly correcting for my mother's behavior. The more my mother celebrated her body, the more I shrouded mine. I bought huge white high-water panties and bullet-proof bras in passive defense against the colorful silk bras and lacy panties and fully transparent teddies that filled her unsanctioned underwear drawer.

When it came to the body, I knew you couldn't be too careful. The Church's cautionary messages, along with my mother's insistence that she and my father hadn't actually had *sex* before they were married, made it unclear to me if you could get pregnant by having oral sex or if you could get pregnant just by being naked in close proximity to a penis.

Since I couldn't perfect my body, I decided to perfect my soul. I became rigid about my beliefs and followed Church doctrine to the letter. When I learned about the evils of modern music, I gave away all of my albums—Eagles, Donna Summer, Billy Joel, and Foreigner—and replaced them with recordings of operas by Mozart, Verdi, and Puccini (as if seduction, suicide, prostitution, and murder were more appropriate themes for the advanced soul). And I refused to entertain the soul-rotting music my younger brother played on cassette: KISS, Ozzy Osbourne, Twisted Sister, Mötley Crüe. Stuff that made you want to drink alcoholic beverages and do god knew what in the dark.

I refused to date until I was sixteen, since Church leaders had assured us Dire Things would occur if you did; and when I did start dating, I made sure to duck out of the doorstep kiss, convinced that doing so would keep me pure and wantable. But I invariably hated myself afterward as I lay awake in bed, trying to turn back the clock, wishing that I'd allowed myself one little spark of indulgence. I was a senior before I kissed someone in earnest, and when I did I was so flush with emotion that I spent weeks immersed in Church literature, trying to determine whether my feelings had been love, lust, or infatuation—as if there were no overlap between them at all.

While I became more neurotic by the minute, my mother fluttered and flirted, admired and adored. One night, she breezed into the kitchen so electrified I thought she might levitate with glee. Entranced by her ensemble, a lab tech had begged her let him take photos of her up the canyon after work. I couldn't say why the pictures made me queasy: her standing in a red chiffon blouse and plaid Pendleton skirt against a backdrop of gold and green leaves; her sitting sideways on a weathered picnic table, her skirt worked just past her knees to show shapely legs adorned by patterned panty hose; her face in close-up, smiling brightly from behind the slim veil of a black fedora.

IT TAKES every shred of energy I've got to look through the closets, and in less than an hour I am flat out of coping mechanisms. The dresses kick up too many half-healed hurts, too much confusion. And so I grab my wedding dress and head back upstairs. No sequins, no silk, no fur, no leather. I leave the silver belt on the bar, the playfulness I felt earlier parading around the kitchen with it hanging from my hips having vanished. I'd ditch my wedding dress, too, if I didn't feel sort of obliged to take it. Staying pure and chaste and virginal until I wed, it turns out, only made lovemaking awkward and uncomfortable. And there was a part of myself that didn't want to be pure at all. A part that ached for abandon. For something wide and wondrous and just out of reach.

Shouting a good-bye from the kitchen, I wait for my father to appear. I've no lost love for my mother's prom dress, which I wore to a dance once, only to split out the zipper before dinner, and I certainly don't want its ugly fuchsia stepsister. The fabric alone would fill my closet top to bottom. When my father asks what he should do with it, I tell him he can send it off to charity, where some resourceful soul can buy it for pennies, chop it up, and revive it as sets of skirts and knickers, like in the *Sound of Music*.

I pretend not to notice the gray bag of belly-dancing costumes, hoping someone will think it is garbage and lob it in the dumpster. But as I kiss my father, he picks up the bag and follows me out to my truck with it, part of my storied inheritance.

EIGHT

An Ecstasy of Weeding

I notice that my emotions have taken on all of the characteristics of a low-pressure system, unstable and counterclockwise, marked by sporadic lulls and gusty upheavals. I have started to dabble in my dissertation again, even though the fire has made the whole enterprise feel alien and irrelevant.

Now and then, I am blindsided by something that feels mysteriously buoyant. Wandering into my office this morning, for instance, I flung open the blinds to blossoms and robins and the faintest traces of joy.

The feeling retreats at the sight of my books, stacked like dusty mismatched saucers across the desk and shelves. But I try to maintain something of its shape and texture as I bring my laptop to my knees, prepared to chisel out a crude introduction to my research.

Problem is, I can't concentrate. A truck rumbles by outside. My coffee is cold. The sun is too bright. The shelves are in grave need of dusting. The screen stares at me like a stubborn teen. My proposal seems to have been written by monkeys. I recheck my e-mail, consider buying new window blinds. By midmorning, having made no progress at all, I throw on some frayed shorts and a ball cap and head into the sun.

Outside, the magpies are in full swing, taunting our black cat from no fewer than five fence posts, each bird luring him with a throaty caw! just before an accomplice calls out a rejoinder behind him. Not one cloud dots the airy blue sky. A meadowlark trills from a willow while I linger at a flowerbed, considering the waves of white petals encircling the still sleeping columbine.

Walking a slow wide circle around our property, I stop to watch the sheep, mowing the stubby grass beyond the cedar fence that falls apart every year. Our mangy ram, Dokken, presides among the ewes, having shed all of his winter wool except for an unfortunate tuft on his ass that looks like a misplaced woolly crown. Our boys named the ram as a joke, a nod to big hair metal bands and to the fact that he'd never been "docked," sheepspeak for castrated.

Once we got the ram, the basics of reproduction could not have been clearer. One night, Arthur burst in the back door shouting that something was wrong with one of the sheep, and we walked out to the pasture to find a dead-looking lamb's head hanging from its mother's hindquarters. Lan laid down the ewe, put his hand inside to release a bony shoulder, and stood back to see if the lamb was alive. We held our breath as the mother sniffed it and were relieved when the tiny body drew a few breaths. As the mother licked yellow slime from its body, I turned to the boys and said, "I did that for you."

Horror flickered across their faces before somebody snickered, and the brittle-brown pasture became the epicenter of joy.

Cheered by the memory, I breathe in dry air tinged with hay and manure. The property wasn't perfect, but it allowed our family to regroup. In the months and years following my affair I fought to stay in the moment, really *be with* the boys, make up for lost time. I couldn't tell if they felt the shift, but I hoped so.

Leaving the garden, I walk a wide circle around the yard, pausing at the mailbox before going inside. I sift through the usual garbage—Valpak coupons and postcards urging me to align my tires and schedule a mammogram—surprised to find an envelope addressed to me.

I check the name on the return address: my cousin, Allen. I can't imagine why he would write. A month since the fire—it's a little late for condolences. Also, I hardly know him. The image I've got of him is long-faced, tall, and muscular, with dark hair and a strong chiseled jaw, clad in blue Wranglers and dusty brown cowboy boots. Which is pretty much the same image I've got of all of the men in my mother's family.

It takes less than a minute for the letter to destroy my nascent happiness. Coldly officious, it extols the Nick Chournos legacy before ordering my siblings and me to get to work. "While your mother's death is regrettable, it does not release you from your obligations. As you know, it was her turn to take charge of the Chournos family reunion this year. This has not changed with her passing. There will be much to do as the date nears, but you need to send out invitations by the end of the week."

Tossing the letter in the dumpster, I project a heartfelt *screw you* toward Syracuse. The Chournoses can take a fat flying leap for all I care. Before she died, my mother had become so obsessed with the family partnership—the governing body that controlled what was left of my grandfather's estate and reduced my mother and her siblings to a bunch of stubborn bawling spoiled brats—that she wouldn't have noticed if I'd been smacked by a bus. In order to have a conversation with her, I had to wrangle my way past acreage and quarrels and cowboys and beauty queens and hypochondriacs, women with tall, ratted hair and "I love ewe!" aprons, and strong, dimwitted men in striped button-down shirts. People I resented insofar as they had become—how did she put it?—her "calling in life."

Her "calling in life," which was related to her "mission in life" in ways I could not fathom, drove me apeshit, as it combined high family drama with the Mormon idea that we made promises to God and each other in some dubious pre-earth life. As there was no way of remembering our promises, I was a nervous wreck as a young woman: How would I know if I was doing it right? When I finally decided that God did not have some special work for me to perform, I felt gloriously unencumbered—I could chart my own course, write bad poetry, study brine shrimp if I wanted. Meanwhile, my mother's fascination with her calling in life grew by the day, fueled by an obsession with the family partnership. And so Allen can take his precious party and kiss my ass.

A cross between *Bonanza* and *All My Children,* the summer reunion was a festival of dysfunctionality that nobody questioned, no matter how weird or progressively strained. Studded with curiously well-dressed women and fresh-scrubbed cowboys, the reunion provided endless examples of "the great and the least, the weak and the strong, in tragedy and in triumph." My mother may have stopped inviting us to her house as she got sicker, but she never stopped lobbying for the reunion as if it were the One True event to which we were inextricably bound by blood and duty.

We were never a family at the reunion. We were second-rate athletes competing for my grandparents' approval, which was kind of like water in the West: so sparse and rare that you hauled out shotguns and zip wire to protect your share. As a young woman, I nearly died of embarrassment every time I had to produce my guitar and sing "The Ballad of the Shape of Things" (a novelty song by the Kingston Trio in which knocked-up girlfriend murders two-timing lover), "Gunslinger" (novelty song by the *Limeliters* in which Oedipal cowboy gets shot to death as part of his karmic comeuppance), and "The Merry Minuet" (hooray for the atomic bomb!). Meanwhile, my cousins shimmied prepubescent shoulders in spangles and spandex for grandparents who—according to my mother—most certainly disapproved.

The tacit rule for the reunion was that it was each family's duty to outperform the family who hosted the year before. Even in the years my mother was at her professional peak, the event stressed her out so completely that I thought she might implode from the sheer force of it. She spent years liberating herself from home and hearth, only to hate herself by the end of the day, having measured herself against the Queen of Domesticity, my aunt Janice, who (it was rumored) cleaned her floorboards with a toothbrush and floss.

The last time my mother hosted the reunion, she looked unmistakably bloated and sickly. Unlike the years she poured herself into a pair of size two jeans, setting off her tiny waistline with a hand-tooled leather belt with bright silver buckle, thus striking envy into the hearts of all of the women who were not a size two, she looked as if someone had blown up a life-sized balloon of her and set it to work. Tiny red blood vessels spidered across her cheeks, and her cheerful blue western shirt, splayed with tiny red rosebuds, looked strange against her pasty skin. Still, as exhausted as she was, she found the energy to guilt-trip us for not planning a skit or a song for the program.

"Can't you girls put *something* together?" she'd asked Michelle and me, as if musical instruments might spring to life in the back seats of our cars. Then she turned on me. "Why didn't you ask Ben to bring his guitar?"

"Sorry, Mom, I forgot," I lied, thinking about how much I'd hated performing as a teenager. "But I think the program's intended for the littler kids anyway."

"Your grandmother is going to be very disappointed," she said, loud enough to include my brothers, within earshot but pretending not to be, who had also failed to equip their children with sheet music and string instruments. "This could be her last year up here. She's ninety, you know."

For a minute, I thought she was going to disown us all right on the spot, and might have, had not Michelle's daughter, Christie, agreed to play "In the Hall of the Mountain King" on a tinny electric keyboard, thus taking it for the team.

UNABLE TO GO BACK to my dissertation, I retire to the back porch, where I pull up a lawn chair and seethe. For a minute, I consider calling Michelle, since she's bound to have received the letter, too, but I'm not sure she will share my outrage. A perky defender of tradition, she didn't just support the reunion; she actually seemed to *like* it, showing up early to stuff the piñata, count jelly beans for the guessing game, and help pre-schoolers paint clay cameos of their pioneering ancestors.

I can't say why Michelle never seemed to mind singing or socializing or otherwise supporting the whole shooting match, but the reason I discouraged my boys from participating in the program had to do with the fact that my mother did not seem interested in them otherwise. She didn't come for their births, as we lived out of state. But even when we moved within an hour's drive of her house, she could hardly be bothered to visit. By the time she gave our youngest a set of embossed scriptures for his eighth birthday, he hardly knew who she was.

When she did visit, it was weird. When I described how Lan had birthed the lamb (minus the part about licking our children), she looked longingly at our small stinky herd and said, "Yes, growing up in the sheep business was *glamorous*," which left me wondering what animal planet she had grown up on.

Once she got wind of my prodigal ways, she started giving me "very expensive" numbered prints by Greg Olsen cast in gilded frames: Jesus with a small boy, holding his hand out to a butterfly, Jesus helping a young woman across a river. As my siblings did not receive such gifts, I could only assume some sort of message was at work—and it was. Looking at where I'd hung them, she nodded with approval, set her jaw, and said, "I will save your children in spite of you."

While the comment irritated me, Lan and the boys shrugged it off. Who cared what was on our walls? As far as they were concerned Jesus Christ might as well have been Karl Marx or a still-life basket of fruit.

Adding to my irritation with my mother was that she replaced us with poodles. She hardly paid attention to the boys and me, so thrilled was she by her pedigreed teacups, which she carried around in her purse. Her favorite: a highly nervous pee-herself princess named Sheba. When we visited, she seemed eager for us to leave. If she talked to me at all, it was part of a larger conversation with her dogs, which she pandered to between sentences with bite-sized strips of Pup-Peroni as if they were tiny Hindu gods.

Illness made everything worse. I knew she was wrestling with some kind of unspeakable pain, but she also seemed able to pull energy out of thin air whenever it suited her. Worst of all had been the afternoon I called to invite her to a concert. Our eldest son, Ben, had taken up the string bass and would be playing a few numbers with the Wilson Elementary orchestra.

I was worried that she might answer in a pain-ridden fog, but she sounded happier than I'd heard her in ages. "Well, it's my daughter!"

"Hi Mom," I said. "Ben's playing in a short concert tonight if you and Dad want to come up. We could grab dinner, if you want. It's no big deal if you can't, but we'd love it if you could."

There was a long pause, during which I imagined her thumbing through a rolodex of Excuses I May Need at a Moment's Notice.

"Well, we'd love to," she said. "But we can't."

"Okay," I said, unsurprised.

"You see," she continued, jubilant. "We just sold Rose Bud today!"

I paused for a moment, wondering how the statement formed a reasonable excuse or a logical conversational segue. "You mean the land out in the west desert?" I asked.

"Yes!" she beamed. "We've been so worried about finding a buyer. It takes a special kind of person to need that ground out there. But we sold it!"

I bit my lip. The partnership again.

When I said nothing, she continued. "Let us know when something big is going on and we'll make sure to get up there."

I slammed the phone into the receiver so hard that fragmented bits pinged off the walls and linoleum. She could have said she wasn't feeling well. She could have said, "For what it's worth, I'd rather not listen to a bunch of grade-schoolers murder *Pachelbel's Canon* tonight." But she had said, "Call us when something big is going on."

Something significant. Something worthwhile

True, I had said, "it's no big deal," but that's because I didn't want to pressure her. I couldn't remember the last time I'd done something impressive enough to attract her attention. But it was one thing to know that I had failed to measure up on the Scale of Things That Were Big Enough, and another thing to imagine that my children were failing as well.

THE PHONE CALL rankled, but I still attended the reunion, albeit in my own half-assed passive-aggressive way. But I finally swore off the party for good after my mother received a letter so venomous I thought the characters might chew through the paper.

I had stopped by her house to check on her after a minor surgery. Thinking I might find her perusing catalogs or placing orders for antiques, I was surprised to see her standing at the bar, gripping a paper in both hands. By then, she looked like a spongy, late-century Elizabeth Taylor, overly made-up and buxom and crumbling.

The envelope featured her name in hateful block letters, while the contents served up spite in all caps: YOU THINK YOUR PALTRY CABIN GIVES YOU SPECIAL PRIVILEGES ON MONTE CRISTO, BUT IT DOES NOT. YOU SQUANDER FAMILY MONEY. YOU HAVE TO HAVE EVERYTHING YOUR WAY. YOU PRETEND TO BE SICK SO YOU DON'T HAVE TO TAKE CARE OF YOUR MOTHER. YOUR FATHER WOULD BE ASHAMED TO SEE WHAT YOU HAVE BECOME.

And so on for two pages.

Cowardly anonymous, the letter shook her to the bone. Her body sagged under it as if it were a handful of half-spent fuel rods. I felt sorry for her then—for her bruised and peeling crepe-paper skin, for her quivering voice, stripped and airy from a recent tracheostomy, for her purple, swollen eyelids and wide swollen cheeks. Taking the letter from her, I folded her in my arms. "This isn't about you, Mom," I said. "It is about a diseased legacy, a petty family, and a person too spineless to talk to you in person."

Holding her, I felt a connection I had not felt in ages. The slim bond forged between us in the days she taught me to make frosting roses, turn a hem, take a pulse. I remembered her holding our first baby, charming a resonant laugh from him I'd never heard before. I recalled boyfriend advice and shopping sprees and blouse borrowing—moments that seemed as if they happened to two different people—before she moved to Roy and everything changed. And I might have forgiven both of us in the kitchen that day, for my growing contempt and her delusions of grandeur, if not for what she said next: "I gave my health for the partnership."

HEART POUNDING, I grab a shovel and head out to the garden, the letter from Allen fueling all the pent-up rage I ever had for my mother's family. Whether the partnership actually *did* sap her health matters less to me than that she seemed so willing to let it.

I know that I need to make headway on my research, but I can't be bothered with *words*. I need something tactile, immediate, grueling. Eyeing the patches of morning glory choking the fence, I set my blade and start digging. I would lather the oval leaves with herbicide and wait for them to wither, but I don't have the patience. Besides, there's something satisfying about teasing out each noxious tentacle and yanking it out by the roots.

An hour or two into my weedy war, I am surprised by an insistent buzzing in my shirt pocket. My cell phone. Propping the shovel against an apple tree, I peel off a glove and crack open the phone, trying to keep dirt from spilling onto the receiver. Keeping it pinched between my shoulder and cheek, I hear my father's voice sounding even and cool, with just the slightest hint of tension.

"So," he says. "We found the money."

"Yeah?" I say, peeling off the other glove. "Where?"

"The police had it all along. In a bag with some other evidence."

The word "evidence" cannot be a good thing, but its significance eludes me as I appraise the wilting clumps that mark my progress. "Evidence of what?"

"Oh, it looks like they found a note," he says in the same way he might tell me that they found a carburetor on an engine. Only the carburetor's full of squirrels and uranium-235.

"Ah, shit," I say, sinking onto a battered railroad tie marking the garden's perimeter. I am not completely shocked by the news, but sorry all the same. A note can only mean that she expected to die or planned it or both.

"Michelle called from the Ogden sheriff's office in tears. I got there as soon as I could. They'd already talked to Christie. The note was addressed to her."

I feel sick for Christie, Michelle's nineteen-year-old daughter and my mother's favorite grandchild. As siblings, we tried not to call attention to the favoritism, since things were pretty raw when it came to my mother's uneven attention, but I sometimes felt sorry for the sunny blonde, tasked with her grandmother's hopes and now left with the worst parting gift on earth. "Oh, Dad, I'm so sorry," I say. "I hope she's all right."

"The note doesn't make a whole lot of sense," he says. "I don't know if you want to see it or not."

"No," I assure him. "I don't."

"She left the money with the note. About eight thousand dollars in hundred dollar bills. She left some jewelry, too, a couple of black pearl diamond necklaces, and some gold coins. It looks like your mom was leaving it to Christie so that she could . . ." His voice trails off, and I wonder if he is reading something or just remembering. ". . . buy a new violin."

I sit, stunned, with my elbows on my knees. "What?"

"The note says that she will need the money to become a concert violinist."

For the moment I ignore the weird sentence and cut to the chase. "Do the police think her death was intentional?"

He pauses. "They won't say. If they rule the death a suicide, the insurance won't pay for the damage. They are waiting for the results of the autopsy to decide."

I can't decide what to think. The news feels surreal, as if I am watching a televised trial in which I happen to know the defendant. "No matter what else happened that day," I say, "she could not have been completely lucid. Christie's never played the violin in her life."

My father hangs up, leaving me adrift in an enormous silence. I want to talk to someone, but don't know who. Below frayed khaki shorts, my knees wear muddy circles etched into my skin. My wrists and arms throb from prying up weeds. My whole body bakes in the afternoon sun. I'd retreat to the shade of the porch if it wasn't so far away.

News of the note breaks something wide open that was just beginning to mend. I don't know what the wound is exactly or if there is a balm for it—gauze? Neosporin? a bright Scooby Doo Band-Aid?—if it is something you suture or leave alone, set straight or let heal kind of funny. I'd call Lan, but I don't want to bother him at work, and besides, there's nothing he can do. Sitting on the railroad tie, I feel powerless, tired, filled with lead. The note hadn't said she *wanted* to die, only that she was *going* to die.

Without warning, the thought of Allen races through my mind. If my mother meant to die, it makes us heartbreakingly kindred. The misplaced pride in his letter makes more sense. To have a sense of family, a place to belong, when your world blew apart.

He would have been fifteen or so when he came to live with my grandparents. I gleaned what I could about his father's suicide from cryptic allusions, since no one talked about it, ever. If I asked my grandmother about the drum kit upstairs or the huge glossy photo of the Bear River marching band, she'd say, "That's Allen's stuff. Leave it alone."

As a child, I knew Allen's father, Monte, from photographs pinned to a bulletin board in my grandmother's dining room. In one, he stood with a copper-haired woman, holding two little girls in eyelet dresses. In the other, he smiled from beneath the brim of a wide cowboy hat. Something about his dark eyes drew me in. Something about his smile made me think he might wink or tip his hat. Before I learned he was my uncle, I thought he was a movie star.

When I finally worked up the courage to ask my grandmother about what happened, she would only say Monte had "troubles." The rest I learned from a newspaper clipping. His body, and the body of his second wife, had been discovered in a car behind Gibson's Upholstery Shop.

There had been a fight. Accusations, maybe. At daybreak, police found the couple in the front seat with a .38 caliber revolver. The copper-haired woman had been shot twice in the chest, Monte once, in the head.

Sitting in the garden, I can't excuse Allen's thoughtlessness. But I also feel a strange seasick empathy for him. God knows what he went through after his father pulled the trigger. No one championed family traditions more fervently. No one idolized our grandparents more completely. And so the letter could be a gesture of inclusion, a way of inviting me into a grownup world where you took the place of a parent, whether or not you were ready.

From my perch on the railroad tie, I notice the pitiful inadequacy of the tools I've been using to heal: the shovel and V-shaped hand weeder, red-handled garden shears and rubber gloves. As my mother got sicker, I sheared off my feelings for her just to stay sane. I was going to be everything she was not. I was going to be healthy and loving and available to my children, even if I *was* commuting to a doctoral program six hundred miles away—an irony that wasn't entirely lost on me. I wasn't going to stop calling or visiting, but I had to sever the part of me that still craved her approval.

The more hurt I felt, the more I retreated into the safety of solitude: long canyon hikes and fastidious organizing. I was a de-junking freak well before the fire. The joke at our house, which wasn't really a joke, ran that all unattended personal items would end up in the trash. Twice, I threw away the back panels to remote controls before someone had a chance to change the batteries. "If you care about something," I said. "You'd better hide it."

Little by little, I started keeping everyone at bay, wielding an invisible sword as if to say, *I will cut you off before you can hurt me.* The word my therapist used had been *sabotage.*

To meet rejection with rejection. That was how you survived. To hide all that was soft and vulnerable and pliant. To be steely through and through. And though it was not particularly clever to say so, it became something of a mantra for me: *Well, Mom's a little freaky.*

Sitting in the dirt and mangled plants, I bury my face in my hands. I had been *cleaning drawers* while she planned to die, for god's sake. I could have been at her side within the hour. I could have held her hand as her pulse slowed to a stop if that's what she needed. *Mom,* I think to myself, *why didn't you call?* And the only answer I can think of is that the feeble cord that connected us had withered or snapped and she knew it.

NINE

The Distorting Mirror

At the end of July, the summer turns dry and merciless, as if God were punishing the fair citizens of the West with a plague in which plants and animals spontaneously combust. Brushfires are breaking out across the Great Basin; firefighting crews and equipment are wearing thin.

Walking past the front window this afternoon, I glanced up at the mountains just in time to see them catch fire. A flash of light winked across the foothills as if the sun caught its reflection in a speeding mirror. Within minutes, a plume of smoke blurred into a constellation of ginger dots. By the time a fat air tanker arrived with a bellyful of retardant, trees and shrubs were flaring up at the rate of one or two a minute.

The flames are so close that the road in front of our house is closed. Power is out; freezers are thawing; and yet everyone is responding as if the whole thing is a giant block party: hauling out grills and lawn chairs, hailing each other and chatting on porches, as if they actually like each other.

It's been three months since my mother died in her burning home, and yet I'm weirdly cheered by the brushfire. In the spirit of things, the boys head off to buy chips while Lan and I grill chicken and crack open warm beer, watching the whizzing lights of the fire trucks, listening to transmissions between the lead aircraft and tanker on a handheld radio. In short: having the most fun we've had all summer.

"I give it a three," I say, watching the C-130 drop a pillowy red stripe onto mostly not-burning bushes. Feeling giddy for the first time in ages, I polish off my warm microbrew and reach for another, imagining that my presence actually matters to the people on the radio saying things like,

"Looks like you've got wind at ten knots up that north-facing slope," and "Roger that."

The tanker makes a wide turn as my cell phone buzzes. Flipping it open, I squelch the Walter Mitty–like impulse to convert the scene into high drama, announcing to the caller that *the boys are doing their damnedest, sir*. Taking a breath, I manage a respectable hello before my father's voice slips through the smoke: "Just wanted to let you know that the results of the autopsy are back."

Relieved to be beerily detached for this bit of news, I try to muster the right kind of attitude. "So, does it tell you anything you couldn't have already guessed?"

"Well," he says, sounding thoughtful and analytic, as if he were consulting a list of board game directions and not a description of his wife's body. "I don't know." For one fleeting moment, I think I hear a shimmer in his voice, but it's gone as quickly as it occurs, a flicker of something on a hillside. "Not really, I guess. It says here that the fire started with burning incense, but no one ever found any."

Of course, I think. *Fire from thin air.*

"The best guess they have is that something on the bedside table ignited some Kleenex and the sparks got circulated by the ceiling fan."

Even with my gently whizzing beer-head, the explanation sounds ridiculous, but I am not about to argue. The news is a relief. No traces of accelerant, no kerosene, no acetone. No evidence of arson. I had heard the investigators hijacked a suspicious brass pot, but it hadn't disclosed anything useful.

"So," I say. "What about the toxicology screen? What does it tell you?"

The tanker makes another pass. A red stripe floats on the air.

"Well," he says. "That's just right here." His voice retreats into an extended pause in which I think I hear the rustle of turning pages. "It says that her blood morphine levels were in the toxic to lethal range."

I think I might enjoy another beer. Or possibly a shot of bourbon.

"She always said the doses of narcotics she took for her pain would kill a normal person. I don't know, Kid. Maybe her levels were that high all of the time."

I mull over the news and brace myself for the report's conclusions. "So, what do they think was the cause of death?"

"Looks like a combination of things. There was soot in her upper airway, so smoke inhalation was a factor. Carbon monoxide poisoning and drug intoxication is what it says here."

Any pleasant effects from the alcohol evaporate as I snap the phone shut. The mountains no longer harbor adventure, just regular people doing their jobs, hiking across the foothills, small against the smoke.

Sitting on the step, I feel a distant ache. I hear the story I want to hear: that my mother's death was accidental. Still, I know that fire needs a spark. That morphine—so much of it—is a marker of pain. But I can't stop wondering what *kind* of pain it had been. The ragged throb of nerve endings or something else? Despair? Rejection? My niece reported that my mother had been inconsolable on the telephone the morning she died, certain that a dark plot was circulating to ruin her—that she had been molesting children, for god's sake. My father would believe the stories and she would be left all alone.

The story had bothered my father so much that he asked none of us to repeat it. My mother's fears had been getting more extreme by the day, but I couldn't figure out why her subconscious would kick out something so cruel. She had weathered her share of rumors in her belly-dancing days. But sexual allegations at sixty-three? Involving *children*?

As far as the fire goes, I've got nothing. I can only wonder what she sensed as she slept. If she felt a strange prick at the edge of consciousness. If she knew. If she had been terrified by the gathering darkness or glad for its final release.

BY THE NEXT MORNING the brushfire is reduced to patchy slivers of writhing smoke. Spotters stay on the lookout for sparks, but things are more or less contained—which is more than I can say for my feelings, which writhe and shimmer as I try to keep them at a bearable distance.

Although I swore I would not attend my mother's family reunion— let alone organize and host the damn thing as requested—I find myself preparing to go. It's not that my feelings for Allen have blossomed into love and goodwill. I still take the letter to be the mark of a dutiful nutjob. But Michelle had stepped up to the plate (or taken the bait; metaphors changed with my mood), and since she promised to do all of the work, I figured the least I could do was show up.

In a normal family, some thoughtful soul might have said "Hey, those girls just lost their mom. How about we don't put them in charge of feeding two hundred people?" But my mother's family had never been normal, and my sister and I had never learned how to stick up for ourselves. We learned from birth that no matter what happened, *you did not shirk your duties.* You martyred yourself for ribbon Jell-O and zesty potato salad; touched up your mascara and filled Tupperware bins full of sandwiches. Although I'd gotten better at saying no over the years (if not *hell no,* depending on the circumstances), my people-pleasing genes still overrode my good sense from time to time, and I figured that's what happened to her.

Months before my mother died, she found an essay I'd written about her father and pulled me aside to ask if I would write about her, too. I'd smiled and said "we'll see" and thought *fat chance.* The story she wanted me to write (which would no doubt celebrate her family's legacy) and the story I wanted to write (which would no doubt slay her family's legacy) were so far removed from each other that I'd have to do the whole thing in quotes by Gertrude Stein: "Out of kindness comes redness and out of rudeness comes rapid same question, out of an eye comes research, out of selection comes painful cattle!"

My mother's conviction that I was destined to write her life history came from a bizarre scavenger hunt initiated by her Mormon therapist. Midsession, the goofy redhead had closed her eyes, traced the air around my mother's body with her hands, and said: "I see something in your home that is essential to your healing! White papers in a red drawer!" After which, my father searched the house for a week before emerging from a sheet music cabinet with the ancient assignment. Why the mystery document happened to be my essay and not, say, the libretto to *Paint Your Wagon* was never determined, but I went along with it. Because what else do you do when your mom says, "My shrink saw your story in a vision"?

But I was not going to write about her in the same way I was not going to attend the family party.

MY CHANGE OF HEART is the sum of painful negotiations. In the bitter push and pull of deciding what to keep of my mother's, I ride the thin edge of acceptance and rejection. At night, after my boys disappear into bedrooms strewn with rocks and sheets and brightly colored lights, I find myself sketching out the stories my mother and I inherited, trying to figure out how they became impossible for us to question, no matter how strange or darkly deformed.

Writing is my way of being extremely selective about the stories I choose to keep. My mother's extremes—her fixation on her father's estate, her mad spending and spectacular illnesses—conspired to create children who were wary: of excess and emotion and each other. My mother liked to brag about how special we were. But the truth was that our family had lost its center. Where my siblings and I looked for a father, we found a man orbiting our mother; where we looked for a mother, we found a woman orbiting her father. Every time we looked for our self-worth, we saw an image of ourselves returned to us through the distorting reflection of our mother's family.

Once, when we were little, our parents had given us two minutes to role-play what we would take from our house in the event of a fire. My mother had hardly started the timer before I'd latched onto my siblings and yelled, "These guys! I want to take these guys!"

My proposal was rejected, as siblings were in charge of saving themselves, and so I grabbed a giant green stuffed-animal snake, which also turned out to be the wrong move. The point of the lesson was that we were supposed to take anything we needed to survive. Which was why we had to make sure our hangers pointed toward the back of the closet: easy release. But I couldn't figure out why we needed clothes so much if we lived to love each other another day. And so, if going to the reunion means salvaging a relationship with Michelle, if being there will allow me to leave my mother's house with my sister and brothers in tow, then so be it.

THE MORNING of the reunion, I bounce along the gravel road to Monte Cristo in my pickup, a bundle of nerves and misgivings. Lan and the boys are home, relieved to be uninvited this year. Clutching a massive thermos of coffee, I crank up an angry mix of alternative metal beginning with "Bitch" by *Sevendust,* hating my decision to attend the party in the same way I have hated myself after too many shots of tequila, or after waking up in someone else's clothes, unsure how I got into them. What seemed like a way to connect with my sister suddenly seems moronically ill-advised.

It's not just the loss of my mother or the lack of friendliness that will hurt, but my lack of loveliness. As a child, my budding self-esteem had been kept in check by people who happened to look like starlets. Genes from my grandmother's sturdy pioneering ancestry had merged with my grandfather's dark Greek features to create human beings who were heartbreakingly beautiful. And yet I had inherited some mongrel features (from my father's side, perhaps?) that gave me all of the stockiness and none of the exoticism.

In reunions past, I tried to look as lovely as everyone else, even if it meant pilfering some rouge and powder from my grandmother's stash of ancient Avon products and wearing brush rollers to bed the night before. My hair was neither long enough to pull into a ponytail nor short enough to wash and wear. No one was going to let me run the propane generator just so I could blow-dry my hair. And so I invariably looked like somebody had rolled a tiller over my head, churning up lumps of tortured curls.

Living at the ranch as the resident gopher trapper meant my jeans usually harbored a bloody severed tail or two that I'd forgotten to give grandma as proof that I'd killed said varmints. Later, when I did the wash, the tails clung to the side of the washing machine like leeches in a spin cycle. Every pocket, collar, sock, and cuff I owned was caked with mountain soil, red and flourlike, as if it were made of pounded bone and blood. And so, when my cheerleader cousins arrived from town, freshly coiffed and glowing, I mostly avoided them, feeling stringy-haired, bubble-waisted, and in all ways marmot-like.

Checking my appearance in the rearview mirror, I try to convince myself that I am no longer the insecure girl of my past—that I have grown up and come into my own. I have showered and spiked my hair and applied just enough makeup to seem naturally pretty. I wear a tie-dyed tank top that shows off my shoulders and flower tattoo, along with a denim shirt to hide my shoulders in case they are off-putting to devoutly Mormon family members. Years of step aerobics and bike riding and marathon running have trimmed my once-buxom self into a

tiny-breasted size four, but I still feel like a fourteen. And so I am as insecure as I ever was, divided against myself, ambivalent as hell.

BY THE TIME I get to the ranch, my mood has evolved from unsteady
to surly, not just because I have spent most of the two-hour drive second-
guessing myself, but because somewhere across the flat my period started
in earnest, and I am bound to have a constellation of red stains strung
across my ass.

Bypassing campers who, I am sure, never had a dorky bodily moment
in their lives, I drive to our cabin, where I hope to salvage something of
my dignity. Within minutes, I am standing at the small dirty vanity with
my jeans draped over an arm, wrenching at the faucet handles only to
discover there isn't any water. I try the valves under the sink, but nothing
happens. There will be no washing or flushing.

Half-dressed, I dash through the cabin looking for liquids, bottled
water, Windex, anything. But there's nothing in the kettle but mineral
deposits, nothing in the ice chest but a warmish assortment of soda pop.
Finally, in a move as resourceful as it is disgusting, I pull the lid from
the toilet tank and soak the stains between the float ball and lift rod. By
the time I am finished, my jeans are not just ruby-ridden but saturated
in a way that only calls attention to the problem. Tying the denim shirt
around my waist, I appraise my appearance: thinning brown hair, check;
tired brown eyes, check; smell of dirt and blood, check.

Hating myself more by the minute, I step onto the dirt road and make
sticky advances toward the lodge, chagrined that every time I come to
the mountain I step into an uncertain teenage identity in which I am
categorically unglamorous. Years of living off lamb roasts and mashed
potatoes had caught up with me by my sophomore year, and I had spent
hours looking at myself in the mirror, wondering what it would be like
to have a waistline. My job at Mack's Family Drive-in had added fifteen
pounds to my already-buxom physique, and I watched enviously as wil-
lowy peers paraded the halls of Bear River High, showing off stomachs
that actually curved inward rather than hanging over their jeans. Anxious
for reassurance, I'd asked my father what he thought about my shape. He
sort of hummed and said, "Well, I always thought you were built a little
bit more like a boy than a girl."

I started watching what I ate—what everybody ate. My younger brothers powered down Pop-Tarts and lamb gravy without guilt. For them, food was something you ate when you were hungry. For me, food was the enemy. The less I ate, the more I thought about eating. At the cabin at Monte Cristo, I thumbed through back issues of the *National Enquirer*, feigning skepticism while covertly committing 1-800 weight-loss numbers to memory. I fought my body and it fought back, slowing my metabolism every time I tried to starve it into submission.

The summer of my senior year was the worst, since I actually said yes when the caramel-voiced woman on the telephone asked if I would enter the Miss Bear River Valley pageant ("a runner-up to Miss America!") as Number 17: Miss Western Trails. The sinister thing was not the stubborn assurances that I was cut out for it, but that I had somehow come to believe that the ordeal might redeem me. If I won the pageant—or even placed!—my mother and I and our whole subpar family could stop hating ourselves.

Obviously, I'd have to lose some weight. My mother prescribed water pills and diet pills, while my grandma Chournos supported me by trying to slim down herself. She spent hundreds of dollars that summer on grainy chocolate weight-loss shakes and excursions to the Gloria Marshall Figure Salon in Ogden, where we kneeled in front of "beauty rollers"—squat machines with wavy hardwood rods that spun in a circle just high enough for us to press our stomachs against. The point of the rollers (said the deeply tanned blonde at the sign-up desk) was to break up belly fat so that you could lose it. If you paid extra (we did), you could stretch out on a machine that jiggled your torso back and forth while you lay on your back in the dark, staring up at a textured asbestos ceiling, marveling at the liquidity of the human body. We smiled for our "before" pictures and waited for the pounds to come off, but our bodies never changed.

In the end, the only thing I managed to do at the pageant was squeeze myself into my mother's green prom dress and walk down the runway without tripping. The swimsuit competition alone had weirded me out beyond measure, as strapping on a pair of stilettos and strutting down the runway half-naked went against all of the shroud-your-body advice I'd ever received. Why it was OK to bare hips and thighs for a panel of judges while it was not okay to go *sleeveless* under any other circumstances was never explained. I felt hopelessly exposed as I pivoted in too high shoes, painfully aware of being ordered and ranked. Middle-aged women in slim dress suits urged me to smile, but I could barely manage a grimace, my lips quivering and spasming as if my teeth had suddenly become as unsightly as my too round stomach.

I'm pretty sure that I came in dead last. I was Number 17, Miss Western Trails, sponsored by a local café that clearly did not get to choose their own candidate: a chunky teenage gopher slayer who failed to explicate the finer points of Utah state politics during the interview (we had a state legislature?) and who had belted out "Joan of Arc" from the *Up with People Song Book* wearing a floor-length polyester smock that could have doubled for a white maternity dress. The picture of globular purity.

I'M HALFWAY TO THE LODGE when Michelle intercepts me with a greeting, noteworthy for its cognitive dissonance: bright happy tones pressed onto seething frustration: "You could at least have stopped to help or say hello before coming up here!"

I don't bother to mention my adventures with the toilet tank, nor do I remind her that I had said *no way* when she suggested that we do the reunion *just this once*. I also do not remind her that I said I would make an appearance only because I loved her. I would help with meal preparation and cleanup, but I would absolutely not oversee the arts and crafts or MC the program or help with the auction or clean up breakfast or play one stupid game of volleyball. What part of *I hate this family* did she not understand?

I give her a hug and apologize, even though my own feelings are buzzing and whizzing like so many frustrated bees. Once I'm home, I will open a fat merlot and drain half the bottle; but for now, I will help as I promised, dismally aware of the time: fifteen minutes down, five hours to go.

Ahead of us, the family lodge looms like a giant industrial wart amid the pines. The glorified Tuff Shed might as well have been the Dome of the Rock for all of the infighting it kicked up from conception to construction. The structure carved years off my mother's life as she quibbled with her family about who would get to use it and when. One of my grandmother's last acts of love had been to read a short speech at its commemoration, dedicating it to her descendants with the hope that it would bring them together. Her speech had been as sweet as it was sad, since the structure had merely managed to solidify old hurts: half of her progeny would beat the living shit out of the other half if they could get away with it.

With a halfhearted hello, I decline an apron and take my place alongside my aunt Janice and some cousins-in-law I hardly know. Aside from brute carbon chemistry, we don't have a thing in common. Our conversation is limited to intermittent appraisals of our root vegetables ("Thin enough?" "Too mushy?"). And so I retreat into my own thoughts, impatient with the small talk, carving and slicing, doing my best not to burst from pretending that there isn't a glaring absence where my mother ought to be.

If any of us ever missed a reunion, I do not remember it. One summer my grandmother went in for a biopsy and awoke with a bloody, L-shaped incision instead of a breast. And still she'd attended that year. I missed the surgery, since I was away at BYU, enduring the Mormon version of Jesus Camp. But my mother described the postoperative scene in pitiful detail. Hooked to bloody fluid drains and IVs, her mother had flitted in and out of consciousness, ashen and limp, calling out "I hurt!" and stirring long enough to add, "I hope somebody loves me."

Although my grandmother later denied having said these things— and, by the time I returned, was handling the whole thing as if she had lost some Chiclets or maybe a sock—the scene had a lasting and profound effect on my mother. And it triggered her pent-up frustration for a father who seemed to prefer ewes to her mother. So, when Janice suggested that the old man be spared the sight of his suffering wife, my mother reeled on her in fury: "She's his wife! He better jolly well get himself here!"

The solid redhead set her jaw and agreed to bring him down the mountain the very next day, even if she did not approve.

TAKING MY LEAD from the other women, I locate a knife and start chopping the freshly peeled potatoes into happy circles and half-moons. Outside, the men are readying the coals for the Dutch ovens. By now,

Michelle is standing at the buffet table conferring with Janice, who wears an orange and white apron with wide brown lace over a white cotton shirt. Clad in mom pants and a white apron lined with red lace and tiny crimson ewes, Michelle plots the placement of salads, making birdlike gestures, nodding. Over the dull hum of conversation in the rapidly filling lodge, I hear her chirp, "That's wonderful," and "I don't know how you do it all!"

On the opposite side of the building, my aunt Cherre is a picture from a Macy's summer catalog, her black hair permed and teased to perfection, wearing a green and gold floral-print blouse with just enough bronze to tie in her tan pants. Breezy and confident, she smiles and laughs as people come through the door, her movements as deliberate as Michelle's are mercurial.

As I work through the last batch of potatoes, I notice my cousins coming and going from the lodge, eyes laced with bushy false lashes and with teeth so white they're almost blue. Not one woman has shown up in a T-shirt, ball cap, or—god forbid—shorts, as if my grandparents might rise from their graves to disapprove. Everyone's hair bears the glossy luster of a Pantene shampoo ad. When Lan's family started camping together, I'd been shocked to see his sisters traipse around without makeup, their hair unkempt or tucked under dusty caps. Had they no shame?

I don't know if our attention to appearance is the product of region or family quirkiness. Being a woman in Tremonton was sort of like being a sheep at the Box Elder County Fair. You got soaped and rinsed and clipped and fluffed; and you weren't ready to parade around the ring until someone took a wash bucket and toothbrush to your anus. When my grandfather compared his daughters to ewes, he wasn't being unkind; he was just stating the most obvious metaphor.

In the lodge, no one says "please" or "thank you." It is as if we are born to our roles. While I ask after Church jobs and children, trying my best to be personable, no one asks how I am.

The stark unfriendliness slams me up against an invisible wall and bores a hole right through my chest. I had always hated the way we interacted at the reunion—the way Michelle and I licked up to other people like submissive wolves. And so it bothers me that I feel so *responsible*—to peel potatoes and placate and put other people at ease.

But something else bothers me, too. I can't remember attending the reunion the summer after Johnnie died, but suspect that I did. Unacquainted with loss, I would not have known how to proceed, either. If I said anything kind—anything at all to acknowledge the loss his children must have felt—I do not remember it.

Every swoop of the knife brings forth a new emotion. A jab of resentment, a glimmer of indulgence. By the time the meal is complete, I am in a black snit. It's not just the lack of gratitude that bothers me, but the whole charade—as if nothing had changed. At one point, Cherre had breezed by Michelle long enough to ask, "Where's your mom?" as if her baby sister were shirking her chores and not fucking *dead*.

Michelle's crestfallen face had said everything, and Cherre felt terrible. When I heard about it, I had been too stunned to speak. While the remark was probably the by-product of grief or denial, it confirmed my worst suspicion: no one feels the sickening weight of our mother's absence but us.

If anything, people seem relieved. In a place with too few resources, where love was sparse if it existed at all, it must be nice not to deal with the headstrong little sister, the spoiled brat racked with pain. The woman who burned up her house to get out of doing the dishes.

By the end of the day, Michelle dissolves into a heap of sagging shoulders and sobbing, not just because our mother is *gone,* goddamn it, but because she had been bold enough to ask if people would please stop dumping garbage in front of our cabin. At the request, some quick-thinking cowboy had yelled, "If you don't like it, get off the mountain!"

I missed the remark, but confronted the cowboy later, only to get a wide-eyed denial. I heard the dumbass out, hung up my dishtowel, and left. If anyone invited me to the reunion again, I would resort to violence.

On the way home, I flit between inventing caustic fantasies in which I tell off certain cowboys so expertly that they wriggle with shame in their ostrich-skin boots and wondering why I care—why I give a shit about whether or not my mother's family respects me, why I always felt homely and inadequate at Monte Cristo and still do. It's been twenty years since I was a chubby teenage gopher-slayer, at least a decade since my waistline overhung my jeans, and yet my self-hatred rallies like a latent virus whenever I get within ten miles of the family ranch.

It takes a stiff stretch of gravel road for the last thought to sink in. Why feel self-hatred at all—latent or otherwise? Why not hate the situation? The weird lack of sympathy? Why not be proud that I'd confronted someone in my mother's family for the first time in my life—that I'd supported Michelle as I'd promised? The most I should feel is some disappointment in myself for ignoring the intuitive nudge that had urged me not to go. But to turn on myself so completely—why?

I learned self-loathing in the same way I learned language: by being immersed in it all day long. My mother may have belly-danced in front of the living room windows, but she often seemed down on herself in an overboard way, especially if the conversation turned to her sister.

An ebony-haired beauty, Cherre had been a cheerleader before she got knocked up and eloped, causing my grandfather to rage and walk out on my mother, as if the trembling eight-year-old were to blame for her sister's misconduct.

It wasn't just Cherre's beauty that grated at my mother for years afterward; it was the feeling that her sister was lovable in ways she was not. In the wake of her father's departure, my mother grew up askew, measuring herself against a sister who had disappeared into legend, a sister who— she was sure!—had been loved by the man who abandoned her. If a week went by in which my mother did not say something like, "Well, I look as pretty as my sister today!" or "So-and-so says I am prettier than Cherre!" I do not remember it.

I felt my aunt's presence every day of my life. Every time my mother bought six pairs of pumps of the sort her sister might buy, every time she shimmied into size two jeans, every time she dyed her hair the same shade of brownish black. My mother's college degrees and medical career suddenly seemed irrelevant when she tumbled them against her sister's beauty and charm.

My mother never said, *Look at how you stack up against your cousins.* She didn't have to. It was the logical extension of her own lopsided rivalry with her sister. I knew Cherre's daughters actually won beauty pageants. I saw them duck their heads in embarrassment if I said hello to them at school (a pattern that—I shit you not—persisted into college). The half-contained tears of frustration my mother shed at not being as domestic as Janice or as gorgeous as Cherre were tears I stored over time, growing askew, too.

Mormon Church leaders championed virtue and inner beauty, but I knew that appearance reigned supreme. The body was the one thing that, according to Mormon doctrine, allowed human beings to become gods. And so controlling the body, perfecting it, was evidence . . . of what? That your inner self was as perfect and circumspect as your outer self?

Everyone knew that marking the body was wrong. Getting my ears pierced in the fifth grade was a huge deal—a sign that I might be embarking on the road to prostitution. Tattoos were out of the question. And yet, breast implants and nose jobs and tummy tucks were fine, if not tacitly promoted.

Flipping on the television a few weeks ago, I was stunned by a news story in which KSL reporters barged into Salt Lake City cosmetic surgery offices as a way of measuring the state's economic health. (Lots of people in waiting rooms: bullish. Few people in waiting rooms: bearish.) And I'd wondered what the reporters might derive if they did a corresponding head count at Valley Mental Health. The days in which I'd longed for cosmetic surgery had been my bleakest. Days that I hated myself so desperately I would have jumped off a bridge if it meant feeling desirable.

I read once that Utah boasts more cosmetic procedures than any other state, and I believe it. Driving on I-15, Utah's central artery, you cannot miss the constant appeals to perfection: dreamy handsome men and slender modest women, faces soft with filtered light. One of the most astonishing billboards features a buoyant new mother holding twin newborns aloft, sporting a waist that could not possibly have birthed them. Every third sign offers some kind of procedure: HANG OVER? (Fistfuls of fat overhanging too tight jeans); LASER LIPO (Hands tugging too-large jeans from a sucked-in stomach); ALL I WANT FOR CHRISTMAS IS MY TWO FRONT . . . (Huge red-sweatered honkers suggesting the word "tits").

I don't think my mother and I received more media messages than other women, and yet we both inherited bodily neurotics specific to our cultural heritage. To be female on the ranch was to be sheeplike and submissive, fluffed and prettier than the next sheep; to be female in the Mormon Church was to know yourself to be worthwhile only insofar as you were flawless and circumspect and pure; ageless and thin and virginal-looking—no matter how many babies you were required to birth.

The first time I went to a temple open house, I couldn't wait to see the sealing room where couples married for time and all eternity. The kindly volunteer explained how the mirrors, hung directly across from each other, symbolized the prisms of eternity. But when I stood between the mirrors, I only saw myself fragmented, imperfect, unlovable, and fat. Forever and ever and ever.

My self-image had been filtered through a flamboyant mother obsessed with her own self-image. But who knew what she saw when she gazed in the mirror? Where she looked for approval, she found emptiness. Her father could not see her at all, fixated with his own image: the poverty-stricken Greek lad turned American success. When my lonely mother got pregnant, he kicked her out of the house, furious that she had tarnished his image.

AFTER GUIDING the pickup across the last stretch of gravel, I pull over and unlock the hubs, relieved to be able to finish the drive without the boxy lurch of four-wheel drive. Outside, the smell of juniper and sage, the ubiquitous twitter of bugs and birds, the sun crouching low past the rumpled skyline, remind me of the years I drove to the end of the canyon and polished off a banana before launching myself down the road for eighteen miles. It took six marathons for me to outrun the chubby girl of my past. At long last, a wiry girl stared back at me from the mirror. A girl who should have been happier, but wasn't.

Ignoring the brilliant sweep of the mountains, pink in crepuscular glow, I cinch myself back into my seat and settle in for the final stretch, trying to ignore the emotions pulling tight across my chest. Slowing for each turn, I mark every familiar rocky escarpment and stunted juniper that shaded me as I raced toward self-improvement, certain that someday—if I was fast enough, smart enough, pretty enough!—I would be proud of myself for longer than, say, forty seconds. Even now, the mile markers leaning in the ground like so many teetering candles remind me of my crowded teeth and crooked smile.

There was always something to hate, if I thought about it. And I hate everyone. I hate the people on the mountain, smug in their happiness, endowed with perfect lives and bodies. Self-important and self-assured.

But most of all, I hate myself.

Feeling edgy and achy and sucker-punched, I steer the truck down the uneven asphalt, pinned to my seat by a weight that has settled across my heart and lungs. If there was a way to go back in time and live my life differently, I would. Given the chance, I would refuse beauty pageants, home perms, and control-top panty hose. I would say no and mean it. I would take back every stupid needy thing I ever said. I would protect my heart more vigilantly. And I would be a better daughter.

The last time I talked to my mother, it had been on the phone.

I called to say that I had to get back to school and wouldn't make it for Mother's Day.

She said she had cut down on her Topamax.

I said I was glad because I thought it made her loopy.

She said she thought so too.

Then I left for Reno, where I spent the rest of the day playing black-jack and slamming back shots of Tuaca.

I DID NOT tell my mother that I had sworn off Mother's Day in the same way I swore off her family reunion. As a child, I dreaded spring, knowing that the world would fall apart one day after church. It wasn't just the music of the annual service that made her bristle ("'M' is for the million things she gave me! 'O' means only that she's growing old"—the first line was forgivable; the second was not), but speeches that extolled the perfect mother. The ride home was usually silent, in which case her jaw was set like a thin metal trap. Then, there was the explosion that sometimes did, and sometimes did not, take place inside the car. "I don't know how they can be talking about a real person!"

During the rant, Cherre or Janice usually emerged as the standard of stay-at-home wonderfulness; and although I couldn't tell if my mother resented or admired the women, I knew that you just couldn't win.

My mother's anger didn't bother me—if anything, I agreed that the speeches seemed sort of stodgy and old-fashioned. It was where she directed her outrage that hurt. If any of us forgot to write a note of appreciation or come up with a thoughtful gift, the gloomy day got even gloomier, despite the fact that the sun was usually shining gloriously. The worst year had been the one in which my father had remembered the requisite cymbidium orchid corsage, only to flub up on the card, which read "Enjoy your Mother's Day, and don't worry about the dishes! . . . They aren't going anywhere!"

The humor, which was utterly lost on my mother, caused her to blow a fuse before church even started, and we almost missed it while she and my father argued loudly upstairs. Michelle saved the day by remembering to buy a little plaque ("If moms were flowers I would pick you!"). I had forgotten the occasion as I usually did, but Michelle was kind enough to say that the plaque was from me, too, since she had also composed a poem. Thank heavens.

Driving the canyon, I don't know whether to blow a fuse, too, or cry. Sick of my mother's moodiness, I finally said to hell with it. I stopped buying Mother's Day gifts and never sent cards. I did not expect my children to remember the holiday and thought she was selfish to think that we should have—as if ten-year-olds counted the Sundays in May. And she could just grow up and get over it.

But her death changes everything, and in the wake of the awful reunion I feel physically ill. For failing to be a good enough daughter. For leaving my mother to her demons.

WHILE I DOUBLED DOWN and split eights and aces, my mother endured her last Mother's Day. My father supplied the details over rubber enchiladas after one of my visits to the burned-out home. "It was getting late," he said. "Almost eleven o'clock when I came in the bedroom. When I got in there she was packing a suitcase."

He put down his fork, resting his chin in his hands. "She said she had to go to Salt Lake to have some special test done or she would die. It was the creepy crawlies, you know, her voices."

I didn't know what was weirder, the way he had said "creepy crawlies" as if they were something everybody got from time to time, like the flu, or the way he lumped them together with my mother's voices, as if they were the same thing.

"So," he said. "I took her into the emergency room. And we got that doctor we got before when her voices said she was going to die."

My eyebrows knit together. Her voices had sent her to the emergency room? On more than one occasion? Eager for him to continue, I did not ask for clarification.

"Well, that doctor just let her have it," he said. "He was not going to wake the technician for some test she didn't need. She could go home or wait until morning."

He shook his head. "After the doctor went out of the room, she cried that without the test she had only ten minutes to live. And I said, 'Dear, there's nothing I can do, so I'm just going to wait right here with you until you go.' I took her hand. When ten minutes were up, she said the voices had given her ten minutes more. When those minutes were up, she said she'd been granted an indefinite reprieve. We sat there, quiet. I don't know who started it, but one of us snickered. Then we both just cracked up. Then we got her things and went to breakfast. I hadn't heard her laugh like that for years, Kid. I thought it meant she was getting better."

THERE WAS NO WAY to tell my mother that I stopped visiting not because I did not care, but because I cared too much. If I didn't care, I would not have been so hurt that she cared more about her abominable family than me. If I didn't love her, I could have gone through the motions of Mother's Day without feeling powerless and angry. If she wanted to feel joy and pride as a mother, why not look at *me*? Was I so terribly disappointing?

But I did care and always had, and I can hardly steer my pickup down the road knowing that I didn't tell her so.

Around me, the world blurs as if a thunderstorm has suddenly descended over the mountains, hammering the fading centerline, watering the soldierlike signs at the side of the road. Rains that do not touch the parched earth, but pour forth from me.

Who knows what might have happened if I had visited my mother. Had I made it a priority, I could have seen her one last time. And I think that if she had felt my love, if I could have proven to her that she was worthwhile and wonderful, if I had stopped by her house with a poem or flower, then maybe she wouldn't have died.

TEN

The Bridge Builder

Just when I think the dusty grip of summer will never end, the days get shorter all at once. There is an unmistakable switch: a crisp edge to the air, noisy gatherings of birds, withering cucumbers and ripening squash, the combined odors of decay and fruition. Even before the leaves take on fevered edges, it feels like fall.

The valley feels softer now. More forgiving, maybe. It would be nice to say that *I* feel more forgiving, but I don't. My path of grief feels less like quiet steps toward resolution than a dodge down a middle school hallway. Now and then I feel the faint prick of something pliant; but it disappears as quickly as it appears. And so I prepare the yard for winter, grateful for the blips between swelter and freeze.

Cleaning out the garden, I throw apples across the fence to sheep that wait for them with wide unblinking eyes. Tonight, I will pile the corn and raspberry stalks in the pasture and bid farewell to the worst summer I have ever known. Until then, I will try to ignore the nostalgia that tugs at me every time I look at my grandfather's covered wagon. Today is the last I will see it standing guard in the open barn. As hoped, I sold the camp to my Uncle George, who is on his way to haul it away.

After the reunion, I had been so eager to get rid of everything that reminded me of my mother's family that I forgot that the wagon once meant something to me. Its wonky green and white presence defined our back yard for almost a decade. Most importantly, it marked time with my children. My little boys spent long hours helping me restore it, pulling nails and shellacking its oak bows and ribs. Together, we had hosted *Harry Potter* readings and warmed hot cider on the tiny wood-burning stove. Even before I fixed it up, I put blue-jammied toddlers to bed in its bunk overlooking the tiny back window. To let it go is to let go of an era in which it was sort of magical.

But the years I enjoyed the camp with my children are over. I never inspect its interior anymore; haven't hauled it up the canyon for years. During a particularly rough patch in my life the wagon became little more than a den of sex and wasps and weed, and I couldn't look at it without wincing. In the essay I wrote about my grandfather—the one my mother's Mormon shrink saw in a vision—I painted the camp as a vehicle of forgiveness. But that was before my mother started paying her shrink to mediate discussions with the dead man. If my grandfather's life inspired such neurotics, it was probably healthier not to be reminded of his humble beginnings. The 1890s carriage needs more than a drafty shed and my ambivalence; my uncle is just the sort of person to pamper it, and I need to let go of the past.

By noon, George pulls into our weedy access road, dragging a flatbed trailer behind a sleek F-350 of the sort that might have given birth to my pickup and then refused to admit it. While he hooks the double-axled nightmare to the winch, I pull my gloves on and off, walking the perimeter of the wagon, pretending to be useful. As the wheels veer unsettlingly near the edge of the trailer, he stops to wrench the tongue in the opposite direction, working silently, wrenching the camp forward. Then he ratchets it down, double-checks the straps, and invites me downtown for a burger.

I am pleased by the invitation, even though I don't have a clue what I'll say to him. Aside from passing hellos at family get-togethers, we've never had a conversation in our lives.

As a child, I idolized George because my mother had. Ten years older than she, he inhabited a place in her psyche that might have been reserved for a teen idol. He made his own saddles, played classical guitar, taunted bulls as a rodeo clown, parachuted from airplanes dressed as Santa for the family Christmas party, and completed a PhD in psychology.

But it's not George's credentials or the lingering glow of my mother's hero worship that appeal to me now. Of all my relatives, he seems the most likely to be square with me, not just about his family but about the Mormon Church. Once I stopped going to church, I felt a rift start to stretch between my family and me. No one was mean. If anything, there was something too nice about our interactions. Maybe I projected disapproval onto siblings who never rejected me at all. But there was no way to express how alienated I felt; no way to explain how radically different the world felt without religious mediation. It was less like being born again than waking up alone—as lonely as it was liberating. And so I am desperate to have someone understand this if nothing else: how it feels to be an outsider in your own family.

The sense that George might be able to understand my feelings stems from a talk he gave at his brother Johnnie's funeral. While we all wagged our heads at the tragic circumstances, George took the podium long enough to say that he never fit in with his brothers, never felt valued by his father for one instant. He did not say, "I blame my father for my little brother's death," but we got the message all the same.

It was as if George had waited his whole life to explain the sad disconnect between himself and his father. But as startling as the revelation was, I wondered if there was more to his feelings of alienation than a failure to fit in. Leaving Utah severed the ties to his father; leaving the Mormon Church strained the ties to his mother. She would not have rejected him; she would have been sad. Which is just as bad in its own way. There would have been the undeniable rift, the understanding that you disappointed the one person in your life who had always accepted you.

When George left the Church, he did so summarily and spectacularly, refusing allegations of sexual misconduct and walking away from a professorship at BYU. When I left, it was more like an awkward scene in a hotel lobby, where one person fumes at the pastry selection, another person presses hands into freshly ironed pockets, and both of them know that the love affair is over.

That my uncle might open up to me about his departure from the Church is a long shot; that he might be able to hear my story—a story I still cannot tell my family—is an even longer shot. But I feel like he's the only relative I've got who can understand how it is to carry the unstated sadness, the mute disappointment, of a father, a mother, a family.

According to my father and siblings, my life choices mean that I will be lost to them when we die, since nothing can save a person who abandons faith once they've known the full truth of the gospel. But I feel like I've lost them already.

Downtown, George and I order up a couple of ranch burgers and take a table in the middle of a crowded café that is mostly failing to look like a 1950s soda shop. Settling into a black diner chair, I appraise the recluse my mother adored. His jet-black hair is shot through with occasional white lines, but otherwise he seems to have aged just like his father. Which is to say, hardly at all. Slim and muscular, he looks like a handsome extra that just walked off a *Deadwood* set, a little too cleaned up and white-toothed for the actual West.

For as long as I can remember, George seemed unusually attuned to the pain in the world, and its beauty. It was as if God had given him the right physical characteristics to be a Chournos, but none of the insensitivity. He *oil painted,* for god's sake—a hobby that must have sent his pistol-packing brothers into fits of laughter. The picture of him on my grandmother's bulletin board baffled me as a child: him standing in a ribbed black robe and velvet hat shaking hands with another robed figure. Somebody told me that the picture meant he was a doctor, but not a *regular* doctor, which made no sense to me at all.

Waiting for our order, I am relieved to find the lingering pangs of hero worship are gone. The years between us seem to have collapsed along with the pedestal my mother put him on.

"I guess you and I are the intellectuals of the family, now," he says, smiling in a way that leads me to believe that he might not think that highly of intellectuals. "I don't know if you've noticed it yet, but getting a PhD only shows you how much you don't know."

"Trust me, I've noticed," I say, recalling the unbearable half hour I'd spent sitting on a long wooden bench under a print of John Milton, sure that I'd failed my comprehensive exams, staring miserably at my shoes while my doctoral committee deliberated. I could not remember a time in my life I'd felt stupider.

"When I was a kid I didn't give a damn about school," he says, smiling. "I flunked out of every class there was. I was going to drop out and get rich like my dad and my brothers."

I restrain a sardonic laugh. The same thing had occurred to virtually everyone in the family—not that we'd drop out of school, but that we were going to be rich.

My grandfather's legacy had seemed so vast, so able to accommodate all of our dreams. And yet the feeling of wealth—or maybe even the tacit understanding that it might not be so unlimited after all—made everyone rigid and anxious. My mother grew downright neurotic awaiting each cash disbursal, spending every dollar before it rolled in. When the last big land deal got hung up in a legal battle over mineral rights, it was as if her whole world caved in: no more grand improvements to her house and—worse—the possibility of owing half a million dollars to a scorned buyer. She received the news in January and died in May, and I sometimes got the feeling that the impending battle did her in.

"So," I ask. "Why didn't you?"

"Only because the biggest, toughest man I knew, the principal of Bear River High, called me into his office one day. I was sure he was going to chew me out for cutting classes, but he didn't. He started to cry."

The memory lights up my uncle's face as if the interview had taken place five days ago, not fifty years. Eyes bright, he leans over the table and locks eyes with me. "And you know what? I'll never forget what he said. He said, 'All of your brothers have dropped out of school, George. But not *you*. What can I do to show you how wrong you are about yourself?'"

I don't know what the principal had seen in my uncle. But the words work their way to my heart as if they were intended for me: "how wrong you are about yourself." If I could put my finger on the sickness I had known all of my life, it was this: that no matter what I achieved, I always felt like a failure. When my doctoral committee invited me back into the conference room to congratulate me on passing my exams, I had not felt pride but embarrassment, sure that the five seasoned scholars had passed me out of pity.

One man had changed my uncle's life. Through the eyes of the principal, he saw himself transformed: as smart and capable and worthwhile. But I can't tell if the string of successes that sprang from the interview did much for him in the long run. There is something not altogether happy about him. Something I used to notice in my mother, something I recognize in myself—something restless and aching; something only temporarily assuaged by achievement and adventure.

"My research in psychology helped me understand my father here," he says, pointing to a finely sculpted head. "But it could not undo the damage here," he continues, moving his finger toward his heart, where it comes to rest between red stitched roses, blooming on both sides of a white western shirt. "I guess you could say the PhD saved my life."

That my uncle needed saving surprises me. He had always been so dazzling. My mother liked to say that George made her "feel like a real person," that he inspired her to go back to school. But she also said he harbored deep insecurities.

I never really believed her. How could someone so talented—a doctor of psychology for heaven's sake—feel insecure? My insecurities made sense. I really was marginal: at guitar playing, at painting, at singing, at school, at all of the things he did with aplomb. Him insecure? Unbelievable.

I nod while he continues, a somber reversal of his earlier animated self. "The PhD didn't make me feel any better about my dad, but it got me away from the Outfit. I told Johnnie that he needed to get away, too, but he just wouldn't do it. Maybe he didn't know how."

Chin to palms, I lean forward. "Do you blame your dad for what happened to Johnnie?"

"I don't know," he says. "If you had a thick skin, you could deal with our old man just fine. If you didn't, well . . ." He shakes his head. "Johnnie called me a few days before he died. He was madder than a hornet about the trust. I told him to leave it alone, to wait it out. But he just couldn't do it."

When I ask when Johnnie began to break down, George pauses. *Was there a beginning to such things? Or was instability just part of the system? A set of inherited impulses that waited for the right moment to flare?* Frowning at a basket full of stubby fries, he gathers a response. "As a kid, I figured everyone thought about suicide since I did all of the time. It wasn't until other kids started avoiding me that I guessed it probably wasn't normal."

I don't know what to say. The revelation is so sad, and yet he mentions his suicidal feelings as if they were a set of unfortunate freckles he'd come to accept. Of the four brothers, three had harbored a death wish; two had acted on it. Sam was the only one who seemed content. The prevailing theory—my mother's at least—was that Sam had been his father's favorite, and that the other children floundered as their father lashed out or alternatively ignored them.

Listening to George undoes years of stilted ideas I've had about my uncles. From my mother's perspective, the men were merely unstable. I don't know if she was more comfortable with the role of clinician than sister, but I don't remember her ever feeling *sad* for them. Sam was the golden child; Monte, a suicidal playboy; George, a gloomy recluse. And Johnnie. Johnnie was the worst. After he died, she admitted to being unable to feel loving toward him as his mental health edged toward the cliffs.

She blamed the emotional disconnect on birth order. The little brother her siblings adored was just old enough to torment her. Left in charge when their mother went to church meetings, he was more likely to chase her with snakes or parade his stash of pornography than help her make mud pies. My mother claimed that he felt menacing to her early on; but it also seemed like the two were stuck in the ages they had been when their father left home—he, a hormonal twelve-year-old; she, a headstrong eight-year-old. After a teenage fight over the family car, Johnnie wheeled on my father and warned him not to date my mother, as she was "the most spoiled little shit" he'd ever seen.

My mother resented Johnnie because he always seemed to be competing with her for parental recognition, but in truth they both were. While my parents were building the cabin at Monte Cristo, Johnnie managed tools and equipment for the Outfit. That she had to ask his permission to borrow something as small as a flashlight infuriated my mother, while her reluctance to do so infuriated him. He was especially suspicious of anything my father did for his in-laws, as if earning their favor meant that there wouldn't be any left over for anyone else. Depending on who you asked, my father was a crackpot handyman who never spent enough to do a job right, and Johnnie was a control freak who squandered money on every little thing. And so on.

As a teenager, I endured such tensions, vaguely aware that my own concerns (losing weight and wishing to god Kirk would kiss me) hardly blinked on my mother's radar. Feeling expendable, I wandered around the mountain with a sling of gopher traps, listening to the *New Testament* on cassette, trying to increase in favor with God and man.

As I was thus engaged, my mother and her brother endured each other. The two kept their mutual irritation in check until something set one of them off and things went straight to shit—like the afternoon both of them arrived to take their father to the hospital, where their mother was preparing to come home after surgery.

While Johnnie fumed that *he* was going to pick his mother up, my mother maintained that grandma had specifically asked *her* to do it, which prompted Johnnie to insist that they would have to take two cars then. Enraged, my mother said that it didn't take two cars to pick up one person, and if he needed to do it so badly then she wouldn't go at all. When she turned to leave, Johnnie thundered, "Don't you leave while I'm talking to you!" and shoved her to the floor.

I did my best to ignore such altercations. Looking in at the struggle was like watching the unfolding of an unpleasant drama in which the comic elements failed to keep people from killing one another. I had the feeling that things were spinning out, but I also thought that things couldn't get worse.

AS GEORGE DOES MOST OF THE TALKING, I polish off my ranch burger and lean back in my chair, idly scanning café walls peppered with Americana. Rosie the Riveter brandishes a bicep at Betty Boop serving a Coke. A stately elk welcomes passengers aboard the Union Pacific Railroad next to a leggy white woman with maracas inviting vacationers to Cuba. Stars and stripes and silver hubcaps. Glossy promises of leisure and industry; peace, prosperity, and mobility.

Annoyed by the images, I shuttle my empty French fry basket to another table and focus on George, who is describing a string of adventures: skydiving and bear sightings; films on which he worked as a livestock consultant. If anyone had wrung the American dream out of thin air, it was his father; and if anyone squeezed glamour out of a dull rural upbringing, it was George.

Although George's stories are the breathless adventurous sort, guaranteed to make my mother swoon, I notice that I do not share her biases. George might have captured my childhood imagination, but Johnnie captured my heart.

There was something about Johnnie's swagger, his silver-buttoned western shirts and snakeskin boots, that flattened me with awe. I eyed the pistol neatly tucked against his ribs, admired the way he left the cabin as if he were going to settle a score. He joked with us kids, gave us rides in his truck, played sobbing western songs by Patsy Cline, Tammy Wynette, and Hank Williams about cheatin' hearts, hidin' out, movin' on. Songs that made you feel happy and wretched at the same time, as if love had stretched your heart so thin its strings would burst like rubber bands. He drove a custom-painted 18-wheeler. He bullshitted on the CB radio. He smirked at my fierce uneven pigtails. That he bothered to notice only made me love him more. None of the other adults acknowledged my presence at all.

I never saw the hostile man my mother described. I didn't know when things started to go south, or why Johnnie and my mother seemed determined to agitate each other. But I felt this in my bones: that his well-being—his identity right down to his core—was tied to his father.

I was pregnant with our second child when my mother called to say that my grandfather was acting strangely. The last time she visited, he had waved an impatient arm at an empty living room, demanding that all of those people in white get the hell out of his house. He'd also started showing affection, which was more alarming to his family than the host of invisible visitors, since they were expected to show up as the veil wore thin, waiting as they did to shuffle you off to the spirit world.

For the first time in his life, the old man started showing something like warmth. In an unprecedented gesture, he pulled my mother to him and pleaded, "Don't let anybody starve, Helen! Don't let anybody ever starve!" The request was strange, but the tender way he drew her to him was even stranger, and his behavior convinced her that he'd gotten wind of the fact that he was about to go, and that he better make amends with his loved ones in short order. One by one, his children and grandchildren came to see him, and one by one—if they were lucky—he whispered something affectionate. For the first time in his life, he told my grandmother that he loved her. He even went so far as to tell some of Sam's family members that they were his favorites—which hardly went over very well with people like George, who returned for the transformation only to find the same ornery sonofabitch he had left behind years before.

Thinking I'd better visit before it was too late, I let myself in the back door and slipped through the cluttered kitchen. I wondered if I might be privy to the tender new man my mother had described, but I wasn't. I said hello and my toddler gave him a hug. Then we stood in silence while I held his dry brown hand. After a minute or two, he simply said, "Well, I guess it's gonna be a hard spring."

Two weeks later, Johnnie walked out of his house holding a man's suit, placed it in the driveway, and set it on fire.

IN THE CAFÉ, George launches into a discussion of the family partnership, but I lose track of the conversational thread. For the first time since my mother died, I notice that fire marked the last day of Johnnie's life in the same way it marked the last day of hers. While her fire had certainly outdone his (and heaven knows how much this might have pleased her), I wonder if it had just taken longer to start. And so I wonder what role fire plays in the psyche, what toxins are released by a flame. What is it about reducing something to ash that allows us to let go?

For a minute, I think I might ask George about fire, but decide against it. When it came to such details I knew not to pry. Told in fragments and cryptic allusions, family stories rarely accounted for motives and never accounted for feelings. And so I can only guess what Johnnie was thinking—what he felt as he watched the suit burn.

I don't know if he arranged the suit first, if he spread its sleeves wide in an embrace, or if he buttoned it carefully, bending the arms at the elbows and resting the cuffs across each lapel. Perhaps he imagined his own body, laid out in its folds. When I heard about it, I imagined him building a small pyre and igniting the wood with a soft flash of kerosene, feeling his life flash before him, fifty-three years of it, working the sheep, driving a truck, floundering at a second marriage. It wasn't enough to want to die. It wasn't enough to want others to die. You had to figure out how to do it.

The suit had belonged to his eldest brother, Monte, the dashing, devil-may-care uncle who shot himself when I was still in diapers. From what I knew, Johnnie had idolized his brother. And so his burning the suit was . . . what? A way of venerating him? Of empathizing? Of preparing himself for a similar end?

I heard that Monte left town before coming apart entirely. No one knew why he disappeared. He had been holed up in a Nevada hotel for weeks when something threw him out of bed—something he took to be the devil. Shaken to the core, he drove home and told his mother, who admitted that she'd added his name to the temple prayer rolls at the same time he'd been tossed to the floor. Mormon temple rites, which culminated in a prayer over the names, were supposed to ensure that help would come. Why the prayers of the faithful unleashed the *devil* in Monte's case didn't make sense, but subsequent events only seemed to substantiate the story. Why else would a man shoot his wife and turn the gun on himself?

I learned about the incident in the Nevada hotel room the same way I learned about my mother's voices and Johnnie's suit-burning: in my father's weird offhand way. As we walked through Barnes and Noble after visiting Michelle one day, he sort of shrugged and said, "Well, I guess it was kind of like that time Monte wrestled the devil," as if it were a perfectly natural thing to say between the cookbooks and genre fiction. I looked at him with my eyebrows askew, and his face melted into a sheepish smile. "Oh, yeah. Your grandmother told your mom that when he died."

I said nothing. As much as I wanted to chalk the story up to family nuttiness, it seemed like something *was* haunting my mother's family. Call it the devil. Call it a demon or disillusionment or despair. It had beaten Monte and Johnnie. And sometimes I think it had beaten my mother, too.

SITTING AT THE CAFÉ, I shift my weight and drain my water glass, surprised by the tilt of the sun. Booths around our small table have emptied and filled until the place empties out in an afternoon slump. I feel honored that George has opened up so spectacularly, but I also feel frustrated. I had hoped to tell him a little bit about myself, but there doesn't seem to be an opening.

Brushing renegade crumbs from the tabletop, I wonder if it would trouble George to know that the conversation reminds me of the ones

I used to have with his father—late-night soliloquies in which the old man barely paused between one story and the next: the harrowing voyage from Greece, the indignities of mine and railroad, the hungry men grappling for food.

While my grandfather's stories cycled back to the hardships he knew as a young man, George's cycle back to his father, a man he seems to revere and resent in equal measure. Listening to him, I feel the familiar tug of frustration that comes from trying to love a spectacular parent—the hopeful impulse to please, the steely resolve to differentiate—all of the ways that one person becomes a single point of reference."]

"The sheep were the last straw," he says, leaning into a cocked elbow. "My dad promised all us boys a herd of sheep when he quit the business. But when it came right down to it, he only came through for Sam. And so that's when I broke with my dad. I told him I wasn't coming home ever again, not even for his funeral."

I nod. I knew that Johnnie had been angry as well—which only infuriated my mother. The girls hadn't been promised a herd to begin with.

The sheer force of everyone's indignation baffled me at the time. Why would anyone fight over *sheep*? Stupid and smelly and infested with ticks. My mother did not have a smidgen of interest in running a herd; and where was she going to put them?

But it occurs to me now that the sheep, like all of my grandfather's possessions, were not items you could tally on a spreadsheet. He might offer you something and he might not, but if he did you took it as a huge honor. He was famous for handing out hundred dollar bills, and seemed to have them stuffed inside his pockets all of the time, as if he'd just held up a bank. While a struggling college student, I'd turned to leave his home one afternoon when he simply said, "Well, you come over here now." Rummaging in a shirt pocket he pulled out a wad and peeled three hundreds away. "You take this with you over to school." Of such gestures, my mother used to quip, "the Lord giveth, and the Lord taketh away!" broadly equating her father with the Savior without a trace of irony.

I accepted the bills at face value, grateful to be able to pay spring tuition, but the gesture meant so much more to my mother. The old man had no ability to show affection, and from what I could tell, no inclination. And so the sheep, like the random cash dispersals, were not just a marker of generosity but a measure of his pride. The closest thing to love he had, and just as hard to come by.

George's version of the botched sheep deal is like listening to a song I used to hate covered by a different artist. Same chord progressions and themes, different voice. When my mother used to rail about such injustices, I sided with George. If a legacy packed so much pain, why not leave it alone?

But the lingering ache in George's voice tells me that he never really left things behind. He might have escaped the Outfit, but he doesn't seem to have escaped the feeling that he never really mattered to his father.

Following his gaze to the empty parking lot, I let a pause settle between us. Love, it seems, is hard to measure in the best of circumstances. There are the usual indicators: the brightness of a smile, the warmth of a hug, the intensity of a whispered "I love you," the ability to listen carefully, as if words were precious and the feelings behind them blown glass. But words could be disingenuous, and my grandfather didn't use them anyway. And he did not smile or notice you at all unless you spilled all of your Welch's grape soda onto the floor. In the absence of the usual indicators, the least of his gifts became precious.

Were calculating the symbolic value of something as easy as calculating the physical cost of an object, my uncles might not have been wounded so deeply. Consider the value of a diamond ring, for instance: there is the cut and color of the stone, its clarity and carat weight. There is the amount of gold in the ring, and the quality of its workmanship. But there is also the story behind it, which is far more important than the ring's material existence. "This ring," says the salesman, waving it under the light, "was smuggled out of Nazi Germany by a Jewish woman who stitched it up under her skin." And it suddenly doesn't matter if the ring is a little dinged, or if you'd initially winced at the price, because the story makes it priceless.

So it was with my grandfather's property. You could put a market price on the thousands of acres of land, appraise the home and cabin and barns and fences and outbuildings. But it was impossible to calculate the symbolic value of each acre, the percentage of The West that still resided in the battered wash-pan, the measure of the American Dream that still lurked in the camp stove and drinking ladle. His worn-out Ford pickup would fetch nothing on a trade-in, but it was likely to cause a standoff if my grandfather tried to give it away.

My grandfather's up-by-the-bootstraps story was important insofar as it seemed to prove that anyone with enough pluck and ingenuity could strike it rich. But it was even more powerful because it had bits of God tangled up in it. The Outfit was more than bread and butter and shelter. It was proof that America offered its treasures to those who, through devotion and diligence, were meant to have them. My grandfather saw his property as a natural result of hard work, while my grandmother saw it through a Mormon version of Manifest Destiny in which the faithful were secured a place in the West. That my grandfather never joined the Church did not seem to contradict her version of the story in the least. "It's the way the Lord intended it," she said to me once, leaning forward in a pink housedress. "The Lord wanted Nick to have this ground, and he takes good care of it."

Because of the way the story got told, I grew up with the feeling that if you were good enough and strong enough and hardworking enough, happiness and prosperity were not just likely, but deserved. Failing to have certain things didn't just mean that you were lazy or weaker than other people. It meant that you must be less pleasing to God.

According to my father, Johnnie endured a rocky relationship with his father, made worse by his dependency on the Outfit for a job, which came and went depending on whether the two were getting along. Finally, Johnnie had wheeled on his father in the west desert one day, grabbing his old man by the shoulders and pleading with him to *goddamn listen for once.* At that he was let go for good.

His father's trust had been the final insult. In it, the family home, all of the sheep, and full control of the estate had been granted to Sam. The girls were to receive half of what the boys got. The paperwork made Nick's biases explicit: who was worthwhile, and who was not. Who shared in his legacy and how much.

GEORGE DOESN'T SAY ANYTHING MORE about Johnnie. He doesn't have to. My parents told and retold his story as if doing so might change the outcome. After the funeral, my father felt a crystalline thought come into his mind, as if someone were speaking the words to him: *Do not concern yourself about Johnnie: I have taken the sword from his hand.* But if God—the only source of such a message—could offer my uncle death, why not offer him hope?

There was no good way to tell Johnnie's story, no triumphant narrative arc. The scattered recollections of his self-destruction vary according to who happened to be where, and I got the whole thing secondhand.

It was the week before Easter Sunday when Johnnie and his wife arrived at church to teach a Sunday school lesson. Within minutes, the couple got into a fight and Johnnie wheeled on the children. The boys were flowers, he said. The girls were weeds. Then he stormed out. When he got home, he burned Monte's suit in the driveway.

That afternoon, Johnnie burst into his parents' home and started shouting at his ailing father. When my grandmother begged him to stop, he snarled, "That's what he did to me when I was just a kid." Then he demanded equal representation on the partnership papers. He was, he said, tired of fooling around. He deserved to be a general partner so he could "lie as important as anyone else." When she tried to calm him, he bellowed that she was "too dumb to know anything," grabbed her neck with both hands, and shook her hard, leaving a band of bruises around her throat. Then he vowed to kill Sam and his family. "I'll lay them low," he said. "You've been told."

In the wake of his departure, my grandmother worried. Things had been strained for so long that it was hard to tell what was normal and what was not, where anger turned into deadly rage. Was her son dangerous or merely unhappy? Would things blow over as they had before, or would something terrible happen if she did not act? Unsure, she called my mother, who said that if no one else was going to call the police, then she would.

The police report claimed that an unarmed female officer showed up at my grandmother's house expecting little more than a family squabble. After speaking with Johnnie's wife on the phone, she called for backup: Yes, he was wearing at least one firearm with the safety off. Yes, he posed a threat to himself and others. And no. No officers would be allowed in the house without gunfire.

Cherre arrived to talk to her brother, while my mother arrived to comfort her mother. There were two homes side by side, one set in solid gold brick, the other planted firmly in its shadow. Between the two, police began marking a perimeter. A few of Johnnie's friends had finally convinced him to come out peacefully, when something set him off. One story ran that he turned hostile listening to his wife make arrangements with the hospital ("They're not gonna lock me up in some basement at McKay Dee!"). Another ran that Johnnie had seemed subdued until his wife pointed in the direction of his father's house and shouted, "Poison! They're all poison!"

Whatever happened, the last tenuous thread holding Johnnie intact snapped. The only warmth left in him flowed from the pure hot heat of rage. Someone would pay for his misery; it didn't matter who. He yelled, "It's all over!" kicked in the door to the laundry room, and headed out the back door.

LOOKING AT GEORGE, I am glad that he lit out for Wyoming and never looked back. It was the safest thing to do, maybe the only thing to do in a place where you were valuable only insofar as you substantiated someone else's story. Who cared if you never felt loved a day in your life? To be affluent in America! To rise above the teeming masses! To be worthy of God's grace! These were imperatives you could not question, even if they eclipsed your own dreams or turned your loved ones into opponents.

The saddest thing about my grandfather's story is that I think he just meant to provide. His children would not know the bottomless hunger he had known as a boy in Greece, the indignities he had known in the mine and the railroad. Being starved for food made sense; being starved for affection made no sense at all. Life was no soft thing. Soft people died. Unlike his own father, my grandfather would leave his children a legacy of plenty, a legacy in which a man could peel away hundred dollar bills all day long, like endless layers of endless onions.

I don't bother to tell George that I severed my ties to his family as my mother got sicker. He doesn't seem interested, and besides, what is there say? That his father's legacy was just as lousy for mothers and daughters as it had been for fathers and sons?

The problem was that there were two things, my grandfather and the *idea* of my grandfather—and the latter was much more important. When my mother looked at her father, she did not see a tetchy old man stunted by need; she saw herself rejected by the most wondrous person she knew. And so I don't think that the man would have cast such a long shadow if he had not been placed on such a high pedestal.

The summer before she died, my mother called me in tears. Why was I so against going to Monte Cristo? Why didn't I want to help renovate our cabin at Monte Cristo? Couldn't I see how hard she'd fought to secure our share of the property, our part of the family inheritance? I wandered around the garden as she spoke, mangling dandelions with my shoe, trying to decide how to respond. In the wake of my pause, I heard a strained whisper: "Don't you want part of our legacy?"

I saw her then, trying to salvage a legacy as she had tried to save Johnnie, running headlong into something that was well beyond her ability to fix. There was the cold April afternoon and dark marks around my grandmother's throat, the two homes side by side. There was a score to settle, a pistol in my uncle's hand, and the exit from the back door of his home. Then, a single gunshot. And my mother running toward the sound of it and my uncle crumpling from the weight of it, and her figure beside him, bent down in the brittle grass, listening for breath, kneeling as in prayer, hands crossed on his heart, pressing and pressing an insistent rhythm, blood pulsing from the wound in his chest with each push, her hands turning dark as she willed life and love and hope into a man for whom they were already gone.

Next door, my grandfather withered under a white bed sheet. There was no sense telling him what had happened. Better to let the old man go in peace, comfortable with the knowledge that he had provided well. Two weeks later, in spite of everyone's efforts to protect him, he woke in the night calling out, "My son, they shot my son!"

And then he died.

If it were up to my mother's papers to tell the story of that spring, you'd think nothing had happened at all. Nothing remains of it. No scraps of writing, no cards or photos, no funeral programs, and—if I remember right—no tears. The mother I remember is not a woman torn by grief, but one making grim-faced arrangements. If she felt anything at all, it was fierce resolve: her family would be represented on her father's funeral program, come hell or high water. Michelle and I complied by singing C. W. McCall's "Columbine," after which she sang "The Bridge Builder." The irony of the song was lost on everyone, as the poem by Will Allen Dromgoole features an old man spending the last day of his metaphorical life building a metaphorical bridge over a metaphorical chasm, into which a metaphorical youth may stumble.

Unlike the old man in the poem, my grandfather had not spent the last years of his life building a bridge, but inadvertently removing all of the supports. The bridge that supported him could not bear the weight of his children, weighed down with their own hopes and dreams. The bridge still looked as if it led to success and happiness, but it did not, and probably never had.

IN THE CAFÉ, I feel George's energy start to wane. I never got to mention my feelings of alienation, but I guess it's just as well. With a legacy like my grandfather's, maybe everyone felt alienated. In a family where no one listened for long, where success was more important than affection, where material blessings were contingent on certain kinds of favoritism, where *things* were the marker of your worth, how could you possibly feel connected to people?

"You know," George says, veering toward the topic of my mother for the first time. "Your mom was smart, and I was a coward. So I encouraged her to become the general secretary of the partnership. If anyone could make things fair, she could, and she did a good job."

For the first time since we sat down, I feel the unmistakable surge of resentment. I can't blame George for my mother's obsession with her father's estate—how could he know that she would lose all sense of where the Chournoses ended and her children began? But he was a psychologist for god's sake. How could he understand the family pathology so completely—so well that he would bolt from it to save his own skin—only to send his little sister into the fray?

True, she had not needed a lot of nudging. Offering her the opportunity to have a little power—a voice!—within the family in which she'd always felt disenfranchised was like offering an alcoholic a lifetime supply of Jameson. When I finally drew a boundary around my own breaking heart—when I said I would not attend Chournos events—she railed and wept until my father called to accuse me of being in "groupthink." With whom, I did not know.

Unwilling to validate George's last comment, I let him fill in the conversational gap with happy chatter. Then I give him a hug and take a last look at the dashing man who flung himself out of airplanes, dodged bulls, and scaled the slick ivory escarpment of academia, and still cannot face his own family.

Vaguely, I know the partnership is regrouping. Since my mother's death, one of her children will need to take her place as our family's representative. My father can't do it. The legalities require blood. Only a direct descendent of Nick Chournos will do, a direct beneficiary within his bloodline. The tradition is as quaint as it is solipsistic. And I will be damned if that representative will be me.

And so I fight my feelings for George. I know how difficult it is to stake out a place that feels centered and stable. I know how lonely it is to draw back from people you love, to try to cobble together a sense of yourself that isn't wholly distorted by another person's dreams and desires.

The one thing I want most from my legacies is the one thing they do not offer: a quiet sense of well-being. A self-worth that is not filtered through the panoptic eye of God or the uneven affections of a preoccupied mother or the American Dream or the hierarchical mechanisms of academia. To feel content. Without heirlooms and titles and achievements and awards. Without anything at all but my own fragile skin, and maybe a little bit of mercy.

ELEVEN

Troubles

As George pulls away with his father's camp, I feel the unmistakable flash of finality. It's not the farewell that bothers me, but endings in general: admitting that a friendship has run its course, recognizing that my children are turning into adults, letting go of unrealistic expectations. There are literal deaths and figurative deaths, and figurative ones can feel just as raw. Grief doesn't come from losing a person, but from all of the hope you invested in them.

It doesn't take a fleet of psychologists to tell me that George and I will never be friends, and while I'm disappointed, I am also grateful for his willingness to dismantle the bulletproof image I've had of him, if nothing else. In the space of a few hours, he did something I've never seen anyone else in his family do—show vulnerability. And so as I stand at the road that shoots northward like an arrow past the fields and intermittent ramblers, tethered to this one spot on the planet, feeling wobbly and small, I try to unclench my heart and let him go.

My mother's siblings had been cautionary tales, not people. With the possible exception of George, every one of them had had a bun in the oven, was suing Trojan, or had in other colorful ways earned their shotgun weddings. Unruly and reckless, Monte and Johnnie got what was coming to them. Their tempers and unstable marriages had not taught me that life was uncertain or hard or unfair, but that you could not be too careful.

Now, watching the camp disappear into a row of poplars, I wonder if you can be too careful. If the flip side of being perilously unruly is being too conscientious. If you can retreat to a place where safety and surety become treacherous, where your own heart of darkness becomes invisible, where being good and pure and steadfast and pleasing everyone is not an extension of your compassion but a reflection of your fears.

As a young woman, I knew that unhappiness was a product of unwise choices. It never occurred to me that unwise choices might be a product of unhappiness.

Sunday school teachers typically taught this concept through twin diagrams: "Satan's Plan" and "Heavenly Father's Plan." In the former, a dark diamond showed actions that moved toward a bottleneck of "Eternal Unhappiness," while in the latter—a rainbow-colored hourglass—actions moved toward "Everlasting Happiness." The choices were simple: Lying and cheating ultimately led to failed relationships, jail, and death; while staying pure and clean, being honest, and refusing coffee, alcohol, and tobacco naturally led to "perfect freedom," "good job," and "good friends."

There was no ambiguity, no crossover. Wicked people could not *truly* be happy in the same way righteous people could not truly be sad—at least for long. Life was full of opposition—that was part of Heavenly Father's plan!—but if you had enough faith you could be of good cheer.

IF YOU WERE TO ASK when our marriage started to fall apart, I could use the zeroly nuanced plot I had once applied to my uncles: We failed to keep ourselves unspotted from the world; we moved away from Utah; we started taking long drives on the Sabbath. We failed certain tests of faith and conduct. We discovered tequila. You might as well say we had "troubles."

I married aglow with the feeling that I'd never bungle anything again. Until then, I felt like a failure at pretty much everything—college, beauty pageants, waitressing, losing weight—but I knew these things were superficial when you tumbled them against eternity.

There was no higher calling than being a wife and a mother. None. And so I forgave my shortcomings insofar as I could and focused on finding a husband. In a daring move, I dressed my buxom self in a black sequined leotard and fishnets and hit up a church-sponsored Halloween dance. By the end of the night, I was dizzy with love. Witty and insouciant, Lan fit all of my most hopeful criteria. A returned missionary and former staffer for Orrin Hatch, he exuded all of the confidence I lacked. Best of all, he seemed to love me as I was.

Determined not to repeat the sexual faux pas of my relatives, I followed the recommended time line for Mormon engagements, which fall between ridiculously fast and dizzyingly so. Having "sexual relations" before marriage meant you couldn't get married in the temple; and not getting married in the temple was like wearing an invisible sign above your head that said, "Shit, guys, we did it!" Non-temple weddings were morbid affairs, held in church gymnasiums, presided over by bishops who inadvertently rubbed in the shame by urging the couple to solemnize their commitment to each other in the temple as soon as they were worthy to do so.

For reasons I never understood, becoming worthy took a full year. Maybe extended humiliation was necessary to prove your worthiness. All I knew was that the threat of a non-temple wedding worked on me, and I became an expert at shutting down sexually, as if God Himself were keeping a running tally of my untoward urges.

During our engagement I tried to remain as pure as possible. The trouble with being worthy was that I didn't know which indiscretions were bad enough to preclude a temple wedding. During a late-night tussle with Lan, I had held my breath in awe as a white wad burst from the woody between my fingers and nailed me right in the eye. Shocked, and pretty sure we'd gone too far, I called the printer in charge of the invitations and put a hold on the order until I could determine if we needed to arrange for another location.

Perhaps our questionable premarital activities signaled that we were two dark souls on a dangerous path—something a bishop would suggest to us later. But I had made a personal commitment to do everything right—a little better than right, if I could. I knew from the *Book of Mormon* that "wickedness never was happiness," but I had not counted on the idea's dark reversal—that if you were unhappy, you must be wicked.

THE BEST PART of being married to Lan was that his love was so stabilizing that I hunkered down and finished college. The worst part was that I couldn't figure out how to rewire my sexual circuits. I had spent so long curbing my lust that it seemed to have stayed curbed. I wasn't sure if I'd even been *infatuated* with Lan, since part of my knowing he was The One had to do with my *not* feeling the wrong kinds of things. He had a broad chest and dazzling hazel eyes, but my feelings for him were mostly platonic. By the time we made it to our nuptial condo in Park City, I noticed that the pressing desire to tear off my shirt was no longer pressing. Which should have been more alarming than if we'd fooled around a little.

According to my mother, marriage was effortless if you did it right. Straightforward and strong like the mountains around us. As a child, I did not need a compass to point out the cardinal headings. The Wasatch Front carved an unambiguous line from north to south, shielding us from the wiles of the world, from godless easterners and dull midwesterners. From what I knew of it, the south might as well have been Vonnegut's Tralfamadore, and California was a shining oasis made up of shapely people in tiny clothes who were certainly going to hell. Between Tremonton and Los Angeles there was Death Valley. Between Tremonton and New York there was corn. Which was all I knew about these United States until we moved to McLean, Virginia.

I'd barely turned in my graduation robes when Lan and I loaded our Chevrolet Sprint with everything we owned—clothes and two boxes of textbooks—and lit out for the East in ways that might have made our pioneering ancestors proud, even if we were going the wrong direction. We had hope and little else. He had a job with a navy contractor; I had a teaching certificate. By the time we crossed into Virginia ("For lovers!" I noted), Utah's steady peaks had long since devolved into mind-numbing flats and rolling hills, fern-flanked highways and fat urban sprawl. Nothing, in short, from which I could take my bearings.

Within a few weeks of our arrival, I landed a job managing a dormitory at the Madeira School, which planted us squarely and pennilessly within the land of power and pedigree. Our new Mormon congregation featured such luminaries as NASA's James Fletcher along with Utah senators Orrin Hatch and Jake Garn. When people got up to testify to the truthfulness of the Restored Church, they also testified to the ways in which the Lord had seen fit to bless them: with Potomac-front property, Bentleys, and surprisingly large diamond rings.

Convinced that happiness was the result of adherence to Church principles, I committed myself to maniacal scripture reading, journal keeping, and tithe paying. But I also noticed that I seemed to be falling short of some unwritten codes that had little to do with these virtues.

There were things that got you ahead in McLean and things that pegged you as an idiot, and I seemed to keep proving myself to be the latter—like the day I asked the dean of students if the school was expensive and she practically burst with derision ("Well, what do you think?!"). Or the time I yelled at the bagboy for stealing our groceries. No one had explained to me that I had entered a brave new world where you didn't push your own cart out of the store, let alone into the parking lot.

I did not have the word for it, but I knew that I was at the bottom of something, and that being at the bottom of this thing made all of the ways in which I did not measure up bloom in colorful detail. I sweated every conversation, sure that my backwoodsiness oozed out of my pores and punctuated my speech. Even with the help of Laura Ashley and Ralph Lauren, I still felt like a klutz, trying to disguise my former gopher-trapping self with all of the right labels. I bought wire-framed glasses with clear plastic lenses as a way of looking smarter, constantly worried that my meager public education would manifest itself in every word I spoke, in all of the history and literature and science that I did not know.

Living in the dormitory made a tense situation worse. Screams of rage and joy exploded at all hours from the tiny telephone booth adjacent to our two-room apartment, and the girls at the school were savvy about the world in ways that simultaneously embarrassed and infuriated me. I flushed boys out of closets and showers and tried to be vigilant about alcohol. But I could never tell if a student was holding a beer or a fancy bottle of soda pop. I wouldn't have recognized marijuana if someone had left a fattie smoldering in the vestibule. Racial tensions sparked feuds; students got fake IDs, headed off to Georgetown bars, and didn't bother to come back all night. One student stole everybody's Secret Santa presents and hoarded them under her bed. Another burst into tears on her sixteenth birthday, sobbing that she was still a virgin, the drama of which was utterly lost on me. I wanted to tell her that sex was actually sort of overrated, but thought better of it. And I doubted she would be interested in a discussion of purity.

Between painting scenery for school plays, inspecting rooms, and doing my duties to God, I played energetic rounds of *Tetris* to take the edge off something that felt like a cross between dread and mind-numbing monotony. Meanwhile, Lan seemed to be having the time of his life.

For reasons I could not fathom, he seemed more interested in sex than usual, which only made me feel tired. In a growing vicious cycle, he initiated advances that I declined, which pissed him off, which made me bristle even more the next time he tried to touch me. When I felt his hand on my breast at three o'clock in the morning, it was all I could do not to haul off and slug him—-and sometimes I did. I had learned to shut down my sexuality before we were married, and the new dynamics of our marriage culminated in spiteful sex that ended with my counting down angrily. If the rocket did not take off by zero, the astronaut was on his own.

If things weren't precarious enough, I got pregnant, as if not doing so would offend God, the angels, and everybody else. Mormon president Ezra Taft Benson had just admonished young couples not to put off having children for "worldly" reasons, such as an education or a career, and he had quoted Brigham Young, who explained that there were spirits waiting in heaven, and that it was our sacred obligation to "prepare tabernacles for them." If I shunned this obligation, these spirits would be "driven into families of the wicked," where they would be "trained in wickedness, debauchery, and every species of crime."

Since we'd put off having children until I finished college, I could not imagine how many spirits we'd already driven into lives of debauchery. Still, I had no special urge to have children and never felt the longing Michelle described as being "baby hungry." Within two months of tossing my birth control pills, I was pregnant. Not because I wanted a child, but because I couldn't think of a reason not to have one.

As I started to gain weight, I noticed that my body had become a public forum about which everyone had some rotten opinion. While Madeira faculty members lobbed pointed comments about how reckless it was to pepper the world with more children, our families in Utah wondered what had been taking us so long.

I had little to offer the girls in the dorm, who mainly regarded me with indifference. No one asked me for help, not even in crises. There was the student who swallowed a whole bottle of pills. Friends found her unconscious in her room and called 911. The most I could do was wait for emergency workers to whisk her body into a waiting ambulance. A few days later, her father came to collect her things. She was recovering, he said. And then he showed me her day planner. Under the date of the preceding Friday, she had written, "Kill yourself today," as if scheduling a pedicure. The man said nothing as I read the message, but I felt the unsaid indictment: *She was so depressed. She wrote it all down. How could you not know?*

But I had no ability to recognize depression, not even my own.

SITTING ON THE FRONT STEPS of our house, I'm not sure I've ever forgiven the poor naive kid trying to survive inside the Beltway by *reading her scriptures.* Which was as effective as improving her marriage by having children. Which was as rational as siphoning off 10 percent of her family income to the Church so that God would bless them with grocery money. Which was only slightly more ridiculous than taking on Church jobs to shore up her crumbling self-esteem.

Weeks ago, I'd finally worked up the courage to read my mother's journals, and the differences between her entries and mine—written on the same day in some cases—had fairly blown me away.

I hadn't planned on asking for the journals. At the behest of my father, I had shown up at the house in Roy prepared to help him weed out the Christmas décor still stashed in the basement: stacks of light-up lawn ornaments, animated angels, and Victorian carolers, as well as countless boxes of themed tree ornaments. By the time Michelle and I had bush-whacked our way through twenty or thirty artificial trees to find an army of toothy nutcrackers and a life-sized pirate-eyed Father Christmas, we were so giddy with astonishment that we started grabbing up everything. Before I knew it, I was the proud owner of a box full of bound volumes, along with a pair of noble pines that might have been made from recycled Mountain Dew cans.

Comparing our journals, I had been shocked by the irony. The mother I thought would be wallowing in pain clearly wasn't, while the girl I had been clearly was.

Where I expected to find illness or the passing throes of self-doubt, I found the Enjoli ideal: the twenty-four-hour woman with the eight-hour perfume. When she wasn't planting hundreds of roses in the front yard, choreographing dance recitals, and reading Leon Uris, she baked bread, set bones, bottled jam, and delivered babies—sometimes in the same day.

Challenges that stressed out other people only served to inspire her. Facing a radical hysterectomy at the ripe old age of forty-one, she pooh-poohed the "war stories" other women told about the surgery and wrote the whole thing off as "a piece of cake," refusing to sleep in the downstairs bedroom my father had prepared for her, as if doing so would make her as wimpy as her best friend, who stayed downstairs for four months after the same operation.

What surprised me most wasn't her energy, which I sort of remembered, but her misogyny. While she raced along kicking ass and hardly bothering to sleep, she railed against women who were insecure, jealous, and moody. At one point she wrote, "I just don't seem to do well with women; partly they tend to be less interesting to me in the first place. Secondly, they are much more often neurotic and emotionally labile or unstable than men. And finally, I seem to threaten them."

Hardest to read had been her depiction of my college years. After a bleak Sunday dinner in which I had burst into tears, feeling as if I could never measure up to Michelle (happily married and named teacher of the year her first year in the classroom), my mother had written: "Sometimes I'd like to shake her up and hang her out to dry!" Later, after my Pinto blew a tire and my father drove twenty miles to help, only to discover that I had a spare and a jack in the trunk all along, she wrote: "The 'urge to kill' department struck again!"

The words stunned me. While I am sure I was no easy child to mother, the impulse to clobber me seemed disproportionate to the crime. It wasn't just the raw anger that caught my attention, but how dissociative it was—as if her emotions lived in different compartments in her body. While the passage probably took its lead from a television ad that was running relentlessly at the time ("It's Joe Albertson's supermarket, but the urge to kill department is mine!"), I also guessed she really meant it.

Like my mother, I tried to project a bulletproof façade in my journal, writing sentences like "Self-pity is a luxury you cannot afford," without ever asking why I might be feeling blue. While my mother's recurring messages had been "Achieve! Achieve!" and "Needy people need to get a grip!" my journals posed dark questions like "Why has God abandoned me?" complete with ready answers like "I guess I probably deserve it," along with perilously weird sentences like "Oh wonderful day, Kaloo

Callay!" (a riff on "The Walrus and the Carpenter"?), in bizarre proximity to "I want to scream."

WHEN I CALLED my mother from Virginia, she positively radiated ebullience. She loved her new job at FHP, a budding health maintenance organization. Loved. It. And felt valuable, really, for the first time since she'd been laid off from her job in Tremonton. So jubilant was she that she thought we ought to coauthor a book entitled *How to Succeed in Marriage Without Really Trying!*

I thought I might mention that I *was* actually trying and not succeeding very well, but I didn't. I wanted her to think how together I was, how citified, strong, and un-needy.

And yet I seemed to botch everything, even the stuff that was supposed to come naturally, like pregnancy and childbirth. From the moment the fertilized egg took up residence in my endometrium, my body became grotesquely functional. I peed every ten minutes, belched and farted like a wrestler, put on too much weight. By my third prenatal visit, the elderly German doctor I'd been seeing refused to finish the exam as a way of chastising me. "You gain more weight by the next visit, and I will not talk to you again then, either!"

The indignity of pregnancy was fully eclipsed by the horror of childbirth, for which nothing prepared me. I'd been in labor for eighteen hours, my cervix refusing to dilate one centimeter, when the fetal heart monitor dropped to zero.

There was a flash of accoutrements as the medical staff raced for the operating room, the sensation of a Barbie-sized Skilsaw zipping across my appendix scar, and a loud wail before someone handed me a warm white bundle.

Eyes wide, the infant considered the fluorescent lights like stars, as if he were as surprised by recent events as I was. Were it not for the shocking physical reality of the tiny person in my arms and the startling rush of emotion, I might have thought the ordeal some kind of joke. To be handed a newborn at two o'clock in the morning on Labor Day, when I had patently failed to perform labor properly.

In spite of the isolation, or maybe because of it, I built my life around the baby. Lan had coworkers. The girls in the dormitory had friends. No one needed me except this small person, with whom I toured the petting zoo, walked the spiral halls of the Baltimore National Aquarium, and wandered the Tysons Corner mall, throwing pennies in the fountain. Feet dangling from a blue Snugli, head against my cheek, he seemed like my only friend in the world.

On the worst days, I called my mother. When I finally admitted to feeling isolated and unhappy, she seemed more validated than concerned. "Well," she said, "I've often thought you were bipolar."

WHAT I LEARNED in Virginia was something I had known all my life: *You do not ask for help.* Not unless you recently lost an eye or your leg got severed by a hay baler, at which point someone would arrive with a casserole and shovel your driveway. If someone asked if you needed help, you said, "No thanks." If someone asked how you were, you said, "Fine, thanks." Only a complete dolt had the temerity to be honest. Staggering around the apartment after the emergency cesarean section, I nearly wept with relief when the Relief Society president called to ask if I needed anything. When I asked if someone might be willing to help me vacuum, she delivered a turgid lecture about how busy other women in the Church were. Then she asked if I needed anything else.

To this day, the exchange still makes me wince. I couldn't see the bait and switch. I only understood that I had violated an unwritten code. No one wanted to know if loneliness ran through your veins like a vast subterranean waterway. No one cared if the spoon you used to slip leaky oatmeal back into your baby's mouth was just *so heavy.* No one seemed to notice if a certain plug had been pulled that allowed objects to refract color and light. Adversity was part of God's eternal plan. It built character. And so you knit your eyebrows and did your best to pull through.

One of the only times anyone from church called me, it was to suggest that I provide a bad example for a Relief Society lesson. The woman explained she would be teaching a lesson on reverence, and wondered if I would wander in late and make a fuss. Eager to be part of things, I made an awkward entrance, the baby wailing on cue as if he knew about our little plot. The teacher paused midsentence while I settled into a chair and soothed the little guy. After a pointed look at me, she explained that we should enter our meetings silently and worshipfully—and on time. Then she went on with the lesson. I waited for her to explain that our entrance had been a setup, but she never did. And so it seemed to me that motherhood only enabled me to perform the wrong sorts of behavior, even as Church authorities demanded I be a mother.

The longer we lived in Virginia, the more I felt as if I were becoming invisible, not just to Church members and Madeira faculty, but invisible as a general rule. While the world's main characters checked watches and donned scarves, I watched the clock tick off the minutes until bath time. If the world were a stage, I would be the maid or nameless extra. A person who entered long enough to say "Tea?" or shout "They're coming!" Sometimes I imagined that I wasn't a character at all, but more like the castle I erected for *Pippin,* hollow and Styrofoam-like. And even though I'd silently praised Pippin for not diving into the flames at the end of the play, I understood how tempting it was to have all of the lights on you, to be heroically larger than life, if just for one moment.

When neither of us could sleep, the baby and I watched *Sesame Street: Bedtime Stories and Songs* until we passed out. On one fitful night, it seemed as if I had just heard Bob sing Big Bird to sleep for the fourth or fifth time when Lan began shaking my arm, "Get up."

If it was morning, it was an awfully early version of it, and I growled the word "later." But he did not stop shaking me. "We need to talk."

I knew what he was going to say before he said it. There was the gray dawn prodding the yellow window shade and a sense of alarm, as if something had triggered a siren deep inside me. I rallied the part of me that was still asleep, that wanted nothing to do with a conversation like this, now or ever, and formed the question to which I already knew the answer.

"Did you sleep with her?"

The sex meant nothing to him, he said. But he felt so bad. Worse than he'd ever felt in his life. He knew he cared more about her than he should—they had been friends for so long!—but he hadn't seen where things were headed, and then it was over and he felt so horribly sorry and he would do anything to make it right.

As he spoke, months of *Tetris* games quietly replayed themselves in my head, dropping cyan blocks, red sticks, and gray tabletops. And it did not matter how quickly I spun them or shuffled them off to the edges, because they only picked up speed, piling onto to the middle of the screen until the words blinked *Game Over.*

Finally, I said, "Well, the baby's awake and there's nothing we can really do about it right now, so you might as well go to work."

He said, "Oh no, I'm not," but I insisted. Things like this happened, I thought, and you took them in stride. And, really, what else was there to do?

And I thought I must have missed a tithing payment or failed to adequately study my scriptures or put off having my children too long or otherwise missed the boat of faith somehow, because no matter how fervently I prayed, I felt nothing at all. Only my own thoughts circling back to me, cast in a line from a half-forgotten Sunday school lesson: "Buy of me gold tried in the fire." And there was fire, I thought, but no warmth; and I didn't know if the flames would cure us or kill us. If the fire would fashion me into something I'd be proud of or not. And there wasn't a soul I could think of to talk to about it.

THE MEMORY VANISHES as a patch of midlevel cumulus slides in front of the sun, turning the side hills to slate. I would go inside to start dinner, but I'm not hungry. If the boys have a sudden hankering for a hamburger, I'm sure they won't mind disturbing me. And so I stay on the porch a little longer, adrift in thought.

If there was a legacy that nearly destroyed me after the endless gray parade of Virginia mornings, it was a stalwart resolve to carry on without a noticeable dip in my demeanor. Lan explained things on a Thursday morning, and I forgave him by Sunday night. I allowed myself a tearful phone call to Michelle and pulled myself together. Once we moved back to Utah, everything would work out just fine.

If I sank into a dark funk, I kept it to myself. If I spoke to anyone at all, I did so with bubbly sincerity. If you had met me then, you would have thought I was my mother: edging toward gold in the Plucky Olympics. I refused to process what my heart already knew. My husband was in love with someone else.

I didn't realize how deeply I had denied my feelings until I took a fiction-writing class years later. Part of my doctoral work, the course was my way of nurturing my creative leanings. Eager for feedback on my first story, I leaned toward my professor in the noisy conference room where clusters of other graduate students discussed their work. I had worked hard on the details and hoped she would notice. Instead, she looked at me with a strangely cocked eyebrow: "You have a suicidal young mother here. How is it she is *fine* by page ten?"

I squinted at the pages. My protagonist was suicidal?

Also noted was that my "sympathetic" male character was actually a dick and possibly a sociopath.

FROM MY PERCH on the front porch, I notice the passing of time. Drivers along our quiet street are flipping on headlights. Lan should be home any minute. The steps are shrouded in shadow; the air has turned crisp and cold. From inside the house come the sounds of the boys blasting each other's cars into smithereens on *Full Auto 2*. Screeching tires and wailing guitars spill out into the night, buttressed by the muted thump of techno. A fusillade of gunfire provokes a wild whoop and muffled expletives. The room dissolves into laughter.

The hilarity in the living room makes me wonder what I have bequeathed to the boys. Ben was born in time to inherit my faith; Arthur arrived to my full-blown malaise. Both of them got pretty heavy doses of anger. They watched their mother evolve from a prim teetotaler into a woman who was capable of smashing bottles of rum in the driveway to make a point. Depending on the phase I was in, they had a stay-at-home mother, a working mother, a mother who disappeared for days at a time to go to school.

If they asked about God, I told them about Jesus or Zeus, depending on my mood. When my father-in-law died, Lan's brother gathered the children together to explain things. Looking across the sea of parents and squirming bodies, he asked: "Can anyone tell me where we go after this life?" When Ben's hand shot up before anyone else's, I wondered what he was going to say, since we hadn't actually discussed it. "I think," he said, and paused, as if he were working it out in his eight-year-old mind for the first time, "that when you die, you come back as something else. Like a flower."

A lovely answer to be sure, but a Mormon pop quiz fail.

I felt two things at once in that instant: the familiar impulse to placate—to say anything to relieve the uncomfortable silence in the room—and the solid thump of pride.

On the steps, I consider my bony knees, slim under faded jeans, less muscular than they were in my marathon-running days, but sinewy and reliable. What strikes me now about the scene at my in-laws' house is Ben's ability to trust his own voice—something I have struggled to do all of my life.

When I think of my greatest regrets, it's not my religious failings that come to mind, but all of the ways I'd been distracted while the boys were growing up. While they leapt into piles of ruby leaves and dragged each other on skis behind a four-wheeler in the pasture, I checked off one achievement after another, as if doing so would redeem the girl I had been in Virginia. Graduate school was part of it. Running was part of it. I did not have to be a vessel for spirit children. I could be muscular and competitive, and Lan's blonde coworker in Virginia could take her store-bought boobies and acrylic nails and kiss my ass.

Still, I do not know how to feel about myself. If anything, I feel sort of raw and *unfinished*. My greatest joys have boiled down to three: Lan, Ben, and Arthur. Watching the sky turn black, I mark the distance to the grassy ditch where the boys flung themselves into the irrigation water until the water turned brown, the thin line of gravel next to the road where they waved cars down with a lemonade sign, the unkempt access road where Arthur caught "Crunchy," a three-foot garter snake, and wound it around his arm as if to entice passing motorists.

Listening to the sounds wafting onto the porch, I picture them now. Arthur is shirtlessly wielding the black controller, eyes dancing with laughter, brown bangs hanging into his eyes, while his older brother sits poised and intent on the glass-topped coffee table in a Rage Against the Machine T-shirt, concentrating through wire-rimmed glasses.

If I could bestow such things with a bright red bow, I would not give my sons ease, but resilience; not surety, but compassion. The ability to look something straight in the eye without flinching. Something they will not have inherited from me, but from their grandmother.

My mother did not flinch when the raw stuff of life was blood and bile, skull and bone. She faced horrors I have so far had the luxury to ignore. And so, as baffled as I am by her journals, I would like to extend the gift I hope to receive from my boys: another chance to be a good mother.

TWELVE

Lath and Plaster Disaster

November finds me back at work on my dissertation. Although I will admit to fantasies in which I retile the bathroom, I'm fresh out of reasons to procrastinate. And so the stacks of books in my office grow like spores with dusty spines: literary theory, history, autobiography. And everywhere, papers. Stapled notes, articles, and outlines; a clipboard bearing the weight of an emerging argument, pages and pages of scribbled notes that sometimes do and sometimes do not seem penned by a rational being. I signed up for the PhD program hoping to emerge butterfly-like from the grubby chrysalis I'd been trapped in most of my life. But I am starting to feel like the academy is as mirage-like and trumped up as Zion.

For me, education is less an *option* than redemption. A way of reinventing myself from the inside out. Husband admits he's in love with somebody else? Get a second bachelor's degree. Sick of teaching middle school? Get a master's. Sick of yourself? Get a doctorate.

Poring over my research, I shift my weight against the spineless wingback, my back echoing the strained progression of my thoughts. Having brewed a third (and final!) pot of coffee, I am fighting a perilously dull sentence involving the word *discursivity* when the sound of the doorbell disrupts the tentative hold I've got on the language. From downstairs comes the sound of a slamming door and a friendly "Hallooo!"

My father.

I do a quick appraisal of my appearance. It's noon and far too late to be wearing my bathrobe along with the same running clothes I wore yesterday (who knows? I might go). I haven't combed my hair, and I'm not altogether sure I've brushed my teeth. If he were to step into my office right now, he would not see an emerging scholar but someone who looked as if she wasn't coping very well with a depressive episode.

Stashing my laptop next to a crumb-flecked breakfast plate on the cluttered window seat, I shout "Be right there!" and bolt for the bedroom, where I throw on a running cap, ditch the robe, and perform some quick tooth-brushing maneuvers. I had called my father earlier to say that I wanted the rest of my mother's papers, but I had not expected him to show up the same day.

Rounding the corner at the top of the stairs, I catch sight of two plastic bins and a black lockbox next to my father, who is smiling under a dapper tweed derby and tan Thiokol jacket, blissfully unaware that his shoes are spattered with drywall putty.

He looks up. "Hi, Kid."

Sidestepping the bins, I give him a hug. "Looks like you've brought quite a load."

"I pulled all of the photos out of those singed albums in the loft," he says. "The other stuff's sort of a mess. And I've got something else for you, too."

"Oh yeah?" I say, feeling curious and wary—god knows what he's got. A singing fish? An antique slot machine? A polar bear dressed as an astronaut?

"Well, you just come on out here," he says, ambling out to the car. There he retrieves a painting wedged between the seats, running the full length of the car. "You seemed to like this."

I note the billowing sleeves and corseted torso. *Cecilia.*

He is right. I *do* like the painting. Despite the myriad ways in which I hate religious art, I am inexplicably drawn to the image. "Still sick of angels, are you, Dad?"

He smiles. "Just sick of stuff."

The day packs an icy punch, but he doesn't seem eager to go back in the house. Above us, a thick layer of stratiform clouds blankets the valley, painting the fields grayish blue. I balance the painting on a shoe, trying to keep its baroque frame from scuffing against the concrete, while he leans his back against the car, looking past me into the northern sky.

"You know it sounds crazy," he says. "But I sometimes get the feeling that she's not gone at all. That she's just waiting around somewhere, and one day she's going to show up to see how it all worked out." His eyes seem to track the horizon, and I notice how thin he's become.

"I guess that makes sense. Since we never saw her body, it's hard to feel, I don't know . . . closure."

"Maybe," he says, looking as forlorn as I've ever seen him. "I tell myself *oh no, she's gone,* but I still find myself wishing she would show up. Just long enough for me to ask how she did it, if nothing else."

"Well, I guess that would make two of us," I say, even though it's not really true. As much as I'd like a decent explanation for the fire, I'd rather no one visited me from beyond the veil. "How's the house coming along?"

"Good," he says. "They tore out everything in those upstairs rooms. Right down to studs. Pumped it full of ozone, coated everything with some odor-reducing primer. Electrical's done. Drywall's done. Just waiting on paint and carpet."

I look at his pleated dress pants, the ones he never changed out of before hauling out a Skilsaw and erecting an extra room. My mother hated the way he never bothered to change—that all of his dress clothes bore the remnants of sawdust and epoxy and grout. She did not seem to understand that the stains and scuffs were markers of devotion. And so I wonder what it is like to be him now, holed up in a corner of the catacombed basement, surrounded by ghosts, knowing that the insurance company is about to return thousands of freshly cleaned artifacts.

"Anyway," he says, "I hope this is what you wanted. There's probably more, but I haven't really gone through the filing cabinets."

"That's okay. This will keep me busy. I've still got a degree to finish, you know."

"I know," he says, looking sort of gloomy about it. "I've been wondering about that. You don't think you're chasing after the sparkling things of the world? You know, like your mother?"

The question makes me bristle. "Sparkling things" is a reference to my mother's patriarchal blessing. Like most Mormon initiates, she got hers as a teenager and knew much of the blessing by heart. The blessing was a rite of passage, an ordinance you could ask for as soon as you felt ready, given by a man specifically chosen by God for the job. Recorded and transcribed, the blessing was both heirloom and compass, a series of promises based on one's faithfulness. Something you passed on to your children and referenced in times of trouble.

The precise wording in my mother's blessing had been: "Let not the glittering nor the shiny things of the world draw thy heart from the Lord, but seek first His kingdom and all else will be added unto you." As her glittering objects multiplied exponentially as she aged, the prayer seemed to predict the future.

Unlike my blessing, which read like a vague fortune cookie ("Good things will come to you in due time of the Lord"), my mother's had been almost graphically specific. Contingent on her faithfulness, she was promised a loving husband and children, along with a home in which peace, unity, and singleness of purpose would abide—which mostly happened. She was also promised that she would be spared sorrow and disappointment, that diseases would not destroy her body, and that her bodily organs would function to their normal capacity for her joy and advancement. Which mostly did not happen.

Since blessings were contingent upon obedience, it was possible to interpret my mother's failing health as a sign that she had put her things before God. But I always got the feeling that her things weren't distractions *from* God, but curiously linked to her relationship *to* God. Proof that she was living the right kind of life.

STANDING IN THE SLOPING DRIVEWAY with Cecilia balanced on a shoe, I try to decide how to answer my father. I would stick up for my graduate work, but I am not convinced of its value. The comparison between my degree and my mother's knickknacks implies that my PhD is trivial and fleeting—so much glass and glue. And who's to say that it's not?

My decision to go back to school belonged to a painfully restless time in my life. It had been a year since my affair, and yet I still felt the sickening weight of it almost every day—the way it tugged at our marriage and dared me to find something to replace it. I needed the solidarity of family. I needed to feel valuable on my own merits—but how? Before I left for Reno, I pleaded with my family to get together *just once* during the summer—and not at the godawful Chournos reunion, either. But everyone was so tired by then. Wrung-out or jaded or caught up in careers and Church jobs and children. So it never panned out. My leaving for school was less about knowing what I wanted than about what I did not want: to live in a place where I felt lonely and purposeless.

I was pretty sure a PhD would impress my mother, since she championed anything that was sophisticated and elite, but I'd also accepted that her praise was something I would never earn. So, whether the degree is a devotion to learning or one more jab at proving The Girl Worthwhile, I can't say.

"Well, Dad," I finally say. "I guess I just needed to grow. And I couldn't do that here anymore."

"Well, Kid," he says. "I guess that's right."

My father has barely pulled out of the driveway before I've hauled the bins of papers to my office and begun hovering over them, gargoyle-like. For the first time since the fire, I feel the rush of anticipation. Part of my brain chalks up my newfound curiosity to dissertation avoidance, but I don't care. I have the sudden crazy feeling that if I can track my mother's pain to its source—pinpoint the moment she got sick—then maybe I can mend us both.

As promised, the contents of the bins are a disaster. Pictures of me as a toothless seven-year-old share a file with a batch of birthday cards, my mother's high school transcripts, and snapshots of grandchildren waving lollipops from a wheelbarrow.

For one ambitious moment, I think I might separate the photos according to year, but there's no way of telling where most of them belong. Early photos capture my mother in varying states of skinniness; later ones merely show her filling out with age. She refuses to look weary or sad in any of them—except one in which traces of tears still show on her face: her silver wedding anniversary. The fact that we (read: her children) had not thrown a big party—had not *remembered* the occasion in fact—seemed to prove that she had spawned a bunch of loveless ingrates.

Tossing the photos from one box to another, I watch for anything that looks like illness, but the photos mostly remind me how exhausting it felt to be her daughter. I am a study in stage-light and shadow, belting out lyrics to "It's a Fine Life" as Nancy's chubby sidekick in a high school production of *Oliver!* She is a study in sunlight and blossoms, dressed in a beaded buckskin dress, standing in an aspen grove at Monte Cristo.

Other pictures of her: skiing, swimming, dancing, singing, horseback riding, backpacking. Other pictures of me: moping. In one photo, I sulk over a sweet sixteen birthday cake; in another I rage at the camera, poised as if I may throw the telephone at the photographer. I knew I hated being a teenager, but I'd sort of forgotten how much.

Uninspired by the photos, I am about to shelve the lot when I come across one I've never seen before: my mother dancing with a handsome dark-haired man. Head thrown back, she laughs, her body bent at an odd angle, her face wide and moonlike. The hand she places on his back shimmers with diamonds and glittering nail extensions, but it also bears a patchwork of bruises and bandages. Looking at the image, I try to remember the context—a Napa Valley wedding, I think, the sort of occasion where she would have died happy: champagne fountains and low-backed gowns, crystal goblets and scattered rose petals. And yet her happiness betrays her. Fully enraptured in the moment, she forgets to conceal the fact that she is dying.

After casting around for my cell phone, I call my father. An obvious indicator of illness, the photo seems like a fairly big piece of the puzzle, and yet I'm not sure I could peg the right decade. There is something so pitiable about my mother's expression that I can barely stand to look at it—something reminiscent of the days she donned scandalous dresses and spun circles across the church gymnasium floor on New Year's Eve. And yet her laugh might as well be a cry.

There is a pause on the line as my father thinks. "I guess that would have been Heidi's wedding—Cherre's youngest," he says, his voice thin against the hum of the engine. "She was so sick on that trip. When we got back home I told her we might as well start making funeral arrangements if she couldn't get her prednisone down."

Of course, I think. *The prednisone years.*

I rack my brain, surprised that I seemed to have blocked out the memory of this dismal portion of our lives. At some point the drug became the one true fact of her existence—the only thing she talked about. And I came to resent prednisone in the same way I came to resent the Chournos reunion and the nervous pampered poodles she carried around in her purse. The drug was responsible for her linebacker neck, cataracts, bruises, and compression fractures, and it was directly related to stress.

Aware of the relationship between stress and the drug, Michelle and I started to engage in bizarre mathematics before every visit: "Well," I would muse, "Thanksgiving is a biggie. And she will be entertaining friends in addition to us. What do you think that'll cost her—ten milligrams or so?"

Flippancy was my way of coping. What else do you do, after all, when your mere presence makes somebody else's body fall apart? My mother explained that she needed to increase her dosage every time she hosted a Chournos meeting or endured drama at work. And once the dosage got bumped up, it tended to stay up.

But there had been a time she seemed to have stopped taking it, too, and I can't say why.

"So, what happened?" I ask, shocked that I remember so little.

A long pause indicates that my father is negotiating traffic or is unsure how to answer.

"Oh, I don't know," he says. "When Kennedy was shot, he had the same thing. You know, spongy tissues, trouble clotting. Adrenal failure. You know, like your mom. She just couldn't get it down."

Typical of my father's communication style, the sentence demands that I connect the dots. The theory we had both heard, via some program on the History Channel, was that nobody had to shoot the president, since the prednisone was already killing him.

"But do you know when she started taking it? Or why?"

Another pause. "There was that trip to California, but she was already on it by then."

Hazily, I recall what amounted to the worst vacation ever. My parents had been airborne before my mother realized she had left her medicines at home. She spent the first day basking in the sunny delights of the Magic Kingdom. By day two, she limped along in anguish, feeling as if her body were being pressed into a meat grinder. Utterly miserable, she checked herself into one clinic after another, where baffled providers shrugged and sent her home. Finally, at the fourth or fifth clinic, a quick-thinking intern suggested some prednisone, which had her feeling perky again in no time.

The ordeal revealed a dependency that had been months—years perhaps—in the making. It was as if her adrenal glands had walked off the job like peevish bartenders, their corticosteroid-making duties having been outsourced to a flashy synthetic.

I hang up the phone, more baffled than before. While the conversation recalls my mother's nasty bout with the prednisone, it hardly answers when she started taking it. And there is the puzzle, too, of why the drug suddenly vanished as a topic of conversation. I can't imagine that the stress-pain cycle just stopped, or that her surly glands got back to work as stealthily as they had stopped.

Scouring the bins for papers, I stack my mother's writing on the floor according to decade, as if doing so will solve some cosmic mystery. There's the predictable pile of high school and college essays, weighing in at thirty pages or so. Then, the stack of journals, about a foot deep, which she kept for nine years. After that, a short stack of disparate papers documenting the last ten years of her life: three-by-five cards and shopping lists, pages torn from Franklin Planners and colorful legal pads, thoughts penned on Coca-Cola stationery and rose-embossed notes—all of them riddled with pain.

The lumpy chronology reveals something I had not noticed before. Between the journals, in which my mother seemed to be invincible, and the handful of pain-ridden notes, there is an eight-year gap in which anything might have occurred.

Curious, I compare the writing that brackets the silence. Her last journal entry records anticipation: her new job in Roy and our move to Virginia. The next thing I have is a note, scribbled on a piece of Procardia XL ("The Value of Experience!") stationery: "Dr. Mark Scott. Fibromyalgia. Felt really horrible [undecipherable] shots, codeine, Tylenol, ice, etc." Ten years later, she is gone.

I SKIM THE PAPERS before zeroing in on specific passages. Something seems wrong about them, but I can't say what it is, only that they tell a story that feels muzzled. While my mother's physical pain emerges in startling detail, her emotional veneer barely manages to shimmer.

Only one document, penned after a sleep study in the offices where she used to work, captures anything like despair. Thick with nostalgia, the pages describe the building as if it were a lover: the communal offices and exam rooms, the patients and colleagues filling the halls, the sound of her high heels clicking across the tile—all of the things that made her feel valuable. She outlines her specialties as a PA: minor surgical procedures, gynecological care, depression, and caring for others with chronic pain. But while she claims to be content, her identity no longer tied up in her profession, the last sentence belies the assertion:

"I am so tired that in many ways I am very glad that I don't have to go in to work. But in other ways, not working and very possibly never being able to work again ~~feels like~~ fills me with great sadness and a feeling that half of my soul has been ripped out."

The words bother me. It's not just the brutality of the imagery that catches me off guard, but the thought of my mother, wary of weakness and impatient with sorrow, penning the loss of her *soul,* feeling small. I imagine her sitting in a pink leather recliner next to the bay windows overlooking the street, watching the traffic rush toward Salt Lake, surrounded by stone-inlaid globes, marble chess sets, and silk roses, the roll-top desk and antique pump organ failing to comfort her. I can't say why she has crossed out "feels like," unless the emotion she meant to describe was too raw—too hard to pin down.

I put down the papers for a moment, noticing my own fragile links to significance. My degrees hanging lockstep on the wall, my marathon medallions, teaching awards, and advanced pilot ratings. Goals that seemed lofty never seemed particularly noteworthy after I achieved them. And what if I did not get a job? What if I were left alone in my own stately house with nothing but my tinny accomplishments to protect me? A framed PhD would only mock my unhappiness if I could not find purpose and work, stripped of the things that defined me.

While I can't decide if pursuing a PhD is a worthy goal or an ill-advised quest, I can say that it turned out to be surprisingly good for our marriage. Being away from Lan made me realize how much I missed him. When I got home, I felt truly present. Our connections were bolstered by having new things to share. And so I can't help feeling sorry for my mother, alone in her too big house. Consumed with pain and a lack of purpose.

PICKING UP FIVE PAGES torn from a yellow legal pad, I reread them. The mother who once pooh-poohed a radical hysterectomy is gone. In her place is a terrified woman preparing for an emergency angioplasty. Worried that her prednisone-ravaged body won't withstand the procedure, she asks for a blessing from my brother, who feels impressed to tell her midprayer that she should take special care during the recovery period.

There are three separate accounts of the surgery in the small stack of papers: a page of fearful preoperative ruminations; a set of jubilant postoperative reflections; and a letter to her brother, Sam, then serving a Mormon mission in New Zealand.

That she wrote to Sam sort of surprises me, as she never seemed to like him and often felt small in comparison to him. So I can only guess that the story felt crucial to her, connected, somehow, to her family.

Taken together, the papers tell a story that goes like this: As if the blessing foretold the future, the postoperative sutures in her thigh pulled through her spongy tissues as she awoke from sedation. Groggily aware of the spreading warmth of her blood, she forced herself into consciousness and rang for nurses, who pressed their hands and bodies against the hemorrhage until they could staunch it with an adjustable clamp.

Unlike the document penned after the sleep study, the account of the harrowing near-death experience showed her renewed faith in God and medicine and—better yet—herself. The Lord was mindful of her. She still had a purpose to serve. And maybe, just maybe, she would regain her lost health.

I puzzle over the letter to Sam. Details of the surgery are the same, as is the triumphant arc. As if to spice things up, she has also provided a line drawing of her next surgery—a treatment for sleep apnea that will require the removal of her uvula, tonsils, and part of the roof of her mouth. But it's not just the weird drawing that catches my eye, but a cryptic allusion just before she signs off: "I really did come very close to dying two years ago; *much, much* closer than I realized at the time. I haven't been able to work at all since."

The sentence baffles me. *What* had nearly killed her two years before? For a moment, I consider calling my father, but decide to wait. Better to make list of questions than badger him every half hour.

Once I feel like I've gleaned everything I can from the documents, I start to gather them up, pausing to take one more look at the most recent one, dated three days before the fire. On a sheet of patriotic stationery, riddled with blue and silver stars, my mother lists goals: "Go to bed earlier, kneel down at nite for prayers, stop buying junk, don't waste time on things that don't matter, start earlier in the am." Gotta do more. Gotta be more. Our life themes.

The subtle self-castigation bothers me—how sick did she have to become to give herself a break?—but I let it slide while I focus on the writing below the list. Under the penned date and time—2:30 PM to be exact—she has written a strangely urgent sentence fragment: "Like telling me that the Lord has taken a special personal interest in me and that's not something very many people get told!"

There is no preamble for the dangling statement, no unifying idea. I can only assume the source of the information is crazy-shrink Andrea. But I can't tell if the tone is one of desperation or hope—if she is assured by the Lord's purported interest or frustrated by a lack of evidence. Following the fragment, she writes: "I will be made well from this very hour so that I can accomplish all of the above tasks and get ready for a mission."

The image of my mother, so aware of her shortcomings, stubbornly trying to heal herself, makes me wish I could wrap her in my arms. She did not need to go on a mission or accomplish a thousand tasks in her disintegrating body to make me love her—I did as a matter of fact. And I would think a merciful God—one mindful of her—would allow her this small comfort.

Holding the note between my fingers, I'm about to file it when I notice a second page clinging to the first by a thin gummy strip. On it, she has simply written: "strange electric tingling concentrated in my L leg, then L arm, then both hands."

The sentence is as creepy as it is cryptic. Heaven knows what a daughter with a PhD in *literature* is supposed to do with such information. It's one of the things I try to avoid thinking about, the sensations she felt as her body went AWOL, alleviated or exacerbated by her long list of medicines, dizzying in diversity and dosage.

Frustrated, I tuck the pain-ridden papers in a pink plastic file. I hadn't expected to solve the puzzle of my mother's pain in one day, but I can't help but feel disappointed by the lack of information. While I finally have evidence of illness, I can't locate a trigger or starting point.

Glaring at the floor, I puzzle over the eight-year gap. I had been in Virginia for four of those years, so there's no way of knowing if she'd gotten sick then. And yet I have the strangest feeling that I *had* been privy to the onset of my mother's pain.

I lived with my parents for two months after fleeing Virginia. I had a teaching job, two little boys, a diaper bag full of toys, and little else. While Lan assured me that he no longer harbored feelings for a certain blonde coworker, I wasn't so sure. When our second baby arrived, he barely managed to stop by the hospital. Foresight or Providence or damn good luck had landed me the job in Utah. If our marriage survived, fine. If it did not, I'd be able to support the boys on my own.

In charge of installing new networks at Thiokol, my father had become a rare nocturnal animal—a tarsier with wide unblinking eyes, nervously regarding the passing of time. So for the first time ever, my mother and I were thrown together as an unmistakable part of each other's lives: she, commuting from the house in Tremonton to her job in Roy, powered by eye-popping cinnamon jawbreakers and TaB; me, trying to grade papers with a colicky infant. When I could no longer keep up with the blue-jammied toddler emptying the contents of the flour jar onto the kitchen floor, or his unhappy brother, my mother scooped them up and read stories.

FORCING MYSELF to take a break, I pull on some gloves and a jacket and head out for the run I promised myself yesterday. My back is cramped and tired, my knees stiff from kneeling over the bins and bits of paper. If I have learned anything from the doctoral process, it is that there is a finite amount of time you can channel into a problem before it stops being productive.

Outside, I feel my breath and heartbeat synchronize, drumming out a familiar cadence. Since my father left, the clouds have gained girth and momentum, and the wind whips up from the south, tugging at my hat. The thin line of dirt at the side of the road is packed hard with the cold, and I think that if I can force my limbs to start moving, it might just jar some memories.

It bothers me that I cannot picture my mother in the months I returned home from Virginia. Only one scene keeps returning to me, but it doesn't have a date. In it, she stands at a bathroom vanity, pressing circles into her scalp, stopping at intervals to tap a rhythm with glittering fingertips, pulling back a clump of hair to reveal a patch of white skin blooming under brown-black roots. "Can you see that?" she says. "Trigger points. Sensitive bundles of muscle that cause terrible headaches." Without flinching, she skewers the spot with a needle, repeating the process from hairline to temple. The most striking thing about the memory is how casual my mother is about the injections, as if she has done them all of her life.

I turn the image over in my head. If it belongs to Tremonton, she would have been grappling with pain when I got home, since she moved to Roy shortly after that. I am almost sure of the cramped bathroom and red cedar walls, the sounds and smells of my childhood home.

I knew my parents were preparing to move, which made my housing situation precarious. On an invitation from my mother, my grandma Chournos had stopped by for Sunday dinner, her hair pulled back in a silver French twist. We'd barely said the blessing on the food when she took one look at the boys and said: "Haven't you guys got a place to live?"

I condensed our little drama. The college students had beaten me to town, and there was nothing available, especially for someone with children. While there were homes for sale, I did not have ten cents to put down on a loan.

"Well," she said, without putting down her fork. "You just come by tonight and we'll see about that."

I dropped by as directed. Asleep on an elbow in front of a muted *60 Minutes,* my grandmother seemed a smaller, sadder version of herself. And I felt smaller too, a girl holding things together with toothpicks and string.

When I woke her, she disappeared into the office without speaking. Minutes later, she emerged with a brown paper lunch bag.

"There," she said. "See what you can do with that." And I counted out eight thousand dollars in hundred dollar bills.

THE WIND WHIPS UP beleaguered fallen leaves as I round the corner to the River Heights cemetery. There is something wrong with the memory—something missing. My grandmother's house had been too quiet.

When I hugged her it was as if she didn't know how to respond. She did not hug me back. She seemed subdued and wearied by my enthusiastic thank-yous. When I promised to pay her back, she merely said, "Don't you try to do it too soon." And I was just glad she'd said something.

The house I bought with the money was a 1924 lath-and-plaster disaster. Within a week, the kitchen ceiling caved in from preexisting water damage. A month later, the gas company condemned the furnace. I removed six or seven layers of old wallpaper, only to discover that the wallpaper seemed to have been holding up the walls and not the other way around. When one of the stovetop burners erupted in flame, an electrician explained that someone had wired the stove directly to the electrical lines on the street, and god knew why the house hadn't burned down. The ceiling fan in the living room slowed down and sped up in response to cosmic forces I could only guess at, and I ripped up yards of stained purple shag to find dark hardwood floors in desperate need of sanding and polishing.

The silver lining to the house was that Lan arrived in time to move in with us. On my mother's advice, I had called to say that I missed him, and the phone call was all that he needed. The drive home, he said, was the happiest he had ever made.

We started our lives over again, flat broke. He was jobless. I had a teaching salary that barely kept us from qualifying for government assistance. But despite our finances, our worst pressures were ideological. President Benson's speech "To the Mothers in Zion" had been circulating widely as an official Church pamphlet. It urged Mormon women to marry, have children, and quit their jobs. Putting off having children to achieve fiscal stability was "selfishness," as was curtailing the number of one's children.

I muddled along that year, teaching, trying to be heroic, picking up socks and grading papers. It broke my heart to drop my children off at day care, and I refused to get pregnant again, not just because we couldn't afford it, but because I could not bear to leave another child in someone else's care. The boys' wailing as I left them at day care haunted me all day, and even though Lan insisted that they did not cry when he dropped them off, I still felt awful about it. Our marriage was like a sapling that had just caught a little sun, but the thing that worried me most was that our boys were suffering because of my selfishness.

Without realizing it, my resentment—at the Church and its countless imperatives, at myself for failing to keep up with vacuuming, grading, and nurturing—had become razor sharp. Lan was not to blame. The boys were not to blame. My irritation stemmed from standards I had not created, but which I measured myself against nonetheless. I had no way of knowing what being a good enough mother meant, since the model I got from the Church was being not good but *flawless.* There was no room for error, no second chance. Your children were your one true calling in life, and if they ended up depressed or confused or angry or broken, it was all your fault.

I struggled silently, feeling like a failure every minute of every day. Then, one day as I was making dinner, it became clear to me that if I didn't take care of myself, I'd have nothing left to offer. For myself or anyone else.

The evening had started simply enough. Lan watched the boys, while I breaded some chicken and tossed it in a frying pan. The most astonishing thing about the day was how normal it was. Things had gone well at school; the boys seemed happy. I sensed a distant edginess, but ignored it as usual. I felt edgy all of the time. It was just part of life, I supposed.

I was thinking I'd give the chicken just a touch longer when Lan appeared in the kitchen and announced: "Looks like the chicken is done!"

And then the world blew apart.

He had merely stated the obvious, and yet I interpreted it as an indictment, as though he thought I was incapable of preparing a meal. I wheeled on him, imagining what it would feel like to throw the skillet through the window. "If you think I can't do it, then why don't you cook it yourself?"

His eyes grew wide. "Hey, I didn't mean anything by it . . ."

Delirious with rage, I cut him off. "So, I'm not good enough, am I? Not good enough for you? Not good enough for the boys? Not good enough to make a stupid goddamn chicken dinner?"

"No!" he repeated, trying to explain that dinner was *fine* and I was *fine.* But I couldn't hear anything beyond the singsong litany that accused me of being selfish and inadequate.

Before I knew it, I was standing on the front lawn, screaming, my car keys gathered in a fist. Lan was silent, his face white. I could not tell if

Ben was standing next to him regarding the scene with wide brown eyes, or if Arthur had crawled onto the porch to observe the commotion. All that was left to me was the white heat of rage, split into a hundred directions, muting the sound of rubber tearing across asphalt.

Weaving in and out of traffic, I talked through gritted teeth as if defending myself to an unseen audience. "If I'm so fucking worthless, you'll be better off without me."

To punctuate the monologue, I powered past a car dawdling in the fast lane and dove back in front of it. I heard the blast of a horn, saw the car swerve in the rearview mirror. I don't know if it was the other driver's irritation that brought me back around, or the immediacy of the close call, but I was gripped by sudden awareness: *I want to die.* The understanding hit with such force and clarity that I dissolved into tears. *God,* I pleaded silently. *Let somebody hit me. Do everyone a favor.*

THE MEMORY UNLOCKS a connection I had not made before, and I feel suddenly lightheaded and queasy. Having reached the edge of the cemetery, I head for the nearest maple and hang on, the air filling with snowflakes, whipping the world into a white blur.

God, I think. *Johnnie.*

To want to die. To want someone else to do it for you. To direct your rage outward when the inner dialogue becomes too painful. We never learned who fired the bullet that killed him. There were no powder burns on the body that would have indicated a point-blank shot. The police stubbornly refused to release the report. And there had been my grandfather's strange last words, cried out in the middle of the night: "They shot my son."

My grandmother hadn't been *subdued* when I got home from Virginia. She was mourning.

BREATHING HARD, I count the months. Johnnie died in April, and I arrived in August. Preoccupied with being a passable mother and teacher, I barely noticed that the place I returned to was reeling from loss. I kind of knew that my first house was a pretty apt metaphor for me: stalwart and strong on the outside, crumbling on the inside. But it must have applied to my mother and grandmother as well.

The structure had weathered decades of compromises. Its tired boards were the by-products of overuse and stress. Its fissures had been concealed, not fixed. It functioned, just barely. It had no protection. Its wavy single-paned windows barely kept out the wind. It weathered years of dents and dings and wear. And still it soldiered on, doing its best to give off a reasonably dignified appearance.

I can't say if my mother was grieving when I got back from Virginia—if she was, she didn't say so. When I asked her about the gruesome resuscitation in which Johnnie's blood had pumped from his chest as she tried to revive him, I expected her to say it was traumatic. Instead, she seemed oddly detached. "I think it was good for me," she said. "Because I got to use my medical training."

WORK, PURPOSE, VALUE. It was almost as if the words were synonymous. Without the first, the other two ceased to exist.

I heard someone say once that "you buy more than when you feel less than." But I hadn't really thought about how it applied to us. My grandmother collecting signatures from Republican dignitaries; my mother collecting diamond rings; me, collecting advanced degrees. And what of the emotions my mother had not allowed herself? Where did they go? The loss of a brother? A father? Her papers skip across sadness, like stones across a stream. Had she said "ripped out my *soul*" because she could not say "heart"?

Snow billows across the sky, blanketing the valley in silence. Like the days in which I prayed for guidance, my questions circle back to me, unanswered. I feel our stories, the weight and texture of them as I turn toward home, the world turning to winter around me.

THIRTEEN

The Room of Blood and Bones

Solving the mystery of my mother's pain is like getting to the end of a crime novel only to realize that the gun had been smoking on the mantle all along. The trouble is teasing out all of the fingerprints. You could argue that my mother took up the weapon herself, like a necklace in a room full of cursed treasure. You could say that the weapon turned on her of its own accord, wielded by hormones or genetics or trauma. But this much is clear: my mother's health tanked in earnest the day she became general secretary for the family partnership.

I owe the discovery to my father, who has visited more in recent weeks than in the last ten years combined, toting pictures and yearbooks and files. With the renovation of the house in Roy nearly complete, it is as if he has emerged from a trench or a hostage situation: a little disheveled and disoriented, a man who blinks in the sun, surprised by the light. And restless. As exhausted as he had been by my mother's determination to turn their home into the Winchester Mystery House (senseless maniacal construction: check; lunatic psychic advice: check; spirits haunting the family: check), the sheer audacity of the venture had sustained him too, and he seems relieved to have something to do.

From recent documents, the story of my mother's disintegration emerges in mosaic, stained-glass slivers from different perspectives. The last time my father visited, be brought a fat file of letters and physician statements documenting my mother's legal battle with FHP after the organization refused to grant her disability. Taken together, the letters describe conditions so extreme that it's a wonder she was ambulatory. But it's not the provider statements that stand out the most, but two letters typed by my mother, since they tell different stories.

Written for the disability board, the first letter describes a dizzying list of ailments, rendered in the heightened language of medical legalese: signs and symptoms and wherefores and concomitants. In it, her pain emerges as a purely physical event, alighting in her living room like an unwelcome raven.

The tone of the second letter is strangely formal, given that she is writing to her brother, George. But what fascinates me is that her pain emerges as *social* event. It takes eleven single-spaced typewritten pages for her to say that her health is suffering in direct proportion to the family nastiness. While she admits to having headaches most of her life, they did not turn into prolonged debilitating nightmares until things started coming to a head with Johnnie. Once she took charge of family meetings, migraines flowered into full-body pain.

According to my mother, family dynamics go something like this: Johnnie's wife makes regular, dramatic entrances (in person and over the phone) to accuse family members of killing her husband. George sides with her, since he feels bad, too, and I guess you've got to blame somebody. Cherre leaves the family meetings feeling physically ill. I do not know how Sam feels about things, or if he feels anything at all, since he seems able to lift himself beyond the drama by his trousers like the Lorax. By choice or by chance, my mother ends up in the middle of things. When she had rushed out to resuscitate Johnnie, she had been intercepted by his wife, who tackled her in a rage and tried to choke her.

My mother tells George that she is fifty-one years old and not afraid to die. What she fears, she says, is living. Not just in a body racked with pain, but with the "blackness and horror" that triggered Johnnie's death. She worries that the same "pit of hate and pathology" will "claim more victims yet," but she hardly seems to think the next victim will be her.

The letters pack a double-barreled kick for me. Sitting on the floor on a crisp November afternoon, I survey the files spread out around me like poisoned flower petals. I want to feel sorry for my mother, but I also want to shake her. If the nastiness takes such a toll, why not relinquish the briefcase of family business that fills her with dread, ignore the duty-filled laptop, forgo the painful exchanges with lawyers and realtors and accountants? Why not follow "it's killing me" with "I quit"? She worries that she will lose her job, describes a growing list of medicines (prednisone, morphine, sleeping pills, lidocaine scalp injections) and alternative therapies (crystals, acupuncture, chiropractic, prayer, Reiki, special pillows, self-help videos). She tells George that she has turned to antidepressants in despair. And yet she clings more desperately to the rope as the noose tightens.

THE DAY IS COLD AND CLOUDLESS, my office chaotic. Fascination with my mother's story has, I am afraid, trumped all interest in my dissertation. Slave of duty that I am, I do not allow myself to puzzle over my father's deliveries unless I've spent at least two hours cranking out *therefores* and *moreovers,* but I stopped giving a shit about my research long ago.

Tucking the papers in folders, I drag my still bathrobe-clad self into the shower, as my father is scheduled to take me to a Chournos wedding reception in Tremonton in a few hours. Given my mother's letters, the prospect of spending an afternoon with The Family sounds as appealing as (if not strangely kindred to) chaperoning a middle-school dance, but I figure I better enjoy my father's company while I can. When he dropped off the last load of papers, he'd barely said hello before disappearing on a date.

What I know about my father is that he is a hopeless romantic and a pleaser, his identity inextricable from that of his beloved. When I asked how he was doing when my mother was alive, he'd say, "We're doing just fine!" as if they were hewn from the same rough stone. And so I am eager to spend time with him, knowing that once he remarries our little alliance will be over.

BY THE TIME I throw on a short A-line skirt, a slim corporate jacket, and some pumps—all black—I hear a car pull into the driveway. A last glance in the mirror reveals a freshened-up withering girl. My marionette lines seem deeper, my body frailer since the fire. The black skirt I wore to the funeral hangs perilously from my hips, threatening to fall down around my ankles. Tracking down a safety pin, I pull the waistband together and pin a deep pleat before swiveling it to a hip where I hope no one will notice. I hadn't planned on attending the reception looking like an ailing funeral director, but it turns out that grief can work havoc on your wardrobe as well as your waistline. Without realizing it, I had thrown out anything frilly or lacy or otherwise wedding appropriate during the postfire dejunking spree and do not have one fluffy gauze blouse or dress to my name.

Concerns about my appearance evaporate as I slip outside, where my father stands next to a new car of the sort that neither of us would be inclined to drive. The color alone catches me off guard, a glittering taupe that, were it a lipstick shade, might be labeled "Nude and Bemused." And so I raise an eyebrow and shoot him an accusatory look.

"A *Lexus,* Dad?"

He smiles. "You like it?"

I inspect the not-quite-purple-or-pink sparkles and smirk. "Well, I guess if you're going out, you might as well go out in style."

My father looks pleased as I walk the perimeter of the car. Me in funeral garb; he in a too thin jacket. I ask after gas mileage and road noise, secretly hating the car. It's not just that my mother's obsession with status symbols snuffed out any desire I might have for such a vehicle, but that I feel a distinct intuitive prick.

My father did not buy luxuries for himself. Hell, he hardly bought necessities. He indulged my mother's obsession for ruby Cadillacs (the last of which boasted a *Lost in Space* voice that relentlessly urged occupants to check the wiper fluid), while he carpooled to work. When he bought the new computer with the widescreen flat-panel monitor, my mother had been so put out (oh, the excess!) that she hardly noticed that he had begun to look waiflike in his patched elastic-waist pants and mismatched shirts, threadbare socks, and fat rubber-soled soles. When she died, the first order of business was to take him shopping for glasses, as the ones he was wearing were so scarred and bent that you might have thought they had been trampled by the firefighters. And so the car makes me proud and sad at the same time, since it tells a story that he does not: he has found someone.

BREATHING IN THE SCENT of new leather as we head out of town, I am struck by the pristine interior, the unnatural absence of dust. Outside, the shops along Main Street thin into fallow fields, dappled with thin strips of snow, bright between dark clumps of earth, the frivolous beginnings of winter.

My father talks as I watch out the window, switching topics in the same way he changes lanes. Which is to say, without signaling. He explains that he gave the S.O.B. painting to Sam, itemizes the things he has kept aside for Cherre and George, fumes about my mother's prescriptions, and muses about retirement. Meanwhile, I watch the world slide by outside—bronze pussy willows and icy canals, crippled barbed-wire fences and sullen black heifers.

As he talks, I notice that we do not mark time in terms of college or marriage or jobs or children, but in relationship to what we now call the "incident." The datum from which our lives are now measured is split into three distinct parts: the weird years before the fire, the stark, heavy days afterward, and the day itself, in which everything teetered on the head of a pin.

"Well, Kid," he says, nodding to a paper wedged between the seats. "I tried to put things in order, like you asked. There's a list right there."

I pick up the paper. On it, a line of typed dates and events, embellished by handwritten notes in three colors of pen. There are the first years of his marriage, bracketed with a penned "No [association with?] Nick," which I take to be the years my mother was disowned. There are college graduations and career changes and moves, set off by arrows that make no sense at all. At the end of the list, he's got a sketch that might be a time line, terminating with a fat descending arrow labeled "Narcotic."

I fold the paper and put it aside. Later, I will line up his dates with mine, but for now I just want to talk.

"Did you know that all of mom's health problems started when Johnnie died? The scalp injections, the prednisone?"

"That sounds about right," he says, maneuvering past the WELCOME TO BENSON sign. Population: horses and handlers. "I tried to reason with her about her medications, but she just got belligerent."

I ignore the non sequitur that leaves the link between my mother's health and the Chournoses dangling. Discussing her prescriptions always left us at the same dead end. What was she supposed to do? Endure to the end? With pain we could not imagine? Nothing enraged her more than the suggestion that she was an addict. Addicts took substances for pleasure; she took them for pain. So what if she squirreled away Oxys by the jarful?

"I don't think there was anything you could have done, Dad. What were you going to do, drag her into rehab? Besides, you know as well as I do that no one could tell her anything when it came to her health."

"Well, that's true," he says. "When she got that liposuction and the rest, I got so mad. I said, 'Your body can't take it, Helen! You've got sponges for tissues.' But she just wouldn't listen to reason."

His voice breaks on the word "reason," betraying the frustration all of us felt when she announced the surgeries. If her body had been whole, we would have chalked up the decision to self-improvement. As it was, I could not imagine a more vicious cycle. If prednisone was to blame for her weight gain, and she needed the drug for pain, then the surgeries—which could not help but cause pain—would only require more prednisone. We had been treating her like spun glass for years, and yet there she was, ready to leap from a high dive into a pail full of water.

My father and I lapse into silence. Scanning the dash, I note the monitoring systems—GPS, rear backup camera, fuel burn and mileage indicators—wondering what it would be like to have a similar set of gauges for ourselves. What if there was an early-warning system you could wrap around yourself like a broad invisible bandage that could make announcements like, "In four hours you will put your foot in it," or "The part of yourself you negotiate here you will never get back." My mother must have known that the surgeries would strike a terrible blow. I must have known, even as I begged her to be cautious, that I was standing on a precipice, too. And nothing she said could have kept me from sailing right over the edge.

The dates in my mother's letters revealed why I had trouble remembering the timing of her surgeries. I had been standing on the porch of our ugly blue rambler when she called to tell me she was going to "get some things done." While she described procedures and praised her surgeon's credentials, I eyed the contours of the rambler across the street—its fenced porch and brown accents, the way its flawless green lawn butted up against the unkempt dandelion-strewn mat belonging to the "earthy" types next door. It was a strangely warm afternoon, searing and bright, despite the red and brown leaves trapped among the withered flowers. I remember asking, "Mom, are you sure?" and her saying, "I know what my body can withstand."

The Room of Blood and Bones   157

By then, I had begun to watch for the red Ford pickup and pale unmarked police car in the cul-de-sac, the way that our neighbor's cowboy boots made him swagger, the way his chest filled out his western shirts, tucked neatly into blue Wranglers. There was something of my playboy uncles about him. Dark eyes dancing underneath cropped brown hair and a schoolboy devotion to Hank Williams Jr. that I found mysteriously easy to forgive.

My mother's scheduled surgeries made me think of my own imperfections: the way my cesarean scars and stretch marks intersected with the lengthy uneven track from an early appendectomy, making my stomach resemble a map of Middle-earth. I didn't admit that I'd already looked into having a tummy tuck, as it would undermine my attempts to talk her out of her procedures. For the first time since I had married, I imagined someone besides Lan appraising my body, and the thought of it terrified and consumed me.

By then, I had stopped going to church. To stay sane, I started to ignore Church directives that demanded I stay home and procreate and lactate. I drove to work every day with my heart in my stomach, tucked the boys into bed, and sucked down coffee on the sly, typing late-night missives to no one in particular, trying to justify my life. I pierced my nose and ditched my garments, and took my Zoloft as directed.

The Zoloft had been my mother's idea. Hands shaking, I dialed her number from a grimy 7-Eleven telephone booth the night I drove off in the car wishing I could die. The sun was going down. Red streaks stretched across the horizon. When I heard her pick up, the ragged unhappiness I had known all of my life came rolling out in one sentence. "I do not know what is wrong with me, Mom."

There was a silence on the line, as if she knew a false step could trip some latent mine. Then, as carefully as I'd heard her say anything, she said, "You're dealing with a lot right now, right?" I thought about our marriage, reborn and teetering, the hundred and sixty student essays sitting on the bar, the two little boys in Batman costumes, and all of the ways I was failing them.

I coiled and uncoiled the telephone cord around a finger as her voice breathed comfort into the line. "I'll call something in for you," she finished. "You can pick it up on your way home."

MY MOTHER started taking prednisone the same year I started taking Zoloft—something I hadn't known until the last installment of papers. I consider sharing this detail with my father before deciding against it. After all, there is no decent way to say, *The faith you love was killing me.* Sitting next to him, I consider the contours of the western hills, the same bony-brown landscape I peered through as my mother explained the role of serotonin. She never mentioned that she was suffering, too. Neither of us knew she had begun to take a drug that would slowly dismantle her body. We solved our pain in the same way you might put out a fire by throwing water at the smoke alarm. The siren stopped wailing, but the building kept burning.

"I don't know, Dad," I say, breaking the silence. "I just don't get the timing on the surgeries. Obviously, the prednisone was bulking her up, but it had been for years. So, why then? Her letter to the disability board says something like 'and as I was getting a bunion repaired I thought I might get some other things done.' But it seems like a thin rationale."

"Oh, it was the same as when she got those breast implants," he says. "I tried to talk her out of those, too. I said '*Why* Helen? You're perfect—*perfect* just like you are.' But she just had to have them, out of the blue."

The breast surgeries had actually *not* been out of the blue, but I don't say so. My father had held back one of her journals for at least a month, and when he did give it to me, he seemed almost furtive about it. The only reason I could see for his reluctance was that he didn't want me to think too hard about the implants, which she got while I was a junior in high school. In the first part of the journal, she had penned her amusement at being asked to join a panel on "the trauma of being small breasted." (Why would anyone dislike small breasts?) Ten pages later, she described meeting her "special friends"—a couple with whom my parents would spend weekends (if not several nights a week as well) for the next fifteen years. Then, after attending a Christmas party in which the friends had exchanged gifts along with the hope that they could show affection without arousing jealousy, she wrote about getting the breast implants she had wanted "for years."

It wasn't the subtle sexual tension that troubled me as I read the journal—if I understood anything, it was the tug of extramarital attraction—but all of the ways I'd felt supplanted by the couple.

The Room of Blood and Bones 159

My mother was not demonstrative. While she appreciated expressions of love (nay: lived for them, demanded them), her own affection took some inferring. It was evident in drives to the mall or the lending of a treasured blouse, in elaborately decorated birthday cakes, home permanents, and hand-sewn jumpsuits. The word *love*—so rare and wonderful in our world you might think it was an ocelot or a fat zebra orchid—was a currency we did not use. And so the sheer number of times my mother had used the word *love* when she talked about the couple in her journal left me feeling physically ill.

From my perch on the wingback, I had thrown the journal across the floor and pulled myself into a tight little ball. It wasn't just my mother's misdirected affection that bothered me, but my own. In the months leading up to my affair, I found so many excuses to visit the house next door that the boys barely saw me. And it sickened me to think that they might have felt the pangs of dismissal too.

I felt nothing like foreboding as I stood in the driveway on that breathlessly clear October afternoon, holding my mother's belly-dancing costumes. Lan and I had dropped by her house with another couple to borrow some things for a Halloween dance. There was something familiar about the moment, as if I had lived it before. My mother was at her best, wearing a floral-print blouse and turquoise capris, brown hair carefully feathered around her face, swollen from prednisone use. I felt a passing irritation with the way she talked to my friend's husband, smiling conspiratorially as if she had known him for years, dark eyes flashing as if she might wink or invite him to lunch. Was she *flirting*? But even as I squirmed, I felt something immutable binding us.

THE IMAGE OF MY MOTHER fades as my father takes the southbound fork of highway toward Tremonton, paralleling the fat gully where the Bear River carves a thin line, thick with dogwood and willow. Ahead, a heap of rusted tractor parts shores up a lone brick wall, jutting incongruously out toward the road. Across the street, the Collinston granaries mark the spot where my mother had waited for my father to get off work, freshly disowned and four months pregnant, knowing her childhood was over.

"It's funny," I muse. "So much of mom's history is a history of her body."

"I guess so," he says. "After those surgeries I about lost my cool. I told that surgeon, I said, 'Look at her! You look at her! She was so beautiful—so beautiful—and you've ruined her. Ruined her!'"

Surprised by the ready emotion in his voice, I wait a moment before asking the obvious question.

"So, what did he say?"

"Only that he didn't want to see me in his office ever again." He takes a breath as if trying to iron out his voice. "I took pictures. Digital ones. I wanted to sue the guy, but your mom wouldn't let me. I'll send them to you if you want."

I think about the offer. By now I have realized that there are things I can handle and things that I can't. I'd barely skimmed my mother's autopsy when I had to go lie down, feeling as if all of the light and life had been knocked right out of me. Still, I figure the postoperative photos can be no worse than what I've already imagined.

"Sure Dad," I say. "Go ahead and send them."

At the Tremonton turnoff, my father takes the road through the river bottom at an impressive clip, slowing for our old house at the top of the rise, where the star-shaped clothesline still teeters behind the apple trees. Past the Kerr's redbrick foursquare, the gold brick of my grandparents' stately bay-and-gable comes into view. Under the wide front window, someone has installed a huge landscaping rock that could double as a headstone, its surface etched in black letters: CHOURNOS. To clear up any confusion about which Chournos is being honored, an image has been blasted into the rock as well—the silhouette of a man on horseback, flanked by a flock of sheep, a mountain skyline, and a lone thin pine.

"Jeez, Dad," I say, feeling suddenly surly. "You think they're ever going to let that man die?"

"Oh, I don't know," he says. "I guess it's all right."

I let the conversation dangle. I can't decide if my father lets the family off the hook too easily or if I level criticism too quickly. If anyone deserved a fat memorial in the flowerbed, it was my grandmother, who at least showed some fondness for the children. Her life had centered on a leathery Greek who might have been Prince Charming given the way she talked about him. She bequeathed her unwavering devotion to a man, an Outfit, a church; and yet my mother and I had inherited something else:

heady devotion to men like my grandfather: successful, self-centered, and spectacularly unavailable.

WE ARRIVE at the wedding in silence. My father pulls the car into my cousin's wide pasture where a sleek pink 1959 Cadillac holds down a flock of balloons. Angling the car so nobody will ding it, he says, "Don't take your guns to town," as if the lyrics constitute a logical conversational segue. Then he smiles at me. "Come on."

I swallow my reluctance and angle my heels across the gravel driveway, relieved that we had not been invited to the temple ceremony. Such invitations invariably evoked questions of worthiness, if not awkward excuses, since you could not attend the service if you did not pass the yearly interview with Church authorities. While you could sometimes get a pardon from paying a full tithe—say, due to financial hardship— unsanctioned beverages were right out, and if sipping coffee made you unworthy, my transgressions were certain to cause an elemental shattering of skin and bone if I got near the door.

Passing a cluster of breathtaking women in perilously high shoes and pink formals, I make my way to the reception line, where my uncle George stands next to Junior, one in a crisp western shirt, the other in a light blue tuxedo. My aunt Cherre tells a group of polyester-clad women that a temple worker mistook the mother of the bride for the bride, and everyone laughs. The highest compliment of all: ageless beauty.

Extending the requisite hugs and hellos, I am surprised to find that I don't want to smack anybody. The irritation I'd felt in the car along with the raw anger I'd felt at the summer reunion seems to have dissipated somehow. My relatives seem like regular folks, not the strangely perfect beings I grew up with. While I still hate the way my mother allowed herself to be sucked into the family drama, I know something about misdirected affection.

Despite my surprising lack of irritation, I don't feel much like discussing the partnership. So, when George cocks his head toward my father to say something about entitlements, I excuse myself to procure a glass of water and a seat on a white folding chair.

Surveying the crowd, I feel myself drawn to my aunt Cherre, who reminds me so much of my mother that I can almost feel her presence in the room: the cadence of her speech, her laugh, the shape of her body, ensconced in pink chiffon. I don't know if Cherre ever understood how much her little sister idolized her, but I feel sort of sorry for her now, shouldering memories of her little sister's envy. And I would resent my beauteous cousins if I did not understand our impulses so profoundly.

The night I wore one of my mother's belly-dancing costumes, I was shocked to see how skimpy it was. I had not remembered the sheer fabric panels held together with a thin elastic band. Ten years of wearing garments had kept me from looking at my body too closely, and I was surprised to see so much of it, white against the silver sequins, my thighs and stomach so blatantly *out there*. Having just finished my first marathon, I was as taut as I was ever going to be, and yet I frowned at my stomach and doubled up on the veils.

The Halloween party turned out to be a bust. Aside from the couple we went with, there were maybe ten other people in the venue, where the DJ lined up the absolute worst of the eighties. After enduring an hour of Starship and Wham!, we fled to a crowded bar where I felt awkward. Having never ordered a beer before, I shrugged at the bartender, who brought something tepid and undrinkable. Unimpressed, I let the beverage grow warmer until someone suggested we move the party to our house.

We played a short game of spin the bottle in the backyard, still dressed in our Halloween finery. The night was unseasonably warm. The boys were in bed. We disclosed fantasies and stripped off layers of clothes, depending on what happened to be on our card. I drew "Kiss the person to your left" and leaned in for a peck from our neighbor, embarrassed by how exposed I felt and shocked at how much I enjoyed it.

Had God been watching, he might have missed what happened next, as it was over so quickly. I was standing at the stereo, gauging the relative merits of Zeppelin and Clapton, when the man I'd just kissed leaned in and whispered "I want you."

It was the simplest phrase in the world. And yet the words ran all the way down through my body, where they settled in my thighs and hips and spun back through my lips where I could taste them. To feel *wanted*. Worthy of love, if not reckless pursuit.

The feeling of desirability was like a key turning in a lock. It did not matter where the door led. I needed the feeling more than I'd ever needed anything in my life. The girl who had always paled in comparison to everyone: beauty queens, cousins, and blonde bombshells—to her own mother, for god's sake—that girl was suddenly *special.*

It didn't matter that Lan loved me in that moment. It was a feeling he could not supply—something I had not felt since we dated. It was wild and dangerous, and for the first time in my life I did not try to suppress the feeling or try to manage it but let it light me on fire.

THE SUN is still spinning a westbound retreat when my father drops me back off at home. After watching him pull out of the driveway I retire to the kitchen, where I pour some wine. A note on the bar tells me that the boys are at Wingers, and so I grab one of Lan's coats, conveniently draped across a barstool, and walk outside to watch the winter sunset.

Pulling the coat tight against my skin, I feel Lan's arms in the space of his sleeves and step out onto the brittle grass. Beyond the waist-high rickety fence, the sheep stand like statues, noses anchored to the feeble remnants of root and stem.

The squat redwood slats remind me of the day Lan and I mended the fence after my affair. No tape, no line, no level. Eyeing the slats above the uneven ground, we passed each other drill bits and screw tips, one of us holding a board for spacing while the other sunk in silver screws. We reused old hardware, pulled rusty nails, said things like "Does that line up?" and "That board's not worth saving," while I tried not to think of how empty I felt.

I felt something flutter past, an orange flash followed by another. Ignoring it, I kept my attention on the work left to do, the rhythm of drilling and fastening. Channeling the git-er-done determination that had earned me advanced degrees and pilot ratings, I felt vaguely annoyed when Lan gasped, "Look at that!"

Reluctantly, I looked up to see hundreds of orange and black butterflies surging through the pasture in waves. They heaved past us heedless, as if yoked to one collective heading, lifting themselves over our feeble fence, bound for some bright destination. Just when I thought they were gone, a new cloud would appear, billowing past the brittle grass and on into the next field before disappearing into the horizon.

For the first time in ages, Lan and I stood united, barely daring to speak. There was something of grace in that moment, beyond the promises of therapy and self-help. Something I might have missed if not for the astonished, "Look!"

Holding my wine, I think about the way the fence echoes the uneven contours of our marriage: the blitz of migrating butterflies, the long walks and crab-leg dinners, the alliance we tried to build with our sons, laughing in the warm oak kitchen, the way we forgave, or tried to.

It wasn't Lan's infidelity that sent me headlong into the affair. It was a longing so familiar it might have been part of my genetic makeup: to be naked and charming and infinitely desirable.

Refusing to be second rate again, I rejected the girl I had been: the dowdy Mormon housewife, lonely and nervous, changing diapers while others sucked the marrow out of life. I ditched my skis and bought a snowboard, took up the flying lessons I had abandoned in college.

I wanted every sensory experience I had ever missed. I discovered alcohol, blasted down the south face of Beaver Mountain with a flask of brandy tucked in my parka, stole weed from a local cop and smoked it in the playroom, screamed through the desert on a Yamaha two-stroke. I insisted on sex at six thousand feet while Lan held the wheel of an oil-flecked rented Cessna, determined to be the person I had never been. Breathlessly desirable and impossible to ignore.

LEANING AGAINST the apple tree in the garden, I feel the wine working its magic. At my feet, our bony cat bathes in the frigid brown dirt. We didn't buy the farmhouse for the kids. We bought it so that I would not have to face the woman who had been my friend, or see the man working a little too conspicuously on the Ford 150 in the driveway across the street.

To take my mind off things, I volunteered to stay with my grandma Chournos, who was recovering from a stroke. My mother was still a wreck from her cosmetic surgeries. Cherre needed to make some appointments. And so I had blasted over on a black Suzuki Intruder, backpack flung over a black leather jacket, hair flying in all directions, feeling older than I ever had in my life.

Yelling a hello over Regis Philbin, I came into the living room and kissed my grandmother, who muted the volume and smiled at me through square pink glasses.

When I asked how she was, she said, "Well, with my fingers," as if limping around with a walker and oxygen was part of some gigantic joke. Then she nodded toward a plate full of doughnuts. "You eat 'em!" she said. "You've got too skinny!" I was still trying to determine whether I could stand to eat one, having lost my appetite for deep-fried fat balls long before, when she aimed a finger at me. "Now you go back to the Church! Don't you get up to that university and forget your heritage."

The words left me speechless. "Your heritage." My heritage was so messy I hardly knew where to begin. It was a god who loved you and a god who condemned you; good and evil spirits vying for your allegiance. It was plural marriage and marital purity; sexual revolution and repression. It was so many dos and don'ts it made my head spin. It was my mother's brazen sexuality and my grandmother's subservience. The injunction to be ageless and angst-less and perfect. It was the understanding that *good enough* would always be determined by someone else. It was faith and works, but mostly works, and I had finally screwed up so badly that I wasn't likely to redeem myself in this life or the next.

There was no way to answer my grandmother, whose one source of strength was her faith. And so I smiled and said, "Don't worry. We're doing just fine."

She glared at me. For a minute I thought she might say something else, but she didn't. Instead, she retrieved the remote control and selected the BYU channel, where Elder James McDonald was lecturing on the dangers of spiritual pollutants.

Sure that I was versed on such pollutants in ways that would make McDonald's head spin, I whipped out a copy of *Madame Bovary*, which I had been reading with the hope that Emma's excesses might correct my own. While I looked for the page where I had left off, McDonald quoted from King Benjamin's address in the Book of Mormon: "If ye should transgress and go contrary to that which has been spoken, ye do withdraw yourselves from the Spirit of the Lord, that it may have no place in you to guide you in wisdom's paths."

The passage made me fume. There were so many ways to get it wrong that even King Benjamin couldn't keep track of them all: "I cannot tell you all the things whereby ye may commit sin; for there are divers ways and means, even so many that I cannot number them." And yet it was your fault if you lost your way, your fault if you did not feel the promptings of some cosmically distant spirit. Like a father who punished his daughter's pregnancy by throwing her out of the house, God would withdraw His spirit when you needed it most. And this god—this god was *merciful*?

I spent the rest of the evening trying to concentrate on Emma's seduction while McDonald yammered about the importance of purity. My grandmother was dying; god knew what was going on with my mother; I was a mess; and the only thing we had to make sense of our lives was the language of sin and redemption.

I had tried to repent so I could "walk guiltless before God." I met with my bishop, who regarded my confession with wide eyes and something like sympathy. Three days later, he called to let me know he'd arranged for my Church court, a meeting in which I would be expected to describe my sins for a group of priesthood officials who would ask about specific details and rule on an appropriate punishment.

The thought of the meeting churned my insides to a frothy peak. Although the bishop assured me that the Church no longer used the word *court* to label the proceedings, there was no getting around the fact that the purpose was strictly punitive. The hearing could not fix the rift in our marriage. It could not mend the part of me that still missed the affair. The brethren could rule on how many months I should go without taking the sacrament, or whether or not I'd need to be excommunicated and rebaptized, but the thing that bothered me most was that the remedy wasn't remotely linked to the disease.

Aware of the book in my lap, my grandmother bumped up the volume, as if to signal that I was supposed to be paying attention. Determined not to listen, but not wanting to upset her, I slipped a finger in one ear, which only created a weird space in which the stories collided. While McDonald lamented the downfall of David, Rodolphe declared his love over the auctioneer's call "for manures!" While David planned Uriah's demise, Emma shuddered at her first adulterous embrace. And I grappled with the memory of a rocky hillside, one of my hands fumbling for a condom while the other held on to a stunted juniper, trying to keep the Coleman sleeping bag from slipping down the embankment.

When my grandmother bumped up the volume for the third time, I put the book down and cradled my ears in my palms, trying to keep McDonald's voice from splitting both eardrums. Bathsheba would lose her husband and child, but her suffering would be eclipsed by David's. Emma would devise extravagant encounters with men who would only forget her. And I would drive home from my first tryst bewildered, vaguely aware of my tired eyes, suppressing a wide and bottomless ache, pressing the gas pedal hard toward the floor.

THE GENTLE BUZZING of my cell phone disrupts the memory, returning my attention to the frozen garden. Across the valley, thousands of tiny lights have winked on in the darkness, presided over by the saintly spires of the Logan Temple, which illuminate the town like turgid nipples. The memory of my grandmother floods me with regret. It was the last evening I would spend with her. We could have talked about cows and sugar beets. We might have stuffed ourselves with milk and doughnuts. Instead, we had been silenced by the thick drone of authority.

Snapping open the phone, I hear my father's lively hello. "Just wanted you to know I e-mailed those pictures," he says. "Dunno if they'll help you or not."

"Oh, thanks," I say, grateful for the sound of his voice on the line. I may have lost a mother and grandmother, but my father remained, steadfast and supportive, no matter how many piercings I got or what questions I asked.

I have the wild impulse to tell him how much I love him. I want to explain that I don't care about the Afterlife as long as we have each other now. But I don't want to make him uncomfortable, so I just say, "Thanks for inviting me along today, Dad. I really love spending time with you."

A pause tells me he's not sure what to say. Although we sometimes add a passing "love you" to a "see you later," we don't normally express affection. And so I imagine him adrift in a sea full of bluebells, wondering how to proceed, when he says, "Well, Kid, that's all right."

Warmed by the phone call, I turn back to the house, the cat dangerously threading himself through my spearlike heels, which aerate the frozen lawn as I limp along. As I don't have anything else to do until the boys get home, I decide to treat myself to some scotch and check out the photos.

In my office, I enter my e-mail passwords, struck by how many times I've keyed them in, breathless, hoping for the right name in the inbox and dejected when it did not appear. Maybe that's what bothered me most about the affair—the way I felt hostage to attention from someone else, the way that silence could wreck me inside.

There was no way to secure endless worshipful attention. Trying to shore up my self-worth by having an affair with a married man was like my mother trying to lose the weight she'd gained from years of pain relief by suctioning her spongy tissues. The remedy made the hole deeper.

My mother's surgeries explained the cryptic allusion in the letter to Sam—"I really did come very close to dying." For weeks, she could not lift a finger without agony. Her pain was so exquisite that no concoction of narcotics even touched it. In desperation, she raised her prednisone dosage to 160 milligrams a day, just to tolerate being alive.

After she recovered—if she ever did—she could not survive on less than 70 milligrams of prednisone a day. The high doses bulked her up even further, filled her eyes with cataracts, and produced yeasty sores that stubbornly refused to heal. She tried returning to work, but couldn't make it through half a shift, even when she upped her prednisone dose to 120. She knew that her failing health would eventually make it impossible for her to work, but she did not expect it so soon, and it broke her heart.

HEART POUNDING, I click on my father's message and open the first of two files. In the photo, my mother sits in a wheelchair, her purse draped across a hospital bed, waiting, it seems, to go home.

If I didn't know the context, I might think she had been the victim of severe domestic abuse. Her body is bulky and rigid, shrouded in a red Nebraska Medicine sweatshirt, her hands limp in her lap and wrapped in Ace bandages. Her head and neck are so swathed with gauze that she looks like a mummy, wrapped in blinding white to the top of her head where someone has tied things off with a little white knot as if she were an unfortunate present. Bruised and swollen, she peers through glasses that sit precariously atop swathed ears. Only her eyes and mouth are visible. There is something resigned about her gaze, something infinitely sad. Her bottom lip droops freakishly to one side, as if she had suffered a stroke.

Closing the file, I open the second, but it mostly baffles me. Dated nine days *before* the first, the photo shows my mother from the chest up, lying in a hospital bed, her head averted, the picture of abject misery. A sharp furrow runs between her eyebrows; her cheeks are swollen and purple with prednisone. There is no telling if she refuses to look at the camera, or if she is too riddled with pain to acknowledge its presence.

I can't be sure where the picture was taken. She is wearing a hospital gown, and the bedding looks sufficiently institutional. The black bedside table with its yellow stuffed bear is nothing I've ever seen before, and so I can only assume she is in a surgery center. I thought she had the procedures done at the same time, but if she had them on two separate occasions, it only makes her decisions more outrageous. Why risk the facial enhancements if the liposuction had nearly killed her?

But I already know the answer.

To feel wondrous and worthy, charming and utterly desirable. My father couldn't supply the feeling—not entirely. Only the distant gaze of esteemed others seemed to fill the void. But the feeling was temporary, I knew.

MY GLASS of scotch sits untouched on my desk. To bargain well-being for esteem. To mistake attention for love. To put ourselves under the knife figuratively and not so figuratively. To let others stake out the measure of our worth. These were things we did without thinking. Nothing shielded us from our flaws so spectacularly, or made them multiply more.

The image of my mother staring through bandages haunts me. The way she looks so small. There is something of a disregarded child about her, something of her own mother flitting out of a postoperative haze, saying, "I hope somebody loves me."

It was not the promise of sex, the room of blood and bones. It was the promise of something better. Intrigue and relevance, maybe love.

When my mother asked me if I'd cared about the man and I said yes, she seemed relieved. "Good," she said. "I'd hate to think it was meaningless."

But it *was* meaningless. When I ran into the man five years later, he was directing cars through a crippled intersection. I popped the horn and rolled down the window. He leaned in and said, "I miss it every day."

The comment illuminated the past like a floodlight. The thing for which I'd bartered my marriage and family had been missing all along. He did not say "I miss *you*." He said he missed *it:* the heady promise of illicit sex.

I used to wonder if my mother had an affair, but I don't think it matters. Ours were legacies obsessed with all the wrong things. Culpability and consequences. Symptoms of suffering, not sources. The powers that governed our lives did not care if we were bleeding inside. They only cared that we paid for our sins as publicly as possible. Our stories mostly failed to promote anything like empathy and understanding. And so they turned us against ourselves—as if that wasn't the problem to begin with.

FOURTEEN

Harold

O n our first Thanksgiving together after the fire, we meet in what
I now think of as my father's home, emptied of its soot-coated
belongings and fully restored. Its grand spaces and cubbyholes seem cav-
ernous without furnishings, and we rattle around in the house like spare
socks in a dryer. No one ventures much beyond the kitchen and dining
room. There isn't anything there, after all: no couches, chairs, or televi-
sions, no shelves or end tables, just large airy rooms with fresh beige carpet and bare walls, painted in a light dusty taupe.

Nothing feels remotely right about the holiday. Just selecting a table-
cloth takes more emotional stamina than I bargained for, and Michelle
and I end up blearily setting the table, listening to Christie improvise
on the piano in the parlor under a towering stained-glass angel, her eyes
turned toward heaven.

Well-meaning people warned me about the renewed sense of loss
that accompanies the first round of holidays, and it's true. There is nothing like carrying on with family traditions, forged through a lifetime of
seemingly insignificant rites—sibling-teasing and food-seasoning and
table-setting—to make you realize how person-specific they are. The
dining room remains as my mother left it, chandeliered and cherry-
wooded, bedecked with floral print carpet that might have been lifted
from a Vegas casino, flanked by a white marble fireplace and a six-foot
painting of Jesus mourning Jerusalem. Its closets and drawers still burst
with fine china and linens, but the excesses only call attention to our
mother's absence.

It does not help that Thanksgiving had always been fraught. I don't
know if my mother had elegant ideas about the holiday that we never

failed to spoil, but somebody was bound to get yelled at for sampling the hors d'oeuvres or clearing her glass of TaB prematurely. As my mother got sicker, the holiday got progressively strained and strange, finally culminating in last year's Thanksgiving, which could not have been stranger.

I should have known that something was wrong when she did not come down to oversee the table setting and meal preparation. Feeling punchy without her supervision, we selected mismatched bowls that dared guests to guess the holiday, tested gravy and turkey with our fingers, and waited for reprisals that never came.

Strangely mellow and distant, she arrived just in time for the prayer, taking her place at the head of the table. I braced myself for her reaction to the table setting, which featured nothing I'd have to wash by hand. No Waechtersbach chargers or sterling flatware or hand-painted china. But she didn't seem to mind.

Around the table, grandchildren poked at Jell-O, poured too much gravy, and needled each other with utensils. Someone yelled, "Pass the rolls" and a warm bun soared the length of the table. I waited for her to object, but she didn't. The fork in one hand skipped idly over stuffing and yams, while the other hand hovered just under her nose. Focused on something in the air above the table, her eyes were wide and sincere. Unnerved, I tried to direct my attention to anything else: the painting of Jesus mourning Jerusalem, the conversation, the potatoes. When I looked back, she was whispering into a cupped hand as if it might be a microphone: "Mary had a little lamb, little lamb, little lamb . . ."

I watched in sideways glances, horrified. When the song was done, she smiled and nodded into a cupped hand, as if sharing a secret with an unseen audience. No one but Lan and I seemed to notice. Michelle described the latest antics of her eighth graders and everyone burst out laughing, at which point my mother looked up and said, "I hate it when I miss something good." Moments later, she called everyone to order. Everyone was expected to be at her home on Christmas morning. No exceptions. When a daughter-in-law burst from the room in tears at this announcement, I tried to explain that we had agreed to meet later because some people wanted a quiet morning with their children. My mother locked eyes with me in a look that spoke of betrayal. Then she retreated back into the shelter of her cupped hand.

I called Michelle later. Had she noticed? Had our mother been behaving strangely for a while, and we hadn't been paying attention?

But we had noticed. Our sailor-like manners weren't disrespect. They were our way of drowning out the pathos we sensed peripherally.

IT'S SOMETHING we don't mention as we prepare dinner this year—the weirdness of the last. My father maintains a calm easiness about the meal, taking time to offer hugs between mashing the potatoes and checking the rolls. As in years past, we test the turkey with our fingers and serve the same food, but everything tastes like ashes.

Anxious for the day to be over, I start clearing the table as soon as it seems decent to do so. While I love spending time with my siblings and their families, the holiday kicks up too many regrets—like fucking up my mother's last Thanksgiving. When we prepared to leave, she looked at me full in the face. "Goodbye to my daughter who is . . . What are you?" She paused to think. "Oh yes, I know. A will-o'-the-wisp, flitting about."

I was struck by her fragility at that moment, by the thin line between rationality and irrationality that she walked, tentatively balancing from one moment to the next.

The term she used troubled me for a long time—"will-o'-the-wisp." A ghostly light that flitted over water, a metaphor for something that led one forward, but remained just out of reach. It was hardly a fitting description for the daughter who stood before her, flesh and bone and hopelessly human, but it was a symbol of what she had always been to me.

AS THE LAST of the pie plates disappears into the dishwasher, my father announces that he would like to share our mother's jewelry with us, and so I put off our departure while he fills the dining room table end to end with rings. Diamonds, black pearls, and star-sapphires, thousands of precious and semiprecious stones I can't name. He invites us to take five apiece, and when that fails to make a dent in the collection, he says, "Take as many as you like." Which also does not leave a dent. Once everyone has a modest pile, he clears the table and fills it with necklaces. Then watches, and bracelets, and earrings.

I paw through the treasures with everyone else, holding the strangest pieces up for examination. But there is too much of it, and I watch it come and go with growing exhaustion. I knew my mother hoarded jewelry, but had no idea how much. Some pieces are old friends, like the huge squash blossom necklace she bought from a traveling salesman who'd heard about her ardor for jewelry and tracked her down at the office. There is the costume jewelry she acquired in the days she sold Avon, the loopy beaded ropes my grandma Chournos strung in the 1970s, and the ruby star sapphire my father bought her for their fifth anniversary—precious because it was expensive, and she still didn't have a diamond wedding ring.

Completely ambivalent, I spend the next hour picking things up and putting them back. Lan selects a turquoise bolo tie; our boys select rings for future loves. And I am just deciding not to take anything at all when my father drapes a hand-carved greenstone koru around my neck.

One of the pieces my mother picked up in New Zealand, the koru comes with a slip of paper explaining its association with new beginnings and harmony. *Ka hinga atu he tete-kura, ka hara-mai he tete-kura: As one fern frond dies, one is born to take its place.*

Feeling the stone warm to my skin, I don't expect I'll ever take my mother's place. But I am left with her strange legacy, whether I like it or not. The stone reminds me that I am temporary, too, and while I can't decide how to feel about this new beginning, I suppose there are worse things I could do than keep unfurling.

RUMMAGING THROUGH THE JEWELRY takes a toll on all of us, and I begin to feel achy and tired. Glancing at my father, I notice that he has begun to look tired too, if not physically ill. His eyes are closed, his forehead shimmering with sweat. If the holiday was taking a toll on me, it had to be grinding him into the ground. Pulling up a chair next to him, I slip an arm around his shoulders.

"Thanks for the day, Dad. I know it was a hard one."

He looks at me and smiles.

"You going?"

"Yep. It's time."

"Well, before you go," he says, "I've got something for you. Come here." He forces himself from the table, where the jewelry bestowal has turned into a spirited test to see who can find the wildest watches. "It won't take long."

Curious, I follow him downstairs where he has made a makeshift office. Flicking on the computer, he asks. "Did you ever get something from your mom called "Denice Dogs"?

My heart skips a beat. "What?"

"Like a file she might have e-mailed."

I look at him, baffled. "She never e-mailed me in her life, Dad. I didn't even know she had an account."

"Well," he says, "I sort of figured that's the way it was." The monitor flickers to life. "I found this the other day while I was cleaning out that old hard drive."

He opens a file, and I look at the screen. A letter to me from my mother that begins "Dear Denicea."

The salutation is weird enough on its own—why the misspelling? Had she been confused? In a hurry? But the strangest thing is that she had written to me at all. While she spent days typing long missives to brothers and lawyers and pissed-off wives, she only did so if she thought something big was at stake. In all my life, she'd never written a letter to *me*. And so I hold my breath as the printer churns out seven single-spaced pages.

Stapling them, my father sighs. "There you go. But I gotta say, it's a little weird."

SITTING IN THE CAR on the way home, I try to contain my curiosity. If the letter is a plea for me to go back to church, I'm bound to be disappointed. But if it is "weird," then there's a chance it will provide a window into her inner world. So far, my mother's papers have fixated on *events,* leaving me to speculate on her longings and fears.

Outside, the sun makes a lunge for the desert, turning the foothills to gold. Exhausted by the day's events, none of us feels like talking. Lan, the boys, and me, with no friends to speak of but each other. Once we stopped going to church, and (worse) when we explained that we did not want to be visited with messages or pamphlets or pleas to come back, we developed something like leprosy or scabies. A condition that caused people to throw tracts and newsletters and fun-size Snickers and small potted plants on our doorstep and run. The messages usually had something to do with God's eternal plan and how much He loved us and how important it was to serve Him constantly and earnestly, which only made me wonder why this omnipotent being was so desperate for our help. And so we had learned to let go and band together, protecting our hearts as well as we could.

By the time we pull into the driveway, I feel wiped out. The memory of last year's Thanksgiving planted squarely over the top of this one makes me wish we could sleep until spring. But I don't want the tragedy to supplant our own traditions. In my heart, I can feel the uncertain arc toward the future, the departure of boys suddenly grown, and so I turn to Ben and Arthur before they tumble out of the car, trying not to sound desperate: "You guys up for decorating the tree?"

Uninspired, they look at each other. Teenage-hood has pretty much spoiled the magic of hanging balls on tree limbs, but they seem to understand that I need them.

Saving my mother's letter for later, I put on some music. By the time I've warmed some cider, I can hear the boys laughing in the living room. Rounding the corner, I find them grouping my mother's palm trees in the wide picture window, along with the two noble pines.

While Ben wraps lights around the palm trees, Arthur adds huge decorative balls (coconuts!) to the fronds, along with a windup gorilla. In the spirit of things, Lan stands our marble Christus (a gift from my mother) next to Father Christmas (a gift from his mother), positioning the two so that they seem to hold hands. Then we unpack our nativity.

The only thing we could afford when the boys were little, the set had been a grocery store special that, due to a glitch in packaging, had two Josephs and no shepherds. The angel came to endless grief, since she never balanced atop the stable very well; her poor wings had gotten so battered from one plunge after another that we thought it might be a mercy to remove them entirely.

The boys park tiny Harley motorcycles next to the wise men, so they all have a way to get home, which prompts Lan to think for a minute before adding an airplane. Then we place twelve light-up Victorian houses (yearly gifts from his mother) around everything, creating a Christmas display that feels a little bit Bethlehem and a little bit brothel.

Admiring our work, I think there's nothing like lining up symbols from your storied past and strapping lights on them to help you understand why you may be neurotic. The competing messages and motifs, the implied shoulds and should-nots, the objects of desire and nostalgia. The white marble Christus eschews the earthy seediness of Father Christmas, and yet you're given both. And so you stand with armfuls of ambiguity, color and shadow, monkeys hanging from trees. If this isn't confusing enough, you are handed this almighty mess along with the assurance that things are not so ambiguous at all.

Cheered by the display, I excuse the boys, who disappear into their rooms, leaving me to my mother's letter. I brew a pot of tea, slip into my robe, and retire to my office, where I turn on a yellow desk lamp and curl up in the tired wingback. The sound of electronics buzzes from behind bedroom doors; the news wafts up from the living room. And I sink into the strangest story I have ever read in my life.

My mother begins by catching me up on the latest partnership debacle: the man who bought the last chunk of property wants his $1.5 million back, along with damages. She is certain that the buyer's crazy gold-digging floozy of a wife has something to do with his sudden change of heart. But what she really wants to tell me is something she doesn't think my siblings are quite ready to hear: her hands have become sensitized to feeling spirits.

I can't decide how to feel about the revelation. As the most skeptical of her children, I hardly make a sympathetic audience. I don't know how she could have missed my contempt for her therapy sessions. And so I feel kind of sorry that she trusts me with her story.

Her newfound ability, she says, first manifested itself through her poodles. Dead for years, they had returned to her in spirit. She reminds me that, like human beings, animals were free to roam the earth after death, and so why wouldn't her dogs return to their favorite place in the world? Her bed! She explains that spirits are electrical energy in a low range, that they have mass and weight, and that she can tell one dog from the other without seeing them.

When she tells her "Magic Lady" about the arrival of the dogs, Andrea closes her eyes. Yes! She can see them, too! There are three: a tiny white poodle (My mother's heart leaps—Sheba!), a poodle of indeterminate color (Usagi!) and another one . . . What is it? Andrea struggles for a moment before the answer reveals itself in an intuitive flourish: "a cute little brown wiener dog."

The narrative is so strange that it hardly seems real, and I would smirk at the details if they weren't so unnerving. Before long, the third dog begins to feel threatening to my mother. Although Andrea insists that the dog is "sweet and little," my mother claims that it feels massive to her— powerfully male and unlike any dog she ever owned. While her poodles sleep peacefully, this dog tramples the bed, trying to get between her feet and legs. Aware of her growing alarm, Andrea tells her to look up the symbolism for the breed, since it might have a message for her.

I close my eyes. It's not just the bizarre counseling session that bothers me—you reveal that a spectral dog is hunting you and your therapist wants to know the *variety*?—but that I feel sort of culpable. She had mentioned the dogs to me once before, but I figured it was just one more odd fascination. I had no evidence that there wasn't a spirit world lurking just beyond our own, and the thought of her poodles seemed to give her such joy that I hardly felt qualified to tell her to snap out of it.

Putting down the letter, I consult my journal. When *had* she mentioned the dogs? She never told me about the threatening one, only that she sometimes felt the poodles curled up on her bed.

A quick search confirms the date: just before Halloween. Without the entry I would have forgotten that it wasn't just the appearance of the dogs that bothered me, but the hope she attached to them. If she could sense animal spirits, then it was only a matter of time before she would be able to sense the souls of people! And if she could sense people, then surely she would be able to talk to her father! "If I could just feel him hug me," she said mournfully, "then I would finally know he had loved me."

I felt darkly outraged as I hammered out the details in my journal that night, irritated at Andrea for fueling such delusions, but now I just feel sorry. It has taken the fire for me to realize how it feels to lose the person from whom you took all of your earliest bearings. And I understand her longing: to know you had been loved by the person you admired most.

Taking a deep breath, I return to the letter. It is as if she is leaving a record of things in my hands. But my hands and heart feel too small for such a story. The narrative doesn't sound delusional, but eerily matter-of-fact. She punctuates perfectly, frets about words she might have misspelled, reflects on the significance of each event. Her syntax and clarity shine. But the content is chilling.

The spirit dogs become her constant companions. When she goes shopping, Usagi (Japanese for "rabbit") waits in the car, while Sheba rides along on an arm like a fluffy corsage. The arrangement makes her happier than she has been in ages—surely, God has sent the dogs to help ease her suffering!—and then everything goes straight to shit.

Pulling her Cadillac into the garage after a piano lesson one afternoon, she shuts off the engine and reaches over to pet Usagi. As she touches him, she feels something slam itself against the car, throwing her against the door. Before she can right herself, the same invisible force slams the car in the opposite direction. The engine is off. There is no natural explanation for the sickening rock of the car.

She prepares to make a mad dash for the house when an electric charge pierces her left foot and starts working its way up her leg. Trembling, she realizes that the dog in the car is not Usagi, but the other one—which, she realizes to her horror, isn't a dog at all, but a human spirit masquerading as one of her pets. She panics: she let the spirit sleep in her bed. What if the degree of familiarity would allow the spirit to possess her body? Mustering all of her courage, she raises her arm to the square and commands the spirit to leave.

At her words, the spirit rushes out of her, and she bolts for the door. Safely inside her house, she calls my father. When he doesn't pick up, she calls Andrea. Listening to the distant ring, she feels the spirit rally, shooting through her foot and moving into her leg. She can feel it ascending: inside her body where it reads as an electric charge; outside of her body, where it reads as a pulsating mass that she can palpate with her fingers.

Unable to reach Andrea, she continues to cast the spirit out, which stalls its progress but does not eliminate it. An hour and a half later, she finally gets through to my father, who begs her to call 911. When he gets home, he promises to take her to the emergency room.

She recoils. What were *doctors* going to do? Put her in a padded cell? She needs spiritual aid, not first aid. If the spirit infiltrates her brain, she tells him, it will be over. She will still be alive, but someone else will be "running her controls."

Panicked, my father flies home and gives her a blessing, which expels the spirit momentarily; but by 9:00 PM it has returned in full force. By the time Andrea calls just before midnight, the spirit has moved into her upper chest where it threatens to cut off her breathing. My father begs her to seek medical attention while her therapist breathes comfort into the receiver. What my mother needs to do, she says, is interrogate the spirit. The more she knows, the more power she will have. *Concentrate,* she urges. *Ask the spirit its name.*

My mother focuses. Andrea closes her eyes. When my mother fails to hear anything, Andrea intuits the answer. The spirit's name is Harold, ruler of armies.

Andrea reminds my mother that we forged powerful bonds before we came to Earth, that in some cases we picked out our own parents and siblings. The spirit, she says, may be someone she knows. *Think,* she says. *Can you tell?*

Desperate, my mother pauses, eyes closed, and the answer comes to her. Harold is her brother. A mighty fallen spirit who chose to follow Lucifer in the preexistence. Forbidden to join the family members he had once loved, he chose to torment them, hoping to make them "miserable like unto himself."

I burn through the rest of the narrative. Harold's presence explains everything: Monte's carousing, George's depression, Johnnie's paranoia. Monte had not wrestled the devil in the Nevada hotel room. He grappled with his own brother, cursed to wander the Earth in exile and intimately acquainted with his weaknesses. Harold had taken the brothers in turn. And now he was after her.

Despite the terrifying presence of the spirit, my mother takes heart. Surely God would not allow Harold to torment her if He did not mean to help. There had to be a reason for his coming! Perhaps her life's true purpose was to eliminate Harold from the face of the earth! By vanquishing him, she could spare her family more pain, save her children. She knew the promise in the Book of Mormon—that the Lord gave no commandments to the children of men without preparing a way to accomplish them. And so help *would* come. It had to.

AS STRANGE AS THE LETTER SOUNDS, there is no part of it that can't be substantiated by our religious beliefs. Except for this: the spirit does not stay away. My mother thinks about her childhood heroes, Alma the Younger and Joseph Smith. When they prayed for help, it came. She cannot believe that God would let her succumb to the powers of darkness even as she called his name, and yet help from priesthood blessings is as short-lived as her prayers. Andrea tells her that her fear gives the demon power, which only increases my mother's concern. How can she not feel afraid?

Emboldened by Andrea, my mother ponders the source of the spirit's power. She recalls that Satan literally means "accuser," an idea she picked up from an institute teacher. This, she says, is the heart of evil: the poisonous impulse to accuse. Harold might be her brother, but he was also the incarnation of blame. Couldn't I see it? If her brothers had not blamed others for their unhappiness, they might have chosen joy. The misery they reaped was the fruit of their accusations.

AS MUCH as I want to agree with my mother as she wrestles the demon, something seems wrong with the interpretation. George had not felt the poisonous impetus to *blame* when he felt the childhood longing to die. Unless he blamed *himself,* which would only beg the question: for what?

While Johnnie attributed his anger to an uneven inheritance—which seemed sort of justified to me—there also seemed to be something much bigger in play, something that went well beyond frustration with his father, something pervasive and pernicious. I could not speak for Monte, but I could speak for myself. In my darkest hours I had not felt *blame,* but something I can only describe as bottomless worthlessness. It was not that I had made mistakes, but that I *was* a mistake, through and through. And so I have to quibble with my mother across a veil I'm not sure I believe in.

Blame is a symptom. It is not the disease.

INSIDE MY OFFICE, I feel the darkness rally. If my mother felt Harold torment her, then he did. And yet she refused to blame anyone—or anything—for her pain. That her brothers had suffered emotionally and she suffered physically only complicated things. As much as I dislike

Andrea's methods, there is something that feels real about Harold, something at the heart of all of our suffering—something that makes "ruler of
armies" feel appropriate.

Returning to the letter, I direct my attention to the last paragraph.
With the harrowing evening over, I expect that my mother will wrap
things up, but she doesn't. Instead, her last words to me are:

"Harold's gone, my job's done and we live happily ever after, right?
Wrong! It probably wasn't more than two days before I felt the four of
us were again not alone in our bed. That coincided with Thanksgiving."

My stomach tightens. The narrative isn't reaching closure. It is arching toward climax—a final confrontation in a battle I will never see. She
started typing the letter on a Saturday, eight weeks before she died. Then
it is as if she got up to answer the door and never came back.

My eyes follow the lines of my desk to the far side of the room where
the painting of Cecilia presides in the shadows like a sylph. My mother's
obsession with angels was no mere spending spree. Who was the winged
figure if not a braver version of herself? A figure to protect her as she
slept, alone against the coming darkness.

FIFTEEN

Cecilia

My mother's gravestone arrives just in time for her birthday, which due to some freakish chain of events turns out to be the same week my father remarries. When we can laugh again, Lan and I will snicker that the courtship had been as speedy as ours had been, and for roughly the same reasons: the chance of premarital pleasure. But for now it's all I can do to watch the landscape roll by outside of the car on the way home from the reception, silently recycling the events of the day, watching the first raindrops of spring dapple the windshield.

I had expected to be irritated by Mormon measures of worthiness that relegated us to the parking lot during the wedding, but I wasn't. There were some things I did not need to see, and my father pledging his heart to someone else was one of them. To be a good sport, I had shown up to the photo shoot at the temple grounds wearing a black pantsuit instead of the requisite dress. A pillar of support and resistance.

The photo shoot had been uncomfortable enough on its own, given our glaring absence from the ceremony. But it paled in comparison to the reception, which ranked among the Most Awkward Events ever. I had just started greeting people when my Aunt Janice harrumphed: "Well, what do you think of *this*?" The restaurant had overbooked and there was no place to sit down. A slideshow featuring photos of the happy couple also featured pictures of their children, cropped and sequenced in a way that erased prior spouses and threw us together as if we had always been part of the same family and the whole thing wasn't radically weird. One of my brothers tried to start something like a line dance to "Tequila!" and my Aunt Cherre had bolted from the restaurant in tears. Which, it occurred to me, I wanted to do.

By the time we left I felt stripped of emotion. My father had been as gracious as possible, but the events only highlighted how raw things still were, and the transition from the celebration to the cemetery puts the whole thing squarely in the Twilight Zone. Sitting sullenly in the car next to Lan, I listen to the hum of the engine, watching the moody March weather bathe the mountains in blue.

EVEN FROM THE ROAD, it's hard to miss my mother's marker. Showy and unique, my father's parting gift to her is just what she would have wanted: a stunning granite angel, winged and wistful, eyes trained toward heaven. While Lan waits, I slip out of the car and pull my wool coat tight against my shoulders, then pick my way across the last slip of filthy snow, carved in uneven ruts by the monument truck.

Standing before the stone, I mark the shape of the angel, rising on tiptoe, palms up, as if awaiting an embrace. A dozen red roses bloom next to her in marble vases, incongruous against the aluminum hues of the day—birthday wishes from Michelle. Still, it isn't the angel's body that draws me in, but her eyes, turned upward as if awaiting a kiss. And so she might be my mother and she might be me, looking aloft as if unaware of our wings.

Her papers have left me with more questions than answers. I will never know if Harold visited her on that last day, if she felt the loving embrace of her savior, the father she longed for so desperately, or if she felt nothing at all. But if I could ask her one last question, it would not be about her transition to the next life, but if she ever felt satisfied in this one.

It's the one thing I can't seem to feel. By now, I have finished the requirements for my PhD, chalked off an impressive list of honors and awards, and yet I feel strangely empty. I don't admit it to anyone, since it would only seem to prove that waywardness makes you miserable. And I am tired of feeling ashamed—as if being proud of myself was the one thing God could not abide.

My grandparents' stately marker sits between my mother's and Monte's, linking children who hardly knew each other. Johnnie had once been buried here, too. Until a family fight sent his body twenty miles to the south. Like my mother, I thought the exhumation was a grand show of petulance, but now I'm not so sure. Why not give the man some space and peace?

To stand before the graves is to feel exposed before my ancestors, owning the person I have become. I do not believe that they are lurking just out of sight, regarding me with wide watery eyes, but I do feel the weight of their stories.

I finally looked up the identity of the angel under my mother's bed, and found she was not an angel at all. My Catholic neighbors would have recognized her immediately: *Saint* Cecilia, Christian martyr, condemned to a fiery death.

My mother would have known the story. She knew every story behind every artifact in her house. And so I am sure that the saint held a special meaning for her. *Cecilia.* Patron saint of music and daughter of Roman nobility, a woman who heard heavenly music inside her as she went to her marriage and martyrdom. A Christian condemned for burying other martyrs, confined to a bathhouse that was set ablaze. A saint who came forth from the fire to preach until Roman soldiers hacked her to death with swords. A saint who refused to be silenced. Champion of the blind. This was the figure that lay beneath my mother as she wrestled the "ruler of armies."

Standing at the gravesite, I consider the strange parallels: a noble family, music, faith, fire. I can't begin to unravel the coincidence of the blazing bathhouse, but my mother's fascination with the saint feels utterly familiar to me. As a teenager, I memorized all of the soliloquies from *The Lark,* hoping to become as fearless and clear-eyed and full of purpose as Joan of Arc, also condemned to a fiery fate.

I follow the angel's gaze to a low band of clouds obscuring the horizon, where the Great Salt Lake ripples in salt-purple waves. I'm sure our fascination with the saints was no passing fancy. We needed the women. But why?

My mother and I seemed to have everything we needed—all of the comforts of life. We inherited her mother's faith, along with the grim resolve of pioneering women who persevered through hardship. We inherited feminine role models and dedicated rule-followers, women so unflinchingly obedient it was hard to believe they were real.

But we had not inherited all we needed. We did not inherit epic heroines. We did not inherit anyone who could teach us to stand up for ourselves, let alone battle something like Harold. As women, we could not invoke the power of God on our behalf. We could not bless our babies before the congregation or even stand in the prayer circle. Our Book of Mormon stories mentioned just one woman by name, and she mainly showed up to give birth to the famous brothers. In the temple, we swore allegiance to our husbands while our husbands swore allegiance to God. Everyone knew that God did not work through women. And so I wonder if my mother needed Cecilia like I needed Saint Joan: to help us feel braver than we felt. Empowered and praiseworthy. Worthy of God's notice and help.

What my mother and I knew without question was that our worth was always contingent. We would be lovable when our eyeliner was right, when we lost twenty pounds. We would please God when we paid our tithing and got our temple work done. We would be proud of ourselves when we graduated from college, had respectable careers, earned a wink from a colleague or friend.

No matter how she tried, my mother would not earn her father's pride. No matter how many commandments I kept, there would always be some that I missed. I could read the scriptures and pray all day long and still fail to create an uplifting environment in my home or adequately develop my talents or plan nutritious meals or prevent diseases or any number of topics in *The Latter-day Saint Woman: Basic Manual for Women, Parts A & B.*

And what if such counsel generally failed to inspire? What if in your heart you yearned to be a warrior? A champion of the blind? The sick? The afflicted?

Well, then you were screwed.

I NEVER GOT TO BE my mother's friend—not like I wanted to be. That role was reserved for more distinguished others. And yet she gave me a gift that I don't think she ever received.

It was August. Not long before the return of her ghostly dogs. I had just earned my commercial pilot's license and she had called to congratulate me—an unprecedented move on its own.

"Your father told me after I got back from getting my nails done," she said. "And I just want to tell you what an amazing person I think you are."

I almost swallowed my tongue. I had learned not to expect her praise, and I had not been disappointed. When I first heard her voice, I shot a habitual glance at the liquor cabinet, preparing to pour the wine that helped me endure her litany of pain. And then her words started to sink in.

"Thanks, Mom," I said. "That means a lot to me."

"I'm so proud of all of my children," she said. "You are all so different and have your own strengths. And in the last few years you have done some outstanding things."

I sat down hard on the porch steps without bothering to pour a drink. A prick at the back of my neck said, *Pay attention.*

"You know, Mom," I said, stunned that her approval made me feel so uncomfortable. "The reason I have done outstanding things has a lot to do with you. You were the first to go back to school and—"

"No," she cut me off. "I don't think so. I want to say this now, because it's true and it feels like the right thing to say. It's not about me. It's about you. And I'm proud of you."

THE AIR between the angel and me shimmers. I feel flayed, defenseless. It had felt so important to write my mother off—so gut-wrenchingly *necessary*—that I never let her back into my heart, not entirely. And yet there she was, defying my expectations, offering me the pride she could not earn. For a moment I feel the wild urge to grab for something solid. But there isn't anything. Just the slate sky, the echo of my mother's voice, and an angel just out of reach.

I don't know if my mother would be proud of me now. I have tried to mark the parts of our legacies worth keeping: my mother's audacity, my grandmother's wit, my grandfather's mysterious softness. I willed myself to be grateful for my share of his estate. But after the first court hearing, I petitioned the judge to waive my rights to my inheritance.

The hearing should not have been a big deal. The judge merely ruled on whether or not the accountant was capable of subtracting whole numbers (he was). And yet the family reacted as if he had thrown a live grenade. People huddled together in the foyer afterward, rallying against each other, their anger surging between the cement pillars like a river;

and I felt the pull and raw power of it and grabbed for my father like a lifebuoy. "Dad," I gasped, "I cannot be a part of this."

Everyone in the huddle had lost someone: to violence and depression and mental illness—to insensitivity and self-righteousness and god knew what else. The fragile, quaking factions had no way to deal with the pain that had built up over time. There were no mechanisms for mediation or healing, and I was too close to the problem to have anything like objectivity. I could be part of the bitterness or do my best to let it go, and so I left.

My father called me later. "All we have to do is go back to the original wording on the trust," he said. "We'll just divide the ground equally, so many acres to each family."

I had been wrestling on some running clothes when he called, and the proposition left me standing with a sports bra half-pulled over my head. "How will that make everything fair?" I said, pinning the phone to one ear with a shoulder and pulling the spandex over ever-shrinking breasts. "There's only one water source and about two hundred people who want it. Dividing the ground will be like dividing Grandpa's body. One family will get the heart; everybody else will be left with waterless appendages, and somebody's going to pop off with a pistol."

"The courts will decide," he said simply.

Astonished by his surety, I said, "You think a *ruling* will make everyone happy? You saw what happened."

It was as if the words triggered a tectonic shift. My father's normally warm voice turned thin and icy. "I thought you'd be more like your mother," he said. "Braver. She would not have backed down or given up. She would have tried to make it fair."

My voice wanted to quiver, but I held it steady. "There is no way to make it fair, Dad. There are too many scars. And I will not participate."

The world shattered as I hung up the phone. Something about the phone call infuriated me, but I couldn't pin it down. The accusation of cowardice? The fact that my father's good sense seemed to vanish every time he had a conversation with one of the Chournoses?

I had not taken Zoloft for a long time. It turned out that I needed the drug only while I was trying to please everybody. When I learned to draw back, say no, consider the cost of an idea before clobbering myself with it, I found something like stability.

And my stability was gone.

I redialed my father's number, so darkly outraged I could hardly see the numbers. When I heard him pick up, a voice I barely recognized as mine screamed at him, tearing across the space between us. There was no calling the words back, no controlling them. I unleashed all of the rage I ever suppressed: for my mother, lost, for the family I despised. I must have told him to go to hell—I don't know. My words were insensible, awful, aimed to cut him to the bone. Raw with strain, my voice finally broke, and when it did I heard my father pleading. "Oh, Kid, I can't tell what you're saying."

I forced myself to be clear. When my voice emerged, it had the same low growl my mother's used to have just before she snapped. "Fighting is the only thing that family's ever been able to do," I said. "I've already lost one parent to them. And you will not shame me with my mother."

In that moment of rage I glimpsed the demon that haunted my mother. And he was timeless and cruel and composed of infinite bitterness. He took the softest parts of us and made them steely, severed every fragile human bond, sent us into the world with our weapons extended. He was at work when I withdrew from others or tried too hard to please. The essence of self-malice.

It wasn't just my father's uncharacteristic criticism of me that prompted me to write myself out of the will, but the person I became in that instant. Sword and shield and utter hatred. Not warriorlike in a powerful way, but someone who lashed out at everyone.

I hung up on my father, and he called right back. "I'm sorry, Kid," he said. "I deserved that." Then his voice broke. "But what if there was an artist who spent his life carving the most beautiful table, and when he died, no one wanted it?"

I knew he was talking about the cabin he built at Monte Cristo. My grandfather had allowed my mother to pick out a site, and my father had built the structure from telephone poles and cross arms he'd salvaged while working for Continental Telephone. Glass insulators provided hooks for jackets and hats, and the crowning touch was a phone booth he'd hauled up the mountain and converted into an outhouse. The wonky A-frame meant the world to my mother, and she hoped it would mean the world to us, too. Maybe once it had.

I breathed in as deeply as I could, trying to release the rage that still felt coiled around my heart. "Maybe the table's not what matters, but the character of the person who built it," I said. "In that case, it doesn't matter what happens to the table or who gets it, because the real gift is not an artifact but a way of living." Shaking, I willed myself to finish. "If your children are secure at all, it is because you gave them love, not land."

THE COLLISION OF MEMORIES—my mother's pride, my father's disapproval—scatters my feelings in all directions. Love and shame, the elemental forces of our world. Like heat and wind. You could not have one without the other.

The shifting states between the two forces created something my father used to call indirect pressure. You knew you were loved, but you also understood that expectations were really, really high. *How* high they were, however, was sort of up for grabs. The bar was set by others. So, you hushed your rebel urges and readied yourself on the lawn, launching yourself toward hurdles you couldn't actually see. The only way to tell if you'd jumped high enough was through the eyes of others. Were they happy? Were they proud? You did not answer to yourself. You answered to Church leaders and heavenly beings, who always seemed disappointed in your efforts while simultaneously assuring you they loved you beyond measure.

I can't fault my father for trying to make things right. I know how it is to be swept up by the sheer grandiosity of a thing—to be a member of the One True Church or part of a unique and special family. But the memory of the phone call still smarts. Around me, the cemetery turns into a glossy sea of stones, the dark gray granite of mother's angel merging with my grandparents' marker and Monte's. There was no way to do right by our stories and stay sane.

I DON'T THINK my father understands how hard it was for me to find my voice—how uneven the journey and how long. When the bishop called to schedule my Church court, Lan took the phone as I wavered with indecision. The Brethren had humiliated him, he said, and they would not humiliate me too. He never forgot his own disciplinary hearing, in which he had been grilled for three hours on details such as the color of the woman's bra and panties. When the bishop threatened to disclose details of the affair to the man's wife if I did not attend, Lan's unbridled shouting filled our house top to bottom. Curled up on our bedroom floor, I listened to the conversation, sick and sobbing, horrified and embarrassed, and so, so grateful.

It wasn't that I had no voice. I had an erratic voice that bounded between extremes, both submissive and darkly outraged. I felt the familiar pluck of exasperation every time I overextended myself, but smothered my irritation in duty.

My inability to say *no* had morphed into a resonant *fuck you*. I can't say where the words came from, only that they rolled from my lips as if I had said them all my life.

The first time it happened, I had been talking to the first counselor in the bishopric on the phone. He'd called to say that the Monty Python–esque script I'd written for the young men and women was inappropriate. "Lou's Brothel and Tavern" was going to have to go, along with the "filling of flagons," the appearance of wenches, and the word "deflower."

Having taken on the job of directing the show against my better judgment, I felt whiplashed. I'd bartered time with my children, put off grading hundreds of papers to write the stupid script; I still needed to put the boys to bed; I had yet to devise a lesson plan for the next day. And so I told him to fuck off and get someone else to direct the damn thing.

The words were so wide and deeply satisfying that I started to tell everyone to fuck off: the slim bitch at the gym who demanded I pay for dinging the bumper on her rust-bucket car; the administrator at toddler gymnastics who criticized my parenting; the police officer who ticketed Lan for speeding in a school zone. And while I did *not* tell my father-in-law to fuck off, he got the message all the same.

It was Easter weekend, I think, and my in-laws' home burst with children large and small. You had to take care not to trip over the infants, strewn about the house like so many delicate throw pillows. Finishing the dishes, I turned to a sister-in-law with a brave new idea: What if Mormonism was just one of many faiths that was acceptable to God?

I thought we had been talking privately, but before I knew it my father-in-law stood between us, holding a *Doctrine and Covenants*.

"Read this," he said, and I did: something about how the rituals of the Restored Church trumped the Dark Age rituals of, say, the Catholics.

I nodded and said "Okay." But he didn't budge.

"Aloud. I want you to read it aloud."

I held my tongue while something inside of me burst like a ball of fire and soared silently into the sky. And just as I thought it might disappear entirely, it burst into a brilliant rage and shot a spray of silver across the stars.

I heard myself say, "I will not read it." Lan heard me say, "This is bullshit." Then I turned from the suddenly silent living room and marched down the hallway where I disappeared into a bedroom, slamming the door so hard it quaked with a wham against the doorjamb.

In the instant that followed, images from a self-defense book I'd read as a child flashed into my mind. One showed the proper alignment of fist and arm so that a blow to the nose would hit an attacker roughly like a two-by-four; another showed the way to aim a kick to the crotch so it would inflict maximum damage. And I wanted everyone laughing or talking in the bright kitchen to know that I was not hiding, but fighting, and the door became every assailant and every idea I had given in to and buckled under and cowered behind. I gathered every bit of strength I had and channeled it into my hips and legs and thighs and kicked a hole right through the flimsy laminate.

STARING AT THE UNEVEN RUTS across my mother's grave, I feel the familiar pang of remorse. If my father were with me now, I would tell him that I know how to fight. I had discovered a foul angry voice. If I wanted to, I could carve a line of carnage with it if someone looked at me wrong. Learning to speak up with dignity was different. For three years, I sat in painful doctoral seminars daring myself to say something. Shaking, I crossed the desert in what amounted to a flying tin can, afraid that I wouldn't be able to talk to air traffic controllers with any kind of authority.

There is no way I can explain to my father how it feels to have to choose—between being divided against yourself and being divided against the people you love. And so I wish he could understand the one thing I wanted my mother to understand. That walking away is not always cowardice. Sometimes it is the bravest thing you can do.

I TAKE A LAST LOOK at the angel before heading back to the car. If I could reverse the harm done by our legacies, it would not be by launching myself into a crusade that isn't mine or speaking up for a bunch of people who need to learn how to listen or chasing one more achievement. It would simply be being able to say, *It is enough.*

I have started writing my mother's story in earnest now, and it is a sadder one than I'd like to tell. Retrieving a paper from my pocket, I tuck it between the roses, watching the drizzle punctuate the lines. Words about her that might as well be about me:

"My mother was a fluke in our small Utah town. It was as if a traveling botanist passed through with seeds from rare and fragile flora, and one inadvertently tumbled to the ground, miraculously taking root between the rows of alfalfa and corn."

SIXTEEN

Principles of Internal Medicine

It takes an hour and a half to drive to Salt Lake City, where I've signed up for a course in Tibetan Buddhism. As I have proven myself to be a lousy Mormon, I've no illusions about being much of a Buddhist, but I'm determined to learn to meditate, if nothing else. After my mother died, one of my advisors sent me a copy of Pema Chödrön's *When Things Fall Apart,* and I spent the better part of a year ignoring it. When I finally did pick it up, I was leveled by the idea of loving kindness. Of all the things I inherited—charity and works and chin-up resolve—being *kind* to yourself was not one of them.

In the spirit of things, I've renamed our cat Sentient Being to see if I'll feel more enlightened about him. It's not just our son adopting an animal that makes his asthma flare up that drives me crazy, but how the cat pulls broad swatches of hair out of his ass if he has to wait longer than a minute or two for attention. Surrounded by clumps of his own fur, he looks up at you as if he has no idea what the hell just happened. Given my feelings for him, it will serve me right to be reincarnated as a neurotic kitty, dependent on the whims of an irritable homeowner.

As I end up at the Buddhist temple before anyone else, I poke my head in the tall wooden doors, wondering if there's a protocol I'm about to violate. Were I in an LDS temple, I'd have been carded by now.

If I didn't feel so awkward, I'd be astonished. The room features none of the markers of worship I've come to recognize: muted variations of taupe, precisely ordered pews firmly bolted to the floor. Following the lead of a woman who comes in behind me, I remove my shoes and take a seat on a bright red floor cushion.

Most astonishing are the colors. The walls breathe a bright yellow arching toward the high ceiling, trimmed in red and gold. On either side of the room, tall windows refract the last rays of the sunset. In the center of the room, a golden Buddha presides amid a chorus of smaller figures draped with red fabric. Lurid tapestries feature deities with crowns, elephant ears, and extra arms. For someone whose familiarity with the gods ends with Jesus Christ and God the Father (who have the decency to appear in tasteful white robes), the figures are fascinating, if not alarming.

Other people trickle in along with a woman in robes, whom I take to be the instructor. She moves like a dancer, seating herself with her back to the Buddha and explaining that she will begin with an introduction to the dharma. In true doctoral form, I approach the information with tweezers and gauze, critically evaluating its pieces, keeping my feelings at arm's length.

We try a short meditation, during which I obsess about whether I should not have worn a leather jacket, after which our instructor describes the journey of the young Indian prince who would become the Buddha. "It is said," she says, "that the young man was destined to become a great king or a holy man, depending on what he saw outside the palace walls."

I sink into the familiarity of the story. Wishing his son to become a great leader, the king does his best to shield his son from suffering, Disneyfying the countryside along his son's traveling routes. Nevertheless, the prince encounters age, illness, grief, and death.

Our instructor asks us to take a minute and meditate on the story. "Breathe in," she says. "Think how it might apply to you." I close my eyes and imagine the young man witnessing suffering for the first time. There is the old man withering under a tree, a woman bent double in pain, a family, their hearts aching with loss, pushing a boat out to sea that carries the body of a loved one.

As the images flash by, something in my chest expands, and I am suddenly awash with emotion. The story does not belong to my culture or practice, but the willingness to behold suffering, to try to locate its sources, strikes me as terribly important. Tears slide down my cheeks and I let them, without resorting to my usual cynicism. When the class ends, I shuffle to the door as quickly as I can, throw on my cowboy boots, and wrap my black leather jacket around me like a shell.

On the drive home, I mull over my reaction. The story is not all that different from other stories of the solitary questing male, which I've learned to regard a little wryly. But it was different, too.

I weave in and out of traffic, wondering how the story managed to get past my defenses, when it occurs to me that the story is all about defenses. The physical and emotional barricades we place around ourselves to keep out the pain of the world. The religions I know best promise a world beyond pain. But this world—the only one we know—is replete with suffering, and I'll be damned if that's not one of the Four Noble Truths.

Maybe what struck me so forcefully is the idea that pain happens to all of us no matter how good we try to be; and that growing up is not about finding a bright future with no unhappiness, but in locating the sources of suffering with as much compassion as possible, even when—or especially when—there is no perfect ending, no miracle cure.

THE HOUSE IN ROY is nearly empty now. A string of yard sales and donations has finally shown my mother's possessions to be finite. Wandering through the garage after a wedding shower for Christie, I appraise the last of my mother's things. Now that so little is left, it all seems precious. Relics from a woman who will always be a mystery to me.

I run my fingers across vases, stemware, and cookware, wondering why on earth my mother had a silver champagne chiller, when my father walks in, grinning. Reaching toward a shelf, he grabs a purple crystal bowl, heaping with glass fruit, and hands it to me. A glass banana perches precariously at its edge, trying to make a jump for it, while something purple—an eggplant perhaps?—juts through glassy oranges.

"You wanted these?"

"Sure," I say. "I don't know why."

Despite the fact that his hair has turned almost fluorescently white, my father seems younger than I've seen him in ages. He wears a tastefully patterned button-up shirt that coordinates perfectly with blue Dockers. Even his shoes match. He no longer harbors a haunted, wild expression, and his glasses hang straight on his face.

"Marriage has been good to you, Dad." I glance at his feet. "New shoes."

He shifts his weight and smiles, looking a little self-conscious about it. "I guess she takes care of me all right," he says. "Won't let me out of the house unless I'm up to snuff."

If a person gets into the Celestial Kingdom by being constant and loving, good-humored and long-suffering, then I figure my father's got it made. I don't think his wives are going to get along up there, but I doubt I'll be around to watch. Still, the image of the two very strong women negotiating a heavenly estate together makes me snicker in ways that probably wouldn't be appreciated by either one of them.

I consider the glass fruit, which does not look rugged enough to weather a ride in my pickup, and ask, "Do you have anything I can pack them in?"

He rummages around the garage until he locates an empty box, and we fold the fruit in wrapping paper discarded from the wedding shower, shimmying each piece into the box until it fits snug against the others. Then he pauses. "I've got something else, if you want it."

Curious, I watch as he pulls out a step stool and reaches for something on an empty shelf, as if he has hidden it there. Coming down, he hands me a slip of paper. "I don't know what to do with this."

My heart races. My mother's handwriting.

Another summer has passed since the fire. Outside, the sun rides low on the horizon, bathing the lawn in green and gold. A light breeze moves with the setting sun, cooling the cottonwoods and toying with the leaves while my father walks me out to my truck. The for sale sign under the twin pine trees reminds me that this strange season will pass, too.

I tuck the box inside the cab while my father leans his elbows on the tailgate, his snowy hair moving slightly in the shifting air.

"I don't know how you got through it, Dad."

He looks past me at the mountains. "It was my Gethsemane, I guess. Everyone goes through one. Maybe more. Some are worse than others."

I focus on the road winding from the driveway and let his words hang in the air.

My mother used to say that it wasn't that we got sick that was remarkable, but that we were so often well. The complex interplay of organs and systems and cells that allowed us to breathe was itself astonishing. Given the biological crapshoot of genetics and environmental factors, the wonder was not that some babies were born with problems, but that so many of them were perfect. It wasn't that bones broke, but that they knitted themselves back together. The scars that marked our bodies were also markers of healing. We were, she said, constantly immersed in a world of microscopic organisms: pollen and germs and viruses that could run renegade in our bodies at any second. And yet they mostly failed to do so. You didn't survive by shutting your doors and windows and sterilizing everything you owned. The best you could do was cultivate resilience, and take your lumps along with everybody else.

Watching my father, it occurs to me that emotional suffering is remarkable, too. Not because it happens, but because we survive it, because our hearts aren't in a constant, battered heap, and because some people come through it with more compassion, not less. Just when you think you'll never laugh again, somebody hauls out a pair of peacock earrings.

BACK AT HOME, I place the latest slip of my mother's writing on my desk along with the rest of her papers. By now, I have managed to read everything: the transcript from the bugged conversation at the police station, lists of evidence and eyewitness accounts, the police report and the autopsy. The only thing I still can't look at for long is the photo of the note to Christie, held by someone wearing blue paper mittens next to my mother's singed purse.

Above my desk, Renoir's *Luncheon of the Boating Party* has been replaced by James Christiansen's *The Oath*, a fabulously framed print of my mother's, featuring a weary physician in Elizabethan breeches and hose pondering the Oath of Hippocrates while scarcely containing an armload of modern paperwork.

I have entered my mother's world, now. Bodies, blood, bile.

To help decipher the autopsy, I enlisted the help of a medical examiner, who took one look at the description of my mother's liver and whistled. That she died that day wasn't surprising, he said, but that she was alive to begin with. One of her coronary arteries was over 90 percent occluded—a ticking bomb on its own—but in all of his years he had never seen a liver so diffusely necrotic and filled with dead cells. "What had she been taking?" he asked. Had she been much of a drinker?

I would have laughed if the irony wasn't so tragic.

No, I said. Not a drinker.

I also consulted a pharmacist, who looked at her list of medicines and sighed. "We see this all of the time," he said. "It gets pretty easy to spot these people."

The comment troubled me. Who were *these people*? People who put their faith in medicine? People bombarded by images of flawless happy others, walking through parks and riding bikes? People subjected to direct-to-consumer pharmaceutical ads that bumped up plucky guitar music over possible side effects, including death? Nameless people who struggled in the darkness of their pain? People plagued with maladies beyond their control?

"There is no way of telling how these drugs would have affected your mother," he continued. "There are six or seven central nervous system drugs alone. If you do the math, you will see that she was on about ten milligrams of intravenous morphine an hour. Two milligrams puts most people to sleep. Given the combination, anything could have set her off that last day. What you've got here is a mulligan stew."

The pharmacist's theory was that health-care providers were their own worst enemies when it came to prescriptions, but my mother was no isolated case. A study conducted by Mental Health America showed Utah to have the highest levels of depression in the nation, while a federal study of painkiller use showed Utah leading the nation in prescription drug abuse. By summer, a KSL news anchor announced that prescription drugs had trumped automobile accidents as the leading cause of accidental death in our fair state.

Online responses to the story made me weary. One camp was composed of those who were sure that the Mormon Church had something to do with it (what were people supposed to do if they couldn't *drink*?). While others argued just as emphatically that the gospel was the one true source of their happiness—and why was it that people had to keep picking on the Church?

Surveying the papers on my desk now, I'm not sure what to think. My mother would surely come back in spirit to clobber me if I suggested that the Church had anything to do with her disintegration. My stressors were not hers. And yet I can't stop thinking that our problems had something in common.

From her earliest years, my mother felt unsure of her value. Her brothers were older and stronger; her sister, prettier. And so she constructed a self that would be impervious to the whims of approval. To show emotion was to be feminine, weak. And so she drove her feelings deep inside her body.

But driving her emotions underground did not make them go away; it only made them manifest in ways that were acceptable. In headaches and hives, in dizziness and deafness and fatigue, in uterine bleeding and ulcerative colitis, in chronic muscular-skeletal pain and virtually every other symptom on the list of diagnostic criteria for somatization disorder, a subconscious process in which psychological suffering presents as physical distress.

My mother would have rejected the idea that her pain had psychological roots. Such a connection would show her to be weak, unstable. It would trivialize her pain, make it *merely* mental. In her head, unreal. It would play into the stereotype she fought against every time a physician grappled for a diagnosis, whenever a pharmacist eyeballed her list of prescriptions.

In happier moments, she shrugged off any number of procedures—hysterectomy, angiogram, tracheotomy—by quipping a line from the New Testament: "If thy right arm offend thee, cut it off!" But her maladies could not be treated in such a way. Her suffering was not due to the failure of her adrenal glands, nor was it due to the failure of any of the organs the medical examiner plucked out of her body and studied like so many ripe avocados.

When she closed her eyes at night, my mother knew she had fifteen minutes before the pain would force her to twist her body into another shape. And in that moment of wakefulness she contended with the forces of evil. *Physician, heal thyself,* she pleaded silently. And darkness answered.

I USED TO THINK that my mother's demon was a hallucination, composed of a worldview that personified evil in such a way. After consulting the pharmacist, I took the demon to be the sum of drug interactions that got worse as her liver got worse at filtering toxins. But I think there is another explanation for the demon, too, which I extrapolate from a soot-stained piece of paper.

Peace, unity and singleness of purpose. For this blessing I gladly endure whatever trials God has given me, the fibromyalgia, the cortisone, etc. Each of us shares the same singleness of purpose which is eternal love for our families and for God. Each of us is very different and our approaches to that end are different. Do you know how much pain and misery and lack of achievement this saves your loved ones? And do you know what it means to a parent to see their children and that misery? Yes, whatever else God requires of me as my earthly test, it is well worth this blessing He has promised and given.

I have no idea who the imagined "you" is in the paragraph, but the promise of "peace, love and unity of purpose" is obviously an allusion to her patriarchal blessing. The patriarch had promised her a lot of things contingent upon her faithfulness, but the part of the blessing she loved best was this line, meant to describe the home she would one day have if she took care in selecting a companion.

According to the paragraph, my mother believed she purchased our peace, love, and harmony with her health. God had handed her the bitter cup, and she had taken it. As much as I dislike the figurative trade-off—why would a loving God demand her health at all?—it suggests a source for her pain. Her body did its best to process physical toxins, as evidenced by her massively necrotic liver. But who could say what part of her body processed emotional ones? My mother would have absorbed all of the rejection of childhood and the pettiness of adulthood, not so that the demon would spare the partnership, but so she would not pass the poison on to her children.

I'VE READ THE PARAGRAPH over and over again in recent months. I admire the way she can pluck meaning from the darkness of her pain. But I can't see why her pain was *necessary.* She posits eternal love as the antidote to misery, but does not speculate on where the misery comes from in the first place, or how her suffering relieves it.

My mother would be happy to know that I've recently attended church. Having been called to the bishopric, my father extended an invitation, and I wanted to support him. I arrived by myself, wearing a too tight Antonio Melani dress I'd picked up for pennies when Dillard's closed, my flower tattoo dancing well below cropped sleeves. I took a seat in one of the side pews where it looked like sinners might sit. Then I sunk into the familiarity of the service, scanning the other attendees: the older women wearing teased curls, the younger ones bouncing babies on shoulders and retrieving toddlers from under the benches. I sang the hymns I still knew by heart, waited for the young men to pass the sacrament. I listened to youth talks on the importance of duty and missionary work. And a speech on the problem of pride.

Announcing that he would be addressing the "pointy end of the Book of Mormon," the speaker reminded us of the genocide of the Nephites. How, in their wickedness, the Lord had left them to their foes. It was pride that led to their downfall, he said. Pride, the true enemy to God. Whenever people turned their backs on their brothers, withdrew, or cried out in protest and rage, pride was to blame. When people fell away from the Church, it was pride.

I found myself getting edgier by the minute. It wasn't just that I disagreed with the premise—pleasure seemed like a pretty good invitation to sin, too—it was the assumption that all non-churchgoers were cut from the same cloth. And something else was wrong, too, something so much bigger than whether or not a person attended church.

I thought of everyone I knew who had left the Church. We did not skip services because we were sitting around thinking how awesome we were—how much greater than God or how wise. If anything, we felt the opposite—something altogether un-pride-like—and tired. Tired of feeling wrong. Tired of trying to keep up. No matter how many times we sang "I Am a Child of God," we felt hopelessly inadequate. If anything, the song made things worse: to spring forth from Deity only to botch things up. The feeling was there when we did not scrapbook or pray or hit a baseball as well as the next person. When we failed to follow gospel precepts without fail. When we let things slip. When we were human. When we snickered when we weren't supposed to. When we failed to feel as happy as everyone else. When we understood ourselves to be hopelessly flawed.

It was not pride I felt as I screamed at my father. It wasn't pride that coursed through me as I curled myself into a tight ball on our bedroom floor as Lan yelled at the bishop. It was not pride that propelled me as I dodged between cars wanting to die. It was something so opposite it was glaring.

The demon was not blame, and it was not pride. It was shame.

TURNING HER LAST NOTE over in my hands, I try to decide how to read it. Scribbled on two sides of a soot-stained envelope from the Aspen Clinic, the note is so sad and strange that I can understand my father's reluctance to give it to me. On the first side, my mother has penned what looks like a strained apology:

"I am sorry you feel that way, so *very* sorry. It's not at all the way I wanted to make you feel. But you won't believe anything I say so I am not going to try to tell you that you're wrong. Hang up. Mental problems in heaven."

Sideways, in purple ink, she has added "20 min."

I can't imagine whom she is writing to unless it is my father, who was anxiously aware that things were spiraling out of control. The last two sentences merely baffle me. There is the apparent attempt to disengage—"Hang up"—followed by the strange observation: "Mental problems in heaven." A critique of conditions in the Intermontane West, if ever there was one.

Her writing continues on the flip side of the envelope, but the tone changes so radically that I can't believe she wrote the words in the same sitting:

So beautiful—in the presence of one of the highest order of angels. Elegance—a very strong part of how I looked, how I acted, and what I was. Best harpist in all of the heavenly host. My voice was one of the greatest in the Heavenly Choir. People would come from all over heaven to hear me play the harp and I did solos in the choir.

As strange as the details are, the longing in the passage feels utterly familiar to me. To be of infinite worth. That her angelic self is so spectacular makes me wonder if it had to be—if the grandiosity of the image was only as large as the hole it needed to fill.

Turning the note sideways, I keep reading. Under the passage about elegance, her writing changes color and direction, reverting to the strained apology: "I don't know why you think that, but if that's [what you?]

choose to believe I can't [change?] your mind no matter what I say." Next to the sentence she has written "2 min" in purple ink, as if counting down. Something has splashed through the ink at periodic intervals, making the letters indecipherable, and I wonder if it means she had been crying.

Resting my head in my hands, I let my heart break apart. All of the half-healed hurts I'd held against her, the defenses I'd built up so that she could never hurt me again, the resentments large and small I'd held on to and nurtured—all of them dissolve into the image of a little girl, helpless and alone, trying to explain herself to someone who won't listen.

Until now, I'd never considered that my mother's insecurities manifested as strengths: competitiveness, achievements, flamboyance. Her self-worth was brittle, held together with wire and glue. Like her bones, supplemented with ibandronate sodium, she seemed steely but was starved to the core. And she was crumbling well before she started taking prednisone.

She did not love herself—that would have been healthy. She loved her *reflection*. And that reflection changed depending on the quality of the source. Her elaborate home mirrored the elaborate inner world she fashioned as a child—a world so grand and good that she could not help but be grand and good herself. Threatened by careless reality, her inner world needed constant validation. The note betrays the wild swings she endured from one moment to the next, trying to make the feeling stay. She was wondrous or worthless. There was no in-between, no solid core of okay-ness.

But it wasn't just the feelings she craved, but the one she could not abide, that drove her, curled inside her emotional midbrain like a sleepy mole. At some point early on—the day she stood on her twin bed in pigtails, perhaps, wearing white bobby socks and a baptism dress, staring past the camera into the hallway, eyes wide as if she'd just seen a ghost— the experience of shame had been so excruciating that her whole body rallied, fighting the feeling like it would fight any other intruder.

Eventually, she became the mother I knew as a young woman: brown eyes flashing under the brim of a felt fedora, bare hips shimmering between the folds of a purple belly-dancing skirt, white shoulders daring someone to stop her as she spun turquoise rings across the church gymnasium floor. Shameless and drowning in shame.

Cradling the last note in my hands, I picture my mother in all her complexity. The woman who left for work in wild-patterned nylons and drew blood in a black leather skirt. The woman who, a year before she died, had thrown herself into a skanking circle to show her enthusiasm for Benjamin's newly formed ska band. Despite her demons—despite her compression fractures, failing organs, and crepe-paper skin—she kicked up white-stockinged feet in peach orthotic sandals, fearlessly bobbing between teenage boys in backward hats, secondhand sports coats, and sunglasses, behind teenage girls in fluorescent tank tops and studded black belts.

Amid bandanas, spiked hair, and bare midriffs, she danced. Clad in cream slacks, her skin glistening under a sequined floral-print sweater, she dared me to get off the sidelines. I felt the familiar twinge of embarrassment—*dear god, Mom, no*—and panicked for her welfare—surely she would die if she fell. Then I held my breath for the two of us and dove into the careening circle, breathing hard to stay apace, elbow to elbow with my mother.

Ben must have been watching from the stage, head nodding to the offbeat, flanked by brass players in striped socks and suspenders. Lan and my father laughed near the door. Part of the circle, Arthur kicked and spun, elbows to opposing knees. And in that moment we were a family.

Sitting in my office, I let the memory wash over me, filling the silence with gratitude. How much of my audaciousness had been a by-product of my mother's? I think about the bins and files and documents, the resilience she found in her pain, her ambition and mine. Closing my eyes, I focus on the only thing that matters, trying to make one thought as crystalline as I can, sending it out to my mother across space and time: *I release you of conditions.*

It's the closest thing to a prayer I've uttered in ten years. It is no grand gesture, but it feels right somehow. I do not feel the heavens open. I do not feel a wild outpouring of grief. I do not feel her respond from the spirit world. Instead, I feel strangely unencumbered. As if I had spoken the words to myself and for one moment believed them.

WHEN I IMAGINE the last day of my mother's life, it goes something like this: My father kissed her good-bye in the morning darkness as he always did. He had started to think that each kiss might be his last, and so he savored it, cradling her cheeks in his hands, breathing in her uneven exhalations, hoping as he had for forty-five years that she would be there when he got home from work. No matter how disoriented she got, or pain-ridden, she was still the girl in the rhinestone cat's-eye glasses, the serious seventeen-year-old standing next to him in the Chapel of Love whispering "I do." He pictured her dancing. He pictured her walking up the dusty road to the cabin. And then he left for work.

A light sleeper, she would have felt his kiss. She did not acknowledge it since she didn't want to wake. For fifteen years, she had lain awake at night, wondering if sleep would come. She never felt completely rested, and the medicines that finally knocked her out made her groggy the next morning. Just a few hours more, she thought to herself, and then she would get up.

By eight or nine, she roused herself. Any longer would have been shameful. Everyone knew that sleeping past daybreak was lazy. Sleeping past nine was unthinkable.

She went into the upstairs kitchen, the one she'd lovingly filled with Coca-Cola memorabilia, and took her first round of medicines on an empty stomach, as directed. In half an hour she would take the rest with some breakfast. Then she dressed, penciled in her eyebrows, and pressed brown curls around her face. It did not matter if she was going out or not. A woman looked presentable. Who knew if someone might stop by?

Her routine that morning had been clouded by something that occurred to her a few days before. She never seemed to get along very well with her daughters-in-law. Could it be that they hated her? Her voices whispered it was so. She could not imagine why they hated her. Maybe they envied her nice things. Maybe they resented her house. She had no evidence for such bitterness, but it seemed so solid and real. As real and true as the mirror that reflected her rosy cheeks and tired eyes.

As she stood at the vanity, the story reaffirmed itself, becoming darker as she imagined how it would play out. The girls would invent a terrible story. And what could be more terrible than if they said she abused them? Everyone would turn against her. The man who stood by her when her father rejected her—the man who had held out his love for her like a handful of magic beans—would leave her forever. He would go to work and never come back.

Her voices whispered that he had heard the lies. And he believed them. So she did what she had always done when things felt like they were slipping beyond her control. She started to write a letter: "I'm sorry you feel that way, so very sorry. . . ." Then the phone rang: Christie making plans for the weekend.

She poured her heart out to her granddaughter and hung up. Had she said too much? Would her lack of discretion make everything worse? If Christie didn't believe her, who would? She had lost her job, her friends, her health; and now she was losing her family. And that was the one thing that she could not bear.

Her voices had told her before that she did not have long to live, and she heard them taunt her now. She had planned on going on a mission to Africa or New Zealand, but that would have to wait. Time was running out, and so she left a note.

Dear Christie,

I only have a minute before I die, because I said too much to you on the phone. But take all of this money. You're going to need it to buy a violin. You're going to become a world famous violinist. These coins are very valuable especially the one with the diamond. The $20 gold pieces are from the years Grandma and Grandpa Chournos were born. The one that says "no motto" is extremely valuable. Also take the big nice dictionary downstairs. I love you!

Then she prepared to die. She could not take her own life. She didn't want to. The voices were punishing her for speaking out. Like Cecilia, she awaited her trial by fire.

She placed the note and money in a blue zippered bag. Christie would put the money to good use. Her granddaughter had come into the world with a gift for music, had played piano since her stubby fingers could plunk out major chords. She had forgotten that it was another granddaughter who played the violin, but it did not matter. Christie would play the violin gloriously, just as she had played the harp. And Christie would understand the significance of the gold pieces. Tokens of her mother and father, symbols of the twin legacies that had shaped her.

She lit some incense and placed it on the bedside table in a ritual only she understood. Then she tucked the small zippered pouch next to her, lay back on the pillows, and waited for the Savior of the World to come for her, the God of love she said was mighty to save.

I LEARNED ONCE that when you died, you got a new and improved body, flawless in every way but one: if you harbored cravings in this life, they would follow you to the next. Like smoking. You would rise up in a breathtaking body with no scratches and dents, but you would still harbor a hankering for tobacco—only it would be a hundred times harder to quit. Why it would be so hard to quit when there were (presumably) no cigarettes in the afterlife did not make sense to me; nor did a God who would punish your new body with old cravings. If God—as a father or judge or shepherd—had a shred of compassion, he would not torment my mother with everlasting prednisone dependence. But the ratio of justice and mercy she deserves depends on how you wield the metaphors. And how you wield the metaphors will reveal the legacy you have been given.

MY CLEANING DREAMS have finally given way to dreams about my mother. In one, I wander through a palatial home of gold and glass, set with a grand marble staircase and long, sweeping banisters. Bright flowers burst from a pot at the top of the stairs, where padded hallways filled with plush carpet diverge into a maze of corridors.

I make my way from room to room, vaguely aware that I am looking for someone, when I turn to find my mother standing next to a cherry-wood bed, hand resting on a slim bedpost, head cocked down and to the side as if she were infinitely tired.

I walk to her jubilantly—does she have any idea how worried I've been? I had imagined something terrible happened to her, but there she is, whole and unscathed and beautiful, in spite of the fact that she looks sort of forlorn.

I take her face in my hands and move it toward mine, so that we look at each other full in the face. Her eyes are lined with concern, but she smiles a little when she sees me, as if she has been worried about me too.

"You are tired, Mom," I say, and she nods, her skin pink and resilient. I pull back the covers and she slips beneath them, and I rest my cheek to her forehead as she closes her eyes.

I retire to the kitchen, where I stir air in a bright silver pot, promising myself that I will never abandon her. So that as long as we live she will not be consumed by pain or fire ever again.

ACKNOWLEDGMENTS

This book began on the shore of Bear Lake, a slip of blue serenity straddling the Utah-Idaho border, where I wrestled with words on a borrowed laptop, baking atop a matted blue blanket, trying to come up with a suitable piece of memoir for the Utah Writing Project. The sun was too hot, the coffee too cold. I was at odds with myself and deeply uncomfortable with my own story.

I trusted few people with my secrets that day. There was my husband, Lan, hanging out down-shore with our two young sons in a battered laminate shack optimistically mislabeled a "condo", Jill and John DeVilbiss, who shared my religious uncertainties; and William Strong, workshop organizer, who inspired me with the idea that stories mattered and that life, like art, was a process. Writing, he said, was like making love: something you continually learned how to do.

By the end of the day, I managed to describe a grainy photo of my sister and me playing dress-up as children: she, looking angelic in a silky white slip and holding a tinfoil wand; me, wearing a cardboard crown and what can only be described as combat fatigues.

There was more to the image than the squatty brown toddler and her sunny sister. There was a problem I couldn't pin down, and a feeling that would take me two decades to name. In the meantime, my voice grew in strength and complexity, bolstered by a growing band of kindred spirits, who formed the foundation from which I could tell this story.

With a spirit as freewheeling and dinged up as my own, Lan became my primary audience and enthusiast, even when the material made him wince. His enthusiasm nourished my words at the workshop and sustained me through countless versions of this book. Along with him, my sons, Ben and Arthur, deserve my deepest gratitude, not just because they endured a mother who spent too many hours dithering with sentences, but because they were privy to the transformations in these pages, which must have been as confusing as they were liberating.

The day at the lake, I feared that my siblings would reject me if they knew all of the ways I had failed them and the faith we shared. This has not been the case. In the years since I started writing, and especially since the loss of our mother, I have felt boundless compassion and kindness. My father has demonstrated that holding fast to a faith does not preclude loving a daughter. My sister and brothers have listened to my misgivings, loved me unconditionally, and buoyed me up in my darkest hours.

Having had little in the way of formal writing instruction, I owe a great debt to fortuitous mentors, who helped me hone my voice. Brock Dethier not only helped me frame my first long argument, but also read and responded to more critical papers, creative forays, and sudden manuscripts than any adviser should bear. Dan Kirby asked all of the right questions about the two girls in the photo. Tom Romano responded to my bleak journal following the death of my uncle Johnnie. Robert Michael Pyle inspired my first essays with enthusiastic marginalia. Bill Francis provided a bulwark of friendship and introduced me to the medical experts I consulted for this book. Cheryll Glotfelty and Scott Slovic celebrated my creative efforts when I was supposed to be writing literary criticism. Thanks to Cheryll, I also had the pleasure of meeting Joanne O'Hare at the University of Nevada Press, whose enthusiasm for the manuscript made this book possible.

Readers of this book will find that I had precious little modeling in terms of making friendships with other women. In spite of this, I have been spoiled by girlfriends who have served as advance readers and life advisers: Blair Larsen, geologist and southern belle, who lured me out of my writerly cave and taught me to socialize; Deidri Neilson, wolfish confidante, who spent hours helping me think through the problems at the heart of this book; Merrilyne Lundahl, whose reading left me breathless, and whose courage makes me weep; Kristen Weaver, who cheered on the manuscript as I was giving up on it; Jane Detweiler and Beverly Lassiter, who provided sanctuary after the fire; Carol Nielsen and Tauna Christiansen, who listened to my early rants and bad parodies; Sheila Terry, who read the manuscript in its infancy; and Teddy Peck, who listened to me read the whole damn thing without a spot of alcohol. As an advance reader, Eleanor Brown offered unparalleled wisdom, humor, and writerly advice. From her, I learned to take my work seriously without taking myself too seriously. Thanks to her, I had the pleasure of working with Elizabeth Winick Rubinstein and Shira Hoffman, who saw this manuscript through its painful adolescence, and without whom I might have continued to misunderstand the difference between thesis and theme.

I am deeply indebted to the outside reviewers for the University of Nevada Press, whose painstaking readings and expert observations resulted in some of the most poignant scenes in the book. I am also grateful to John Mulvihill for meticulous editorial feedback and to Dan Inman, whose tears told me the book was finally finished.

Last, I would like to thank the members of the Chournos family: George, Cherre, Allen, Sam, and my cousins, who may seem maligned in these pages. Any scars we share are products not of ill-will, but of love..